Archetypes of the Soul

Our knowledge of the soul is only fragmentary.
Remembering this fact might help us to consider
the possibility of developing a psychology of the soul,
based on the assumption of an autonomous spirit.
Carl Gustav Jung

Varda Hasselmann
Frank Schmolke

Archetypes of the Soul

Translated by Terry Willey

Original title:
Archetypen der Seele by Varda B. Hasselmann / Frank Schmolke

© 1993 by Wilhelm Goldmann Verlag, München,
a division of Verlagsgruppe Random House,
München, Germany

English translation copyright © by Varda B. Hasselmann / Frank Schmolke
Translation by Terry Willey
First published in German in 1993 by Wilhelm Goldmann Verlag, München,
a division of Verlagsgruppe Random House, München, Germany
3nd revised printing 2010

ISBN 978-3-442-22000-7

Contents

Foreword
to the English-Language Edition

This book presents a translation of messages received from the SOURCE by
Dr. Varda Hasselmann, a German medium, and her partner, Frank Schmolke,
during some 150 trance sessions over a three-year period. The information transmitted by the SOURCE (»Die Quelle«), a wise transpersonal entity from the
causal plane of consciousness, does not require blind belief but can be tested and
proven. Indeed, the SOURCE urges us to question and test the information.
What is transmitted can be verified and be of concrete use to those who choose to
apply it.

Archetypes of the Soul provide extremely precise insights into the structure
of the world of the soul. That such a structure may in fact exist was first revealed
by another causal entity called Michael. The Michael messages have since been
expanded upon, made clearer and deepened by other chanelled information and
especially by the entity called the SOURCE. First transmitted in the German
language, this translation seeks to make the material available to readers in
English-speaking countries.

Based on information contained in this book, Varda Hasselmann and Frank
Schmolke developed a method of teaching people to recognize their soul pattern, or
MATRIX, which the SOURCE says the soul chooses before an incarnation: The
Soul Role, the Chief Characteristic of Fear, the Development Goal, the Mode,
Mentality and Reaction Pattern. The Soul Role—that of King, Priest, Sage,
Scholar, Warrior, Artist or Healer/Helper—remains constant throughout the
course of a soul's incarnations and beyond. All other elements vary from lifetime
to lifetime. The soul age advances steadily, according to the natural ability of the

soul to master a particular incarnation task and to assimilate the lessons it has chosen to learn from it. This advancement is not the result of »being good«, but happens all by itself, just as a body ages from minute to minute. The SOURCE is a soul family, an entity composed of Sages and Scholars who have completed their earthly cycle of incarnations.

Seminars based on these teachings have served as a type of scientific laboratory in which the validity of the teachings of the SOURCE regarding the MATRIX can be tested and proven. These seminars have been attended by thousands of people from many countries. Among the participants have been countless psychologists, doctors and therapists but also lawyers, ministers and artists who have reported that they are successfully applying the knowledge of the archetypes in their work. Knowing the archetypical soul pattern of one's children, siblings and parents, of one's friends and colleagues or students helps to love and understand them more deeply. To assume, even theoretically, that all of them are ensouled beings with a meaningful, unique and inspired MATRIX, makes it impossible not to respect them.

The MATRIX system, based on the forty-nine Archetypes of the Soul, is not a therapeutic method. But it is a practical tool that can be applied in different therapeutic approaches and in every other dimension of life and work. A jazz singer with the Soul Role of a Sage will perform more audience-oriented than a singer with a Warrior Soul, who wants to fight for a better world with every song; he will also have different admirers and students. A carpenter with a Scholar soul produces chairs and tables more pragmatic and usable from what an Artist soul carpenter with his inborn desire for originality would make. A doctor with a Priest soul talks to an invalid with more compassion and personal sympathy but maybe less authority and power of conviction than a doctor with a King soul would do.

The SOURCE's teachings lead to a profound understanding of, and essential tolerance for, oneself and one's fellow-man. And the teachings convey the reassurance that whatever has been created throughout the history of mankind is *not lost, but still valid. It forms the basis for future lives. Our incarnated souls are the ones who have all helped create the earth in our many lives and whose own souls in new bodies will inhabit it in the future.*

As another millenium begins, more and more people are looking for new dimensions in their understanding of themselves and the world. It is significant that these teachings of both Michael and the SOURCE have appeared at this time. Our SOURCE explains the reason for this teaching:

»The Godly principle is love and understanding. Love merges with understanding in the Godly.

In their reality humans are often separated from this unity. But their souls know the bliss which arises within a being—even if only for a second—when love and understanding become one.

We offer you these teachings about the soul, of which we are only the conveyors not the creators, so that you may more often experience the possibility of cognition and love at the same time. Whatever we say is guided by both principles. You can sense this, you can experience it. Everything we say can be comprehended by your minds and not only by your emotion.

As modern human beings you have access to the wider dimensions of your soul only in exceptional circumstances. This applies first of all to the enlightened children of materialism and rationalism, who, more than others, need new access to their second, irrational half which needs not necessarily to be rejected by their analytical and logical minds.

Our desire, therefore, is to make the reality of your soul's dimension in love and cognition accessible to you in an appropriate way so that you can again bring into harmony all that you have sought and worked for in this life and in many thousands of years.

You know much about the laws of your earth and your physical existence. Humans constantly make new discoveries. The extent of your knowledge expands with break-neck speed. The sphere of your abitlity to love, in contrast, falls short.

We want to create a balance without belying scientific knowledge or diminishing its worth. We want to show you that your cognitive faculties can also be applied, through the method of love, to all the areas of your soul's existence. We want to lead you to understand the soul's dimension, which makes up your existential half, not as a formless, mysterious and occult sphere but as another realm in which you can travel with the same vehicles that you use in your material, mind-oriented world, in order to understand it. We want to show you that you can walk on the same streets and visit the same places. This is not a mirror world or a simple territorial counterpart, but a spiritual complement whose worth you've almost forgotten and whose remembrance we can reawaken with an ease which astounds both you and us.

Our task, therefore is to convey the teachings of these worlds of the human soul and to make you conscious of their particular reality. This is the purpose of our work. Our inner-most desire is to reunite the comprehensive with the individual, to link the universal consciousness to your personal consciousness, and especially your cognitive consciousness

This isn't because we are so kindly and generous and are speaking to you from a place that is far above yours, but rather from an inner necessity which evolves from the universal system of archetypical energies we belong to. We have to do what we are doing. We don't have a choice. You are the ones who can choose. You still live in a dual world which we've already left behind. You can love or not love, realize or not realize, understand or not understand. This possibility is closed to us but we don't regret this. Everyone is in the right place and does what is necessary. If you discover that our teachings are useful to give meaning to your life and your existence and to understand your world better, then we will have achieved what we wanted to.

We're satisfied if you sense that love and understanding have become a little stronger and more powerful in your being.«

This book is also intended as a token of profound gratitude for a publication which many years ago started us out on our spiritual journey. »Messages from Michael« by Chelsea Quinn Yarbro contained extremely fascinating information about the core and nucleus of what since then has become the purpose of our lives: the exploration of the structure of the soul. The mental revolution which in our view the »Messages from Michael« contained inspired us and led us to leave promising academic careers in order to pursue the study of what has since been revealed to us by a causal entity we call the SOURCE to be a complex system of soul archetypes.

We want to express our thanks to our excellent friends Terry Willey, Dr Bob Hooper and Monika Pitterle who contributed with their work and affection to making the Archetypes of the Soul available to English-speaking readers.

While reading this book on the Archetypes of the Soul, please remember: These messages are faithfully rendered in their original oral style and wording. And neither the soul nor an archetype have a gender. But now, allow the SOURCE to speak to you.

Dr. Varda Hasselmann   Frank Schmolke
Munich, Germany 2004

The Source's Introduction

Each person's soul pattern, the MATRIX, is like his genetic pattern. Both direct him at every moment. As a rule, this occurs unconsciously. Like the genes, the MATRIX automatically fulfills its functions. If, however, you can find conscious access to your soul pattern, doors will be opened to your inner world which otherwise must remain closed. Such conscious access provides an overwhelming richness of answers to the one great question which touches every person who's moved to follow a spiritual path. This is the question of self-knowledge, the question »Who am I?« But it is important to understand that the soul pattern differs basically from the psychological pattern although there are a number of points of contact because, as long as you possess a body, the soul can only manifest itself through your psyche.

A MATRIX describes your core, the essential, the unique, that which you bring with you and which makes you what you are. It's the result of a decision by your soul and therefore has a purpose which differs fundamentally from the significance of the psychological pattern which, to a certain degree, can be altered or influenced. The MATRIX contains a blue-print of your total, pure potential and the possibilities of your soul development in each individual life, in a certain existential context. It's also a reflection of your basic energy. The psychological pattern, in contrast, is already a result of what has been experienced in this life and in former lives. It consists of events and their assimilation, of traumas and shaping. It produces reactions and behavior. It limits you instead of showing the possibilities of your broadest radius.

As long as a soul is present in a body, the soul pattern must also manifest itself psychologically. But it should be pointed out that this manifestation isn't similar to the reactions of the psyche, which stem from compulsion, fear and history. Instead, the soul pattern describes freedom, a large frame in which you can develop. It presents a dimension in which you can truly be yourself instead of being a product of circumstances.

All the constants and variables of the MATRIX create this freedom through a polarization, which should be viewed not as linear, but multi-dimensional. These poles, denoted by plus and minus ($+$ and $-$) describe the fluid spheres of love and fear, of more love and less fear, of more fear and less love. And your freedom consists of navigating between these poles, of applying your consciousness and awareness to locate your position in this sphere, to judge and to understand.

You have at your disposal the absolute, continual, total, enormous and highly-differentiated multi-dimensional sphere between the poles of love and fear. This is both a comfort and a guideline at the same time. Your desire to grow, your will to develop, your longing to make progress along the path, creates an orientation map which helps you find your way in this sphere that is your home land.

The MATRIX is a pattern of your inner world. This world differs from that of the physical and psychological world, but it's not an anti-world.

All three dimensions—the physical, the psychological and the spiritual—are connected to each other. They work together and can be harmonized. The difference consists in the fact that the soul dimension was created during your disembodied state in the time and space between lives, while the psychological dimension stems from the existence of your being during the embodied state. Therefore, the soul pattern is imprinted with more love and purpose than your psychological pattern. Spirit, mind and reason help you to understand, to observe and learn. Thus you can become conscious.

Even if all aspects of your physical and psychological being could be described, another dimension of your existence would remain veiled. This dimension concerns the requirements and prerequisites of your soul identity, an identity which embraces all lives in the body and retains its validity beyond corporal existence. Our intention is to bring you closer to this third dimension, the imperative, irrefutable reality of your soul pattern, and to open the possibility of a deeper, more intimate relationship to your soul. Every word we employ to describe the Archetypes serves this purpose.

The Matrix of the Soul
and Its Seven Elements

Table: Archetypes of the Soul

Soul Age VII	Infant Soul	Child Soul	Young Soul
Centering VI	**Emotional** – sentimental + sensitve	**Intellectual** – hair-splitting + thoughtful	**Sexual** – seductive + productive
Mentality V	**Stoicism** – resigned + tranquil	**Skepticism** – distrusting + investigative	**Cynicism** – humiliating + critical
Mode IV	**Reservation** – inhibited + restrained	**Caution** – anxious + prudent	**Perseverance** – fixated + persistent
Goal III	**Delay** – withdrawing + reviewing	**Rejection** – prejudiced + discerning	**Submission** – subjugated + devoted
Fear: Chief Characteristic II	**Self–Deprecation** Fear of Inadequacy – self–abasing + modest	**Self–Sabotage** Fear of Joyfulness – self–destructive + self–sacrificing	**Martyrdom** Fear of Worthlessness – victimizing + selfless
Soul Role I	**Helper/Healer** Principle: Supporting – servile + helpful	**Artist** Principle: Inventing – artificial + original	**Warrior** Principle: Fighting – overwhelming + convincing
ENERGY	**1** sky blue	**2** butterfly yellow	**3** blood red

Quelle: Archetypen der Seele, Varda Hasselmann/Frank Schmolke, Goldmann Verlag, 1993

Mature Soul	Old Soul	Transpersonal Ensoulment Not Part of Incarnation Cycle	Transliminal Ensoulment Not Part of Incarnation Cycle
Instinctive – thoughtless + spontaneous	Spiritual – telepathic + inspired	Ecstatic – psychic + mystical	Moving – hectic + untiring
Pragmatism – rigid + practical	Idealism – vague + visionary	Spiritualism – gullible + verifying	Realism – guessing + perceptive
Observation – watchful + vigilant	Power – patronizing + authoritative	Passion – fanatic + charismatic	Aggression – belligerent + dynamic
Standstill – immobilized + pausing	Acceptance – ingratiating + kindhearted	Acceleration – confused + comprehending	Dominance – dictatorial + leading
Stubbornness Fear of Unpredictability – obstinate + resolute	Greed Fear of Privation – insatiable + demanding	Arrogance Fear of Vulnerability – vain + proud	Impatience Fear of Omission – intolerant + audacious
Scholar Principle: Learning + Teaching – theorizing + knowing	Sage Principle: Communicating – talkative + expressive	Priest Principle: Consoling – overzealous + compassionate	King Principle: Leading – tyrannical + dignified
4 grass green	5 sunny yellow	6 ocean blue	7 purple

Soul Roles

⑤
Sage

– talkative   + expressive

②
Artist

– artificial   + original

Expression Level

⑥
Priest

– overzealous   + compassionate

①
Helper/Healer

– servile   + helpful

Inspiration Level

⑦
King

– tyrannical   + dignified

③
Warrior

– overwhelming   + convincing

Action Level

④
Scholar

– theorizing   + knowing

Assimilation Level

I The Seven Essential Soul Roles

The essences or essential Soul Roles are the inner-most core of your soul identity. They link you as a human being with natural laws governing soul development and learning which are valid throughout the entire universe.

All seven essences complement each other. None is more important than the other, none is better or worse. Each element contributes to the success of the whole and nothing can prevent it from making this contribution in accordance with its very own function.

Your essence is your core soul identity which binds you more than all other aspects of the MATRIX to the great whole. By this we mean that the essence of each of you has the same universal worth as the smallest identifiable particle in the universe.

This essence is a bearer of universal energy. It cannot disappear and therefore your essence is valid, not to say eternal, as long as the phenomenon of soul families, their dispersement and fragmentation, as well as the desire for reunification of the individual souls and their new integration into the larger associations with their soul populations, remain valid. As long as the manifestation of individuality in the world of souls is decisive for learning, the principle of essential Soul Roles is also valid.

All souls represent universal principles which are valid not only on your planet Earth. All entities in their fragmented condition need support, consolation, leadership, communication, forming, discussion, instruction. This does not apply to those who are no longer, or not yet, fragmented.

The event of fragmentation before any physical life is just as wonderful as the effect all those seven essences continue to have in their association with their soul families on the astral and causal planes of consciousness. There is a joint desire for growth which exists from the beginning to the end of all existence. This also remains valid during the period of fragmentation.

Your souls take on one of the following roles: Healer/Helper, Artist, Warrior, Scholar, Sage, Priest or King. It remains the same during all of its manifestations and incarnations no matter on which planet or in which cosmic manifestation. It's your role from the beginning to the end of your experiences in a human body. It provides identity and stability and is in no way restrictive, which it might at first appear to be. For each MATRIX which is chosen and assembled for each individual life, as well as the inexorably increasing Soul Age with its development stages, provide you an immeasureable, undreamed of bandwidth, such a diverse potential that you can exhaust all areas of experience which are possible in a human body.

The depth and breadth of the essential roles allow you to sense and realize the identity of your individual souls. And this identity differs from all other souls in the universe because of the uniquely individual development process during an incarnation cycle through completely independent and unique experiences. For if some core didn't forever remain the same, you wouldn't be able to recognize it again. When you speak of eternal life and eternal existence, of the immortality of your soul, you mean essentially, without realizing it, the immortality of your constant unchanging Soul Role.

There are myriads of associations of seven soul families in the entire realm of the universe. If an association is prepared to strive for a special form of learning and decides to manifest itself on some planet or some level of energy, it breaks up into individual soul families. These soul families each contain differing numbers of essences: two, three or, more seldom, four. We, the SOURCE, for example, have the energies of Sages and Scholars, whereas MICHAEL, a sort of cosmic cousin to us, is made of Kings and Warriors.

All seven Soul Roles combine their power in an association or clan of seven soul families. But when they begin to experience fragmentation in one of the individual Soul Roles, a completely new way of development and experience in the body begins.

The essence or Soul Role links the individual soul to the Whole, to the AllOne. As long as you incarnate in the physical world and fluctuate between the astral world and your earth, you're subject to the demands of time and space. You never entirely lose contact with the dimensions of timelessness and endless space, since your essence retains that connection. The role is the only MATRIX element which isn't bound by the limitations and conditions of the physical world and is in a position to preserve that which you've forgotten. It represents your soul's memory.

You've forgotten and you must forget without giving up all premonitions and hopes. Religion means finding a way to make all hopes for eternal existence become an inner certainty.

Energy I

The Helper/Healer

Principle: Supporting

– Servile   Helpful +

Many people unjustly fail to appreciate the Soul Role of the Healer/Helper. They fail to realize that the role of the Healer and Helper, as well as being the most wide-spread, is also that which makes life on your planet well-organized and practicable. Healers make the world go round, they ensure that life in human communities works, that people take care of each other beyond their animal instincts. Self-Sabotage

Those who don't appreciate the role of the Healer in your society and community aren't doing themselves any favour: first, because contempt never brings anything positive, and second, because the important functions of this soul essence only begin to produce results when other Soul Roles become cognizant of the tasks of the helpful Healers and gratefully accept them.

But even the Healer and Helper himself has the tendency—based on the modest, simple and sometimes self-deprecating energy of his Archetype—to disparage himself, to find himself unworthy of being noticed by others or to be taken seriously in the important tasks he carries out. Therefore, he often misjudges his own worth and role in society. He labours under a misunderstanding that in order to help, he must stay in the background and debase himself like a menial servant.

This isn't helpful. On the contrary, a Healer is only capable of happily shaping his life close to his soul essence when he recognizes his service as something worthy and understands that this service within society and the community is indispensable. Because of a lack of respect from others, the Healer/Helper fails to appreciate himself and tends toward self-denigration because he often doesn't understand how important self-respect and respect for his services are for his spiritual development.

The Healer supports what others wish and desire. The Healer serves irrespective of whether the task is good or bad, the master »just« or »unjust«. And he finds his dignity therein. When he can experience his service in love, he'll realize that his service is not a burden but a joy and an enrichment of his life.

We find it necessary to emphasize that the Role of the Healer is an archetype role and no horror scenario of a person who must agree to everything, who must toil until death for his bread and wages, who is a slave because he has no rights. He has the right, above all, to refuse to serve when he considers this necessary to preserve his dignity.

The concept of the words »Helper« and »Healer« describes the fact that this soul-essence feels fulfilled in support and service and is ready to perform duties which would be disdained by others but which nevertheless are necessary and have global significance for the advancement of the whole. That service can be performed as queen or prime minister serving the nation or as a cleaning woman serving an old man. This kind of service is healing in a world full of conflict. It is healing because it does not ask for immediate reward. Healing through helping is a spiritual task in the service of mankind.

The Helper/Healer is truly happy when he or she can find self-development in the service of another person, a community, an institution or an office. To serve means to neglect somewhat one's own selfish interests, to place the greater whole in the forefront, to perfect this greater whole to an ideal which nevertheless is tangible and comprehensible, even to the extent that it can be felt physically, like a caress or a helping hand.

Therefore, the Healer/Helper prefers to serve a real person or a group of people who are in a position to maintain a relationship with him, who are not impersonal or as abstract as, for example, an idea. Healers don't like abstractions. They want to build an individual and personal relationship with their object of support.

If a Healer loses himself in service, when he can't feel himself for all the feeling he has for others, for relatives, his company or charitable institutions who have assigned him a service or social task, he's in danger of losing hinself. Then he can no longer take note of his own needs; he risks atrophying into a colourless and insignificant individual. He's no longer capable of carrying out his tasks to the degree to which it's desirable for the development of his soul. It is best to serve with radiance.

It is not submissive, obedient, servile service, the fading into anonymity or the complete withdrawal into artificial unselfishness which will help the Helper's soul develop. Accepting circumstances in true humility and true love rather than with resignation will bring fulfillment.

And if a person, whose task as a Healer is serving and supporting, doesn't learn in time to avoid those who would force him into positions of complete dependence and loss of dignity, he will, without realizing it, distance himself from his essence and won't be able to fulfill the necessary tasks he's set for himself in this life. It's therefore of vital importance for a Helper and Healer, to set limits, whether it be for a person or institution. These limits must begin at the point where the healer is in danger of losing his joyfulness, his affirmation, his radiance and his positive acceptance of what is being demanded from him.

He who thinks he can achieve a place in the sun through excessive servility or shadowy service, whether it be in his personal belief system or in a superimposed social system, is badly advised. This place in the sun, which, by the way, is guaranteed to every soul, will be most quickly reached by those Healers who accept their task with joy. But the shadows will increase the more a Helper/Healer retreats into subservience, tries to hide, tries to make himself invisible and, in such a way, turns his capacity for love into unspoken self-debasement or into a hatred for those whom he serves. To serve with love will help every Healer/Helper develop.

And, with love, to reject what is no longer bearable, which leads to antipathy and negativity, will help him develop even more quickly.

Healers in a way have it easier than other soul-roles: they'll find enough opportunities everywhere and in every respect to serve and support, to uncover the needs of their soul-essence, to find and satisfy them. This also means that they can readily find possibilities within society of performing their service in dignity without expending or losing themselves.

A Soul Role which has the most possibilities of expressing his essence, and this is the case with the role of the Helper and Healer, will sometimes be able to pass through the many lives he needs for his development at an accelerated pace. And, therefore, within the soul-family, the Healers are often those who complete their development cycles the most rapidly and then, in their disembodied state and on the astral plane, stand ready to serve and support the siblings of their soul-family, to accompany them, to protect them and to help them in whatever way they request.

Success in the external sense means little to the Healer. The inner contentment which he feels when his services are accepted positively and have positive effects, are, as a rule, reward enough.

His religious feelings concentrate on serving the Deity with great devotion. God or the gods are friendly masters to him, someone mighty and good who helps in need and distress and who will forgive sins out of his natural goodness, just like himself.

Many lives which you as humans have chosen to master are not pleasant but are often filled with great exertions and considerable torments. But a soul which, on the basis of its constant attempts to act and strive and serve in a manner true to its essence, has a certain bonus in that it will have to spend less time than others learning through suffering and sacrifice.

Energy 2

The Artist

Principle: Inventing

– Artificial   Original +

The Artist is a Soul Type who doesn't want to leave his life behind without having created something for the world which expresses his soul's true nature and his individuality as purely as possible. More than others, the Artist strives to create something visible, demonstrable, original, something which proves that he exists and that he had a right to exist. He wishes to create something that has never existed in this form or with this content. The new, the unexplored, all that astonishes and surprises, is his domain.

And it doesn't matter whether the soul of an Artist resides in a stone-age person who hews a rock in such a way that it can be used for new purposes, or if he is the inventor of the wheel, the designer of a machine, a composer who aligns notes to produce a new sound, or a poet who creates a new pattern of verse which gives his words a new and unique expression. The main aim is to create something new—not to repeat, deepen or improve upon something that has been created by others.

All Artists have many pictures in their heads. Sometimes they feel overwhelmed by all the images, fantasies, ideals and works of imagination. Watching them, they giggle at themselves. They can be extremely witty and easily see the amusing side of all things. Most of them are endowed with a sharp perception and good intellect. They develop a reputation of mental clarity. And Artists can be very witty.

When an Artist is plagued by the fear of not being able to offer something new, when he feels hindered or inhibited by other aspects of his MATRIX (like Self-Sabotage, Self-Deprecation or Martyrdom) in creating something unprecedented he'll nevertheless attempt to invent just something. But everyone, with the exception of himself, will notice that his invention is superfluous, rigid, that it enjoys little success, that it strikes others as a pretence and doesn't create true happiness but only strengthens the fears and illusions of the environment. Many representatives of this Soul Role are found in the advertising industry or at inventors' exhibitions, patent offices as well as in the music sector, in show business, and among impersonators and sidewalk pavement artists. They're the ones who doubt their own abilities, who fear they're not original enough to create something entirely of their own and, on the other hand, aren't fearless enough to draw the consequences from this lack of real creativity.

If an Artist falls into artificial artistic expression, regardless of whether this be an engineer, a scientist, a craftsman or a teacher, he estranges himself from his own being and his own creative, inventive power. He behaves as if he's doing something original but his achievements are artificial, sometimes even unnatural, and create more tension than happiness.

The medium in which an Artist creates something new is not important to him. An Artist's soul essence can be expressed in the creation of a new cooking recipe as well as in the development of a space exploration project. The main thing is not the content or the resonance which spurs the artist to create something, but the desire and satisfaction that he finds when he feels that he's bringing together elements and factors which until then had co-existed without ties or contact. In such a way he gives them a new meaning.

Many scientists and artisans have Artist-souls. They're not the well-behaved practitioners of their craft, but rather those whose spirit actively desires to bring change and novelty to their work. Artist souls are also found among many people whose spirit won't let them rest until they've created something unusual which leaves a lasting impression on the people in their own environment and, if possible, on a larger group. Therefore, two things are important for an Artist: the childlike happiness and satisfaction which he finds in the creation of his work and the admiration of his originality by other people. Rather than applause, the Artist seeks recognition.

This Soul Role is satisfied and close to his own being when he creates forms out of the need to give his work an aesthetic harmony reflecting his own inner beauty and harmony. The objects which an artist essence creates are completely arbitrary. They can come from the material or the spiritual world. This soul can just as happily express its Artist role in the design of his living-room as in the choice of his clothes, in a successful surgical procedure, in the construction of a street or bridge, in the design of a garden, in the education of children, in composing a sermon, in the drawing up of an order of battle or through a harmonious, aesthetic construction of his own personality and the circumstances in which he lives.

In this way, the essence of an Artist can make all areas of his existence in all lives an expression of his artistic being. That's his goal but this is also the reason for his frequent doubts since this essence is fastidious and is seldom satisfied with what he's created. He often fears that his creations are insufficient, that everything should be different and much better. He takes pleasure in them only for a brief time, then—like child—he's seized by unrest and wants to destroy everything he's done and begin anew. And he always suffers internal pressure to be, or to create, something special, something original. It's precisely at times like these, when he gives in to these pressures, that he's easily led onto the level of artificiality.

When you observe Artists at these times, you see men and women who strive to individualize themselves through extremely original clothing styles. This individualization, however, is sometimes so artificial that it gives the impression of something frenzied and strange. Self-stylizing can take two directions. One is an exaggerated perfection which leads to a conspicuous appearance and looks like the product of a design school student or model agency. The other seeks originality in a non-conformity in which one's appearance, hair-style and dress are showy but neglected.

The desire for uniqueness sometimes manifests itself in torn clothing, uncombed hair, or the neglect of cleanliness as an omnipresent protest against all norms and customs of the surrounding society. Of course, the desire for successful self-expression does not always have to take these extreme forms. Nevertheless, extremes of extravagant elegance or self-neglect are mostly evidence of an Artist-soul's imbalance.

This deep dissatisfaction, which results from a failure in the positive realization of the soul essence, torments many Artist souls because they're unable to discern their particular potential for artistic expression. What they do, what they create in order to express their essence is not taken seriously by themselves. They scorn or ignore the small, inconspicuous possibilities. At the same time, they admire all others who, in some way, are artistically expressive or active and they're filled not only with a longing but also resignation which could be expressed by the words »I would like so much to be able to do that, too, but I really don't know how.«

In order to overcome his own perceived inability to express himself through the accepted forms of art, it's extremely important that an Artist understands that one can express oneself artistically in thoughts, in writing letters or in artisan crafts as well as in more strictly-regarded artistic endeavours. Even if a person can neither draw nor compose nor create artistic objects, that doesn't mean that he has to abandon the idea of expressing his artistic essence.

A number of these Artist souls also find self-development in admiring, understanding, promoting or selling the artwork of others. This is a completely acceptable form of development of the Artist-role but it doesn't represent the final form. However, it can be of great worth for the

Artist-soul to spend his life working with the artistic creations of other souls and other essences, learning to know and love them, in order to one day burst forward with its own inventive creativity much like a child is born from the protection of his mother's womb in order to begin its own independent, unique life.

The Artist needs considerable variety in his relations with other people and especially in his sexuality. His richness of expression can only blossom when he escapes the threat of routine. His spirit and fantasy constantly need new stimulus and therefore he needs friends and partners who share his pleasure in the new, the unaccustomed and the unusual.

The religious inclination of this Soul Role is exemplified in a completely original relationship between himself and the Godly in whatever form it may be adored, depending on the individual's soul development. He strives to create an image of the Godly from his own personal perspective. His image of God becomes a holy work of art. Since this image must deviate from that of the crowds, the Artist-soul jealously preserves his personal godly image, which means everything to him, for himself. He protects it from exposure and treasures it like a jewel, which may only be viewed through his eyes or by him alone in secret.

The Artist incessantly shapes his reality and life. The contribution which this essence makes to the great whole and the development of its significance consists of finding previously unused and unexplored possibilities of self-expression and, through this self-expression, to give new expression to the whole of human, worldly and cosmic developments.

Energy 3

The Warrior

Principle: Fighting

– Overwhelming   Convincing +

If there were no Warriors the desire in your world for progress and change would be lacking. The Warrior soul is never satisfied. He wants things to be other than they are. He wants to apply his total energy to his tasks. He is prepared to fight for his goals with all that he is and has.

The Warrior is both active and passive. He's active because he's never at peace. Action enables him to find fulfillment. He's passive because he happily lets himself be harnassed by others to achieve their goals. The Warrior often depends on others—for example, on kings, but also on Artists, Priests and Helpers/Healers—to use him in their efforts to strive for and achieve what they consider worthwhile. He seeks to, and indeed does, take pride in the excellent execution of his duties. He doesn't need applause. As reward he needs honour, decorations, posthumous fame and respect for his dignity. If a Warrior is threatened with having his honour sullied or his dignity taken from him, he's offended more deeply than any other essence.

This Soul Role will always take care to behave in a manner he deems honest and honorable. Yet the Warrior also places high value on obedience and loyalty to his master. He works actively for the interests of others. He fights happily for »widows and orphans«, as well as for justice and against injustice. He fights for more order, more knowledge, more truth, a greater overview. But he must take care not to fight against something. When he fights for something, he draws on his deepest strength. But when he fights against something, this strength is stripped from him. The Warrior is the most energetic and vital of all the seven Soul Roles. With the term »energetic« we mean not only energetic in action and deeds and endowed with strong willpower, but also intense and empowered. He enjoys enormous body vitality.

Often he'll be governed by inner warfare. For if he can find no reason to fight for or against something in the external world, he'll wage a battle within himself and cause internal conflicts in order to have something on which he can test his power so as to not lose the feeling that there is something worthwhile for which he can fight. For fight he must.

A Warrior doesn't easily become resigned. He loves victory, but if he loses a battle, he will feel deep shame. Therefore he tries to avoid defeat. He won't give up. A Warrior-soul will battle until death in order to achieve his goals, whether it be a fight for work, a relationship, his health, his faith, his freedom. Nothing is too much for him. He'll give his last drop of blood in order to achieve what he's chosen as reward for his victory.

The need for victory and the desire for victory are important themes for the Warrior. He quickly feels useless and superfluous if someone indicates that victory doesn't matter, that not everyone shares his courage and readiness to fight. He seldom understands why others behave in a contemplative, passive manner or bide their time. Why are they so little ambitious? Why don't they want what he wants? Why do they sit there, doing nothing?— It surprises him that most people find him overwhelming.

And he can't believe how anyone can act without rebelling. It's difficult for him to accept that there's unfaithfulness, treachery and resignation in the world. The resignation he does experience is always connected to subordination to an order or to a commanding officer, when they don't ask him to do the right thing or force him to do the wrong thing, out of loyalty. His loyalty demands that he remain true to whomever he has made his master. But he's also master of himself, a responsible Warrior in the jungle of life.

A Warrior soul finds it difficult to rest. For whenever he rests, new desires for victories arise, and fantasies appear before his eyes about new goals for which it pays to fight. If you take away the Warrior's pleasure in victory, you'll destroy his joy in life. A Warrior must battle, he must be victorious in order to direct his energy into the right channels. Other soul essences often fail to understand this. They wonder why a Warrior tries so hard and does so much for what could have been achieved in other, easier ways.

But a Warrior wants actively to conquer. An easy challenge is boring to him. A victory achieved without his personal involvement or contribution means nothing to him. However, a Warrior also needs a cease-fire and peace. More than others he must take care to observe periods of armistice and peace and see that he doesn't feel superfluous when the canons of life are still.

When a Warrior is resting, he must take care that he doesn't continue the battle in his dreams. A cease-fire, when he observes it, will give him new strength and show him what is worth fighting for and what isn't. The right goal is important, but he sometimes has a tendency to fight for unnecessary and superfluous interests. If he realizes that it's not the battle alone which justifies the fight, but that there are goals which are worth fighting for and others that are not, there will be much progress.

A Warrior must also learn that he doesn't have to be a lone fighter. He views himself fondly as a solitary guerrilla, for this supports his idea of honour and an honorable victory. If, however, he's enlisted in life's army, then he not only enjoys honour but also protection. The Warrior soul both fears and wishes to be alone. But when he acknowledges that others can fight on his side, he can rest more often. Or he can test his battle courage together with others in a way that he never would have been able to do alone. The Warrior can only sense his own reality in comparison to the reality of other souls, in the measure of their strength.

Since the Warrior thinks so much of his own activity, it's easy for him to force others who are less active to follow his example. He should take note of his desire for power and question whether a forced victory is really so desirable and whether it wouldn't be better, and of longer-range significance, to achieve victory through politics or persuasion. For he's is in danger of being led by his own desire for battle and victory into forgetting that violence and victories achieved through force and fear are never long-term victories but those which lead to rebellion and revolution. He can learn to convince others of his goal and thereby achieve a true victory. That is his goal. He should not forget that even in war and battle, love brings the greater fame and the higher honor.

Energy 4

The Scholar

Principle: Learning/Teaching

– Theorizing   Knowing +

The Scholar Soul Role distinguishes himself from the first to the last day of all his lives, as well as between lives, by being especially interested in learning and in gaining knowledge in order to become knowledgeable. Knowledge shoud not be confused with wisdom. A Scholar wants to pass on this knowledge to others and teach them how they, too, can gain knowledge to heal their souls and to acquire ultimate certainty.

A Scholar wishes to be acknowledged and praised for what he knows. Although he doesn't depend to such a great degree as the sage on the admiration of his fellow man and contemporaries, the Scholar does want to be listened to and respected for his insight. The Sage wants to draw his own synthesis. Details have little interest for him. A Scholar, in contrast, takes more pleasure in keeping the details of his knowledge distinctly separate and to be able to call them forth at any time. The fragmentation, analysis and observation of individual aspects of life is more important to him that the deduction.

The Scholar soul concentrates on learning. And when he's learned enough, ideally he'll find the courage to teach what he's learned. His ability to aquire knowledge depends, first of all, on encountering knowledgeable people. He must turn to them in order to learn something. This can be manifested in the broad field of science, in philosophy or the study of old languages; it may come alive in an old woman observing her rheumatism in order to find the right dosis of her pain killers; or in someone who finds out that crops are influenced by the moon cycle or in someone else who likes to take his motorbike apart. But it's also possible that the Scholar will meet a person who'll teach him something important in an entirely different, inner sphere. The Scholar as a soul essence is focused on constantly acquiring further knowledge of all aspects of existence. But one day he will find fulfillment in passing on this knowledge to others and sharing it with them. It's essential to him to first acquire knowledge in order to then become an authority.

A Scholar in essence always needs times of retreat, times of distance and time to find himself. Only then do his theories become true knowledge. This retreat, this distance, are alchemic means to transform empty theories into the gold of authentic knowledge.

It's important and meaningful for a Scholar to choose a specific area of learning or branch of study and to specialize. He wants to learn as much as possible about a particular subject, no matter what it might be. In so doing he can concentrate on a particular sector of life in order to delve into its depths. It's immaterial on which area he chooses to focus. He needs to find out as much as possible about what interests him. Only when he has conquered and assimilated as much as possible—and he's prepared to sacrifice much to achieve this—can he develop the confidence to acquire knowledge in more areas. Since he must deal with the products of other's knowledge in his own search for knowledge he easily risks accepting their ideas instead of testing them himself. His knowledge then becomes purely academic or theoretical. He must study and experiment, apply and test, otherwise his teachings will be trite and lifeless. He likes to think and to apply the results.

This Soul Role does not always specialize in areas which are generally regarded as Scholarly. A Scholar can also be a person who's interested in the sport of swimming. He'll then attempt to acquire all practical and theoretical knowledge about all facets of swimming, the technique, the history, etc. A Scholar can just as well be a teacher of needlework, who's enthusiastic about knitting and tries to learn as much as possible about knitting patterns and techniques, to experiment with them in order to pass on this practical knowledge to others. The Scholar concentrates on completeness. His world is made up of teachers and students. A Sage who did the same work would soon choose from all the knitting patterns his favourite one and would then happily talk about it's advantages. He would be less interested in the technique and more interested in the result. He would ask his students, or rather his audience, to produce a sweater that's really nice and warm.

The Scholar, in contrast, wants to command as broad, exact and as fundamental a knowledge as possible and is proud to be able to draw upon this knowledge at will. He finds fulfillment in being an authority, no matter in which area. He likes to explain. His goal is to transform empty theory into knowledge. In order to acquire this knowledge he is prepared to sacrifice a great deal. It is less difficult for him than for others to limit himself in many ways, and therefore he prefers to look at things from a certain distance, from a telescope or through a microscope and in so doing, to be disturbed as little as possible. Therefore, other people are occasionally a disruptive factor for him.

His enemies are those who ask him questions he cannot answer. His shame and contrition at an obvious lack of knowlege is almost unbearable. He fears no criticism of his person, but when it comes to his competence, he is extremely sensitive. When he is relaxed and in the loving plus pole of his essence, he can easily promise: I'll look it up in the library. But when he is in the fearful pole, he'll rather start theorizing and distorting facts to save his skin.

As a rule, and contrary to the common concept of a university professor, a Soul Role Scholar doesn't have to fear eccentricity. He possesses a practical mind and likes to experiment, test and research. The danger abates when he realizes that knowledge and theory are two separate things, when it becomes clear to him that his teaching will be happily accepted when he's filled with joy and love. When he's enthusiastic about his own teaching he'll be able to pass on this enthusiasm to others. At the same time there will always be a certain coolness about him. He is basically dispassionate. He may be an enthusiastic teacher but his enthusiasm remains reserved and distanced since fundamentally he only needs himself and some kind of object. He doesn't depend on his fellow man to share his enthusiasm, whether it be for a stamp collection or a geological study of the earth. He'll guard his enthusiasm like a quiet fire and is not inclined to fan the flames or turn it into a volcanic eruption in order to attract the world's attention.

Being dispassionate doesn't mean that the essential Scholar has no temperament or warmth. Nor does he fail to relate to his fellow man in a loving or even erotic manner, in fact quite the contrary. It simply means that it takes a Scholar a bit longer to develop trust and intimacy and that you can reach him through love when you either support or at least do not ridicule the Scholar's constant inclination to learn, to research, to find out or to collect. When the Scholar feels understood and accepted, he's a devoted, loving person, whether it be in a partnership or in a friendship.

There are exceedingly orderly, fussy, somewhat compulsive Scholars who are uneasy when everything isn't in place, when they don't have everything under control, when they can't find every card in their filing cabinet with their eyes closed. Then there are those Scholars whose papers and life are in terrible disorder but who aren't disturbed by it since this is a prerequisite for the inner order which comes about as a result of the chaos. The first type is a Scholar who isolates himself, who regards others, with their desires and wishes, as a burden, as an energy which distracts and disturbs him. This often includes family members whom he tolerates more than loves and whom he can only bear when they don't interfere in his affairs. The chaotic Scholar, in contrast, seeks contact. He thrives in discussions and conversations. The more varied, the more colourful or diverse his contacts with the world are, the clearer become his thoughts. Both, however, are united by the feeling that they are part of an endlessly long chain stretching from the past into the future which has been formed by all people who have ever learned anything worth knowing.

Every essential Scholar therefore takes his place in a row of predecessors and successors who, on a vertical level, free him from his aloofness and also often his isolation. He fondly looks back into history and discovers there his friends in the spirit and his soul relatives. He longs to uncover the core of earlier, ancient or even primeval knowledge, the secret forgotten teachings of his predecessors, in order to understand them in a newly integrated way. In so doing, he becomes a mediator of traditions and knowledge that would otherwise have been lost. The Scholar assimilates; he represents input and output of human knowledge.

Thus he represents through his interest in the past and present a continuity between the old and the new, and that is his real function among the seven Soul Roles. Through his ability not only to collect, to study, to test and to experience, but to integrate the results into the knowledge of his time and place he does his soul work. This includes valuable as well as seemingly unimportant things. A Scholar will always be fascinated in some way by the knowledge of healing, the world outlook, the arts, philosophies and fables, the music and architecture of past times. He's inspired by whatever there is to study, to learn from. Old books and witnesses to the past will stimulate and enrich him. He will integrate them in the knowledge which he himself has acquired during his present incarnation.

The Scholar's spirituality is aimed at acquiring certainty. Depending on his Soul Age, he addresses this burning desire at first at the influence and authority of those who claim to possess certainty, deity or the clergy, or his own shamanistic practices. Later he'll seek certainty that his God and a natural order exist. In a still more advanced soul age he'll look for certainty and a feeling of security in the cosmos and the universe. Finally, there will be nothing more important for him than to develop an inner certainty that something of him will remain immortal when he leaves his last body. This ultimate certainty represents the harvest of many lives and is so safely stored in his spirit that the Scholar will share it with a multitude.

A Scholar in soul essence will always be enthusiastic about ancient religious traditions and obtains stimulation as well as confirmation from the holy books of the past and from foreign peoples. Scholars are the ones who cultivate the heritage of spiritual development. They preserve, publish and translate, they gather evidence of everything which they consider important and, more than all other essences, even the Priests, they often have a sense for the hidden, the secret, the difficult-to-decipher messages in old texts, and not necessarily those of a religious character. The Scholar always needs time, quiet and the possibility to withdraw in order to assimilate and integrate the information he's received through his spirit, his body and his psyche. Therefore, he should make a point of systematically ensuring that he, even as a familiy member, reserves enough time for contemplation so as not to feel over-stimulated or overfed. Only that which has been assimilated can be passed on.

The Scholar will never be satisfied with propagating undigested or untested theories. When he acknowledges the meaning of his Soul Role for the advancement of mankind, he'll be less timid in spreading the certainties that he has won and thereby will anchor them in the minds and hearts of his fellow man.

Energy 5

The Sage

Principle: Communicating

– Talkative   Expressive +

The Sage is wise because he knows that wisdom isn't everything. The Sage is wise because much that the Scholar must take seriously, the Sage is unable to. The Sage is wise because he doesn't depend on wisdom alone. He seeks wisdom in ways which aren't easily accessible to other soul-roles. His desire is to remain in very close contact with other people because his fellow men, whoever they may be, make life comprehensible for him. The Sage learns in an interchange. His being blossoms in communication.

The Sage soul is interested in examining and discovering how the world, humanity and others close to him react to his existence. He needs an echo. No matter how modest, he doesn't like to be ignored. He always assures that he'll be noticed, whether it be through words, body contact, action or silence. Some Sages will tend to use silence or a few very well-chosen words, rather than too many, to draw attention to themselves. But the goal remains the same. They want to be noticed.

A Sage in essence likes to settle down with a cup of tea and just talk, preferably about people. The Artist's mind is more volatile, more intellectual and philosophical. The Sage's philosophy is that humans will be human and need to be accepted as such. And while the Artist is witty and sharp, the Sage is humorous. This good-natured humour is one of his most conspicuous traits.

Sages, in contrast to the the inventive Artists, specialize to a greater degree on improving upon innovations, reproducing in order to convey something new—for example, as an actor reading the work of a poet, or as a musician performing the work of a composer—and in this way to express and present himself.

They have an overview of the whole, while Scholars, in contrast, take delight in details. The Sage looks beyond the detail. He is very good at summarizing. He's driven by the need to understand and look beyond the visible. He wants to create a comprehensible and comprehensive whole from the individual elements of his experience and of life. His knowledge stems not from theory but directly from the source of his life and experience. Because of this, he often feels repulsed or betrayed by institutions of learning.

The Sage is wise enough to know that he can't recreate everything from the beginning. He therefore happily and gratefully accepts the work of other people in order to create something to his personal liking. He's happy when a poet writes a poem which he, the Sage, can recite. He considers himself fortunate to bring to life on an instrument the work of a master composer. And every conceivable thought-out idea in which he can orient himself and which he can use as a small mosaic stone in the picture of his inner reasoning, any addition to his world wisdom, will be further developed by him and will be led to a destiny which often is completely at variance from the original purpose.

This Soul Role desires to learn and profit from the experiences of mankind. How he assimilates the experiences of others depends on the individual, but communication plays the primary role. This can also be accomplished through observation, reading or through questions. The Sage will always be dissatisfied as long as he fails to understand. So, piece by piece, he'll digest whatever challenges and interests him. He wants to comprehend the world and won't rest until he's done so. He wants to penetrate all the human insight that has been gained over many centuries.

But contact and communication are not restricted to the outer world. A Sage will never be wise if he lacks contact with his innermost being. A Sage can learn much from himself when he examines and accepts his own feelings, reactions, experiences; when he observes what he has learned in this and previous lives, thereby drawing a conclusion and creating a synthesis which is valid only for him and no other. He is also a humorous observer of mankind. You can recognize a Sage by his special ability to tell jokes. His laughter is often loud and hearty. He can laugh at the world and at himself. For him, life is a comedy.

He needs interchange and seeks contact with those who have similar or different experiences, whether this be through a person, a book, through history or the present time. He seeks as much as possible to draw together all the facets that he's explored.

His desire is to express his being, his personality in a thousand different ways. He wants to express himself and he wants to impress his fellow man. It isn't the singular achievement or originality at any cost that satisfies the Sage; this is not where he seeks his salvation. Because of his experiences, the Sage has a great subconscious overview. He sees things not from a distance (like the Scholar) but certainly from above. He sees more than others because of his special ability to; he's not an analyst. He wants to create something new and wise from the fragments of his collection and his ability to comprehend allows him to create, from individual elements, a whole which he finds valid; this whole can then be presented to others as a convincing product of his perception, and merit applause.

We've already said that the Sage can only then be truly satisfied when what he produces with his ability to synthesize is noticed and honored by others. When a Sage is seized by the fear of not getting enough attention, he'll fight for it by trying especially to impress those who ignore him. He'll do everything to gain their attention and, since he's motivated by the fear of being ignored, he often happily overshoots his goal and makes sure that he's noticed, but in an unpleasant manner. That often matters little to him since he has, in any case, achieved his goal.

Sometimes you see people on the street who talk loudly, who show off at parties, who speak to themselves in public but who fail to make any real contact with other people. You're surprised when someone who is usually quiet, suddenly, in an inebriated state begins to chat as if a dam had broken. You are puzzled when a person whom you don't even know suddenly breaks loose in a flow of words which is so overpowering that one can hardly stop him. You quickly become bored by this extreme loquaciousness despite the fact that the stories you hear sometimes are very dramatic. But one senses a strange energy of fear behind the relating of the tale that makes you feel uncomfortable. This is someone who wants to draw your attention to himself but who has lost contact with his own nature. These are Sages, who, because of the pure fear of being overlooked, aren't able for a while to express what could win them recognition. They live a second-hand existence and behave in a way that gets on people's nerves because their need for communication is shallow and inexhaustible. The minus pole of this Soul Role is talkative, the plus pole expressive. When a Sage is in his plus pole, he is »a person you'll never forget«.

A Sage can be deeply sympathetic and accepting of the shortcomings of his fellow beings. He also easily forgives himself for not being perfect. That is one aspect of his wisdom. He's able to use his communicative talents wisely in order to foster real communication between himself and others. He's a good listener, deeply interested in what you have to say, he can summarize and express well what he's understood within himself as resonance. His preferred means of expression are words and he uses them to create a link between himself and the world. But his ability to express can also be employed in other areas. He can satisfactorily use it in a focused and impressive way and communicate a synthesis of his knowledge just as well through painting, medicine, architecture, psychotherapy, music, acting, or through management activities. Usually he'll prefer professions or activities which allow him a direct, communication-oriented means of expression. You'll find Sages on every stage, in many government offices and in all political parties and as cashiers in supermarkets. And, since a Sage loves to bring people together, he's usually considered a pleasant, well-liked conversational partner, guest or host. His need for recognition and acknowledgement will be directly fulfilled when he follows his urge to create ties between people, no matter who they may be. He's often a good speaker and a stylist of expression, because he loves words. He knows that every word matters. He gives off an aura of trusting kindness as long as he avoids using too many shallow words. When he notices himself getting too talkative, he should ask himself: What am I afraid of—at this very moment?

His spirituality is based on a direct personal experience of the Godly and a direct communciation with the higher sphere. It is his heartfelt desire to establish a dialogue with his inner voice or with the forms of expression of inspired love which he senses through communciation with other beings.

But he always makes it something very much his own. Dogmas, traditions or written rules mean little to him, his own immediate experience is everything.

The Soul Role of the Sage makes its contribution to the great whole by directly expressing what others study, feel or postulate, what they fight for or find true. He differs from the Artist in that he develops his means of expression in close contact with other people and the world. His ability to communicate also creates ties between representatives of other Soul Roles. He is a bridge-builder. The insights and wisdom which he gains from his direct experience and which he communicates are an enrichment for all.

Energy 6

The Priest

Principle: Consoling

— Overzealous   Compassionate +

The Priest is a Soul Role who experiences what isn't present, tangible, or real in the graphic sense. But it is indeed present in his perceptions and in his ideals. He feels himself the agent of godly grace, of a godlike sympathy, of cosmic compassion. The Priest always wants to be where he isn't: in the higher, better and purer realms. And he also wants to help others realize that—out there, up there—is a purer, better, higher realm.

The Priest wants to serve a higher ideal but he also has a great desire to convey to others what he feels for this ideal by consoling, cheering, sympathizing and counselling them. He wants to help by advising. He wants to help create clarity by explaining even the mysteries of religion. It would be erroneous, however, to assume that his explanations must always encompass spiritual or religious subjects. Quite the contrary: a Priest-soul can also be active in providing a clarifying conception in political subjects, in environmental affairs, as a proponent of a certain life-style, as a promoter of a certain form of nutrition.

No matter where the Priest sees his ideal he seeks to promote it and is all too often convinced that his conception is the only valid one. This is the problem of the Priest-essence. He views those who don't share his ideal with a certain disdain. He thinks he owns the truth and nothing but the truth.

Tolerance is not his strong point, although it could be. As a rule, Priests, especially those of the Child, Young or Mature Soul-Cycles, are to a certain degree intolerant of other views and other ideals. The Priest often fails in his desire to convince others of his longings and truths. And then he feels helpless and alone. Loneliness very often leads to fear. And when a Priest feels fear, he will do everything—occasionally even to the extent of using force—to convince others of his viewpoint. He will act zealously and prosetylize, and it's immaterial which subject he chooses. But it will always be his own ideal, his conception of something which ought to be more beautiful, greater and better.

A soul in the Role of a Priest is by no means always a Priest in the religious or professional sense. But more often than other Soul Roles, he chooses a profession which has priestly functions.

The Priest wants to console. He does this exceptionally well when he finds someone who has lost their faith or contact to God and who, nevertheless, is searching for a higher truth which he senses deep inside but can't comprehend. That's the reason why in your time there are many priests in the field of esoterics, counseling, psychology, psychiatry as well as among those who are proponents of people sleeping on patent mattresses or in rooms free of disturbance. Most of those seeking to improve the world and the over-zealous happiness-makers are priests in essence. You will recognize them if you are aware that the ideals of the priest-role do not necessarily have to be in religious, godly or cosmic spheres, but also in small and mundane areas.

A Priest doesn't have to be a social worker or a pastor. More often he doesn't feel comfortable in activities dealing with church institutions and their dogmas. In former lives he has seen too much of that! On the contrary, the Priest-soul has such an obvious tie to his personal truth that he often, in great disappointment, realizes that established religions don't represent the truth as has been revealed to him. More so than other essences, he distances himself from the established faiths and attempts to find contact to the higher realm within himself. As a rule, the Priest has lived many lives in which he carried out the most varied priestly functions. He may have been a Shaman, he could have been in a Buddhist monastery, or he could have been a nun or monk in the Christian faith. He could also have been someone who only served on the fringes of these confessions, such as a temple servant, a sexton, a temple-builder, or someone who, following services, cleaned and cared for the church. The Priest feels happiest of all in magical or sanctified rooms or places. During his travels he'll always feel drawn to old temples, cult sites or areas which have a magical resonance. He's especially sensitive to sacred vibrations and it is almost normal for him to feel part of two dimensions, just as he has two legs, one of which stands on the earth and the other steps upward to a higher dimension.

The Priest's relationship to religion is always a little unusual. More than all other Soul Roles he repeatedly chooses in his many lifetimes professions which bring him into contact with the schools of faith around him.

But Priests can be found everywhere, there is no place on your earth where compassion and consolation are not needed. The Priest's Soul Role differs from that of the Healer in that he is less actively involved in helping, but rather stands ever ready to listen, sympathize and advise.

The Priest isn't unhappy when he suffers. Here there lies a great danger which can stop him from fulfilling his positive development. The Priest doesn't suffer like a martyr sacrificing himself, but as one who is prepared to bear the suffering of others. He easily confuses compassion with suffering. Suffering in the place of someone else is a form of love that has little to do with compassion. When a person is suffering and the Priest feels a need to share this suffering, the only thing that results is that two people are suffering. But when he discovers how healing true compassion can be, it's much more likely that soon no one is suffering anymore. The Priest must take care, therefore, that he doesn't identify too deeply with those he wishes to assist and counsel. He isn't called upon to make everyone's suffering his own or to take the world's suffering upon his shoulders. But the Priest is often in danger of doing this. He does it when he fears that he cannot face his God unless he makes himself a sufferer, because he has been told that suffering is the key to heaven. This attitude is found not only among Christians, but in almost all world religions.

If a Priest wants to live his positive pole which is compassion, in complete love he must avoid coming psychologically or physically too close to those whom he wishes to help, otherwise he can no longer differentiate between himself and those in need but falls into a state of symbiosis. Love requires a distance that allows one to really see others. One of the greatest problems of all Priest-souls is setting limits, since essentially they are those who transcend limits, especially between the human and the Godly.

The Priest has difficulty feeling comfortable and secure in the material world. He regards money as a necessary evil. He fears a descent into the banal, the unspiritual, when he feels it necessary to earn his living without being able to help and console anyone or to promote his ideals. If he has to work on an assembly-line or do another activity which hinders his contact with other people, he'll be unhappy unless, at least during his free time, he's sought out by friends, colleagues or relatives who are in need and whom he can comfort and to whom he can give loving advice.

People with a Priest-essence are often very severe with themselves. They strive for the highest ethical ideal. They relentlessly evaluate their morality both in the inner and worldly sense. Because it's important for them always to be in the right, they become dogmatic and and over-eager. Their readiness to confront their own mistakes with more indulgence must be developed. Therefore, it's of special importance for Priest-souls to show mercy toward themselves. Only then can they be truly merciful towards others.

Confusion, a feeling very familiar to Priest-souls, is often covered-up. It's painful for him to find in retrospect that his ideas and goals were not as fine or noble as he would have wished. He feels under attack from others, and fears any type of criticism, since human errors and mistakes fundamentally seem to threaten his pure relationship to the perfect deity. In order to avoid this, he prefers to put other people into question and, in so doing, enforces his own truth on them, no matter how incomplete. The greater his fear that his ideals find no resonance, the more he'll over-zealously prosetylize his knowledge and his goals. For it's all the same to him if he is convincing someone of the great idea of atheism or communism or fundamentalism, as long as he himself believes it to be the ultimate truth.

Priests often don't even notice that they are telling small or big lies, because it is difficult for them to admit even to themselves that they don't live up to their own exaggerated idea of holy truthfulness.

A Priest begins to learn compassion when he really starts to empathize with the needs of himself and others, to understand how others feel when they're stripped of their own beliefs when he acts as a missionary and are forced to adopt truths not their own.

Compassion is also called for in regard to very earthly, purely corporeal needs which Priest-souls would preferably disregard purely because of ideological reasons. Included among these are the basic needs of food, protection, sexuality, comfort and material well-being. The Priest-essence regards sexuality as especially suspect since it belongs to what he views as the lower instincts. He needs it but doesn't want to need it. It would be of great significance and spiritual worth for Priests to respect the body, to care for it and to satisfy it. Enjoying sex as well as delicious food binds the Priest-energy to the body and, although the Priest would like to deny this or to find it unspiritual, it does him good. Because he's a dreamer of the otherworld he needs to be grounded more than the rest of the Soul Roles. When a Priest, out of a sense of idealistic pretensions, tries to limit or suppress his sexuality or other lustful areas of his life, he distances himself from humanity and, correspondingly, from the plus-pole of compassion.

The Priest is a Soul Role which is simultaneously oriented above and below, towards heaven and earth. The ties to the material world are problematic for this soul during any incarnation. But the Priest should make sure he is well-grounded because he otherwise easily risks becoming a religious fanatic or a fanatic in all areas. This fanaticism is a part of the manifestation of his archetypical fears. He can easily become arrogant and aloof since he's always convinced that he alone knows the truth.

If you observe someone who pursues his goals with great zeal and often shows arrogance instead of tolerance, then you can be assured that this is an eager Priest who'll do everything to achieve his own aims and will show little compassion toward those who represent different beliefs. Then you can lead him back to his love pole of priestly energy if you appeal to his compassion and, in a tender way, make clear that he doesn't need to fear not being heard or noticed when others don't share his subjective truth. And you'll also be able to recognize a Priest when you feel a particular kind of comfort and relaxation, trust, understanding and acceptance of your being in his presence. The Priest, when he's acting with love, is a good listener; he will keep your secrets; he gives good advice and compassion and has a comforting, uplifting and healing influence.

Energy 7

The King

Principle: Leading

– Tyrannical   Dignified +

There aren't many who have the Soul Role of the King. Many people need good leadership, few are needed to be in leading positions. Therefore, you'll not often meet a person who could be identified as a King. But when you do, you'll recognize him more quickly than other Soul Roles and your relationship to him will be clearer than with other roles.

This is because a King has a peaceful, dignified, imposing and commanding presence independent of whichever temperament or MATRIX he has chosen for a particular life. A King fills a room whether he wants to or not. He doesn't have to do anything in order to draw attention to himself; he may not like it, but he's a person who can't easily be overlooked. The King soul tends to choose a physical stature in most, if not all, incarnations exceeding the higher ends of the norm. Only seldom does there appear a small person with a King's Soul Role. But even in such a case, people are surprised by how impressive and imposing he or she is.

A King need not speak or act in order to be noticed. He appears majestic regardless of his physical stature. But when he does speak or act, he'll easily earn the respect and attention of those around him. Something like a court or following naturally arises around him without him even having to raise his voice. A King who screams in order to be noticed is assuredly not in his Soul Essence a King. As a rule, when they don't become tyrants in their families or firms, Kings are generally beloved. They are admired and can sun themselves in this affection to an extent that other essences seldom experience. This is like a reward for the constant exposure and great responsibility which they're constantly prepared to assume. Their authority and dignity will be recognized without them having to do anything special to earn it.

There are so few Kings because among the soul essences no one else is as prepared as the King soul is to take on that much responsibility in each life as a matter of course. Responsibility is the key word for the role of a King. As you know, every person, of course, bears responsiblity for himself and also for others. Every single incarnated soul has its own lessons to learn regarding the theme of responsibility. But the King makes responsibility his basic theme not only in all his incarnations but also in the social duties which he fulfills throughout all his lives as a matter of course. This, too, places a certain burden on him.

The King rules best when he's not tyrannical but when he takes the advice of clever advisors in order to rule his Kingdom. Therefore a King in practical, everyday life is a figure who is very seldom alone. On the contrary, he tends to be someone who finds it difficult to find a minimum of solitude. He may feel lonely in a crowd, but that is another question. He'll always be surrounded by people who compete for his attention as well as by advisers, upon whom he depends for counsel, who are so devoted that they find it unpleasant to be far from him. People like to be courtiers to a King.

He needs good friends and will find them in every life if he isn't too tyrannical. He will remind other people of their own dignity. A King, however, is also someone who knows how to combat true enmity in a dignified way. He's aware of his role, his calling, functions and duties in a way that has nothing to do with his personal degree of self-confidence. When a King acts with love, he rules even a small realm (like an office or a shop or a petrol station) justly and wisely without forcing his rule on his subjects, but he's also to such an extent cognizant of his duties as King that he won't delegate to his people decisions they're incapable of making. A King in essence is like a good father who allows his sons and daughters great freedom in their development but doesn't send them out into life without orientation or guidance. He sets limits which ensue from his own experiences and enforces rules and laws—not as if they were God-ordained.

Only seldom does a human with a King's Soul Role on your planet actually assume a throne. That is an exception. The few Kings hardly have an opportunity in more than a handful of lives to assume political positions of power which would best fulfill their essential needs. This also means that King souls are required and disposed to manifest themselves in all activities, professions and functions where even only a semblance of responsibililty, power, control, influence or model is required. You will find Kings as bank presidents, intensive care nurses or mothers of eight.

A King will often feel inclined to choose a life in which he can, incognito or in disguise, gather the experience he needs in order to rule in a wise and just way. For a King who knows nothing about the life of his people can never exercise his rule justly and respond to the needs of his subjects. If a King dons other costumes, for instance, that of a Warrior, whom he would normally command, or to study the life of a Helper/Healer in order to find out how someone feels who serves rather than rules, how someone feels when they have no power at all to make decisions, or when he joins the ranks of his priests, he'll fulfill his self-chosen place with great dedication and responsiblity. And you'll then sense that the King, no matter which profession he pursues or which position he has assumed in life, will always radiate an inimitable dignity and even, as a half-starving beggar under the bridge, still remain an imposing figure of authority whose presence one doesn't forget.

Will-power is a dominant trait in all soul Kings. He gets what he wants and doesn't even notice that this is exceptional. If a King becomes fearful of his dominion or his right to rule, he easily succumbs to the temptation to turn his authority into tyranny. If he fears that he's not being listened to and that his power and dignity aren't recognized, he will insist that notice is taken of him. Then he will do everything possible, even unjustly or cruelly, in order to impose his wishes. His fear makes him self-righteous and deceives him into believing that he's right in every matter, thus preventing him from listening to the reasoning of others or taking their needs into consideration. He's so convinced of his basic inborn right to be as he is and to do what he wants that he can no longer budge from this position. When he fails to receive constant recognition from others, he's forced to provide himself with confirmation and admiration. Since he's accustomed to being exalted by his subjects, he can hardly renounce this. He loves to exude a certain grandeur. If he fears not being given attention to the extent he needs, his authoritative radiance is transformed into a tyranny which promises to give him everything that he believes due him. He gives off airs and parades before his rebellious knights without noticing that he has lost contact with them. Often he becomes pompous. In his fearful isolation he ruffles his feathers like the sun-king, makes decisions without consulting his advisers and avoids all communication which might put his authority into question and pose a threat to his rule of tyranny. Such behavior presents problems for people dealing with this Soul Role. They sense that the King can no longer be reached when he's isolated by fear. They have to give him time until he feels the desire to reestablish contact in order to replace his tyranny with the magnificence of a true, loving, enriching union.

Kings prefer to be in positions where they can rule and command—a general, a conductor, a head of department, an abbot, a film director, the head of a political party, a police chief. The don't like positions where they have to report and obey.

It's obvious that when a King feels threatened with revolt, he'll fight for his throne and realm. And if, on the basis of his individual soul history, he feels predisposed to abdicate, then he's a figure of special greatness. He voluntarily renounces sovereign authority and tyranny and will temporarily move in spheres where voluntary renunciation is regarded as a reward. A King in exile gathers his strength and his friends in order to eventually again justly administer his duties and resume his responsibilities in human society.

When a King reaches the cycle of a Mature Soul or surpasses it, he'll sometimes leave a deep impression in the history of humanity since so many will then belong to his kingdom that it will hardly be possible to count them. And he'll sometimes lead large groups of people, he'll bring about powerful movements, or may, with preference, become a famous philosopher or political leader in order to teach others who feel drawn to him and his majesty all that he has gained from his numerous travels in the many realms of existence.

Chief Characteristics of Fear

⑤
Greed
Fear of Privation

– insatiable   + demanding

②
Self–Sabotage
Fear of Joyfulness

– self–destructive + self-sacrificing

Expression Level

⑥
Arrogance
Fear of Vulnerability

– vain   + proud

①
Self-Deprecation
Fear of Inadequacy

– self-abasing   + modest

Inspiration Level

⑦
Impatience
Fear of Omission

– intolerant   + audacious

③
Martyrdom
Fear of Worthlessness

– victimizing   + selfless

Action Level

④
Stubbornness
Fear of Unpredictability

– obstinate   + resolute

Assimilation Level

II The Seven Chief Characteristics of Fear

Each of you has fears. They live with you and every day you are directed and guided by them. A life without fears is something you often desire. It appears to you tantamount to paradise. But when we speak about the Chief Characteristic of Fear, we don't mean common fears. For the Chief Characteristic of Fear is part of the soul pattern and therefore an important, indispensable factor of your soul development. No one can live without it.

Don't insist that this basic fear must eventually disappear. The desire for a life free of fears is understandable, but as long as a soul resides in a body, you won't be able to exist without fear. And some fearful memories will even be carried over into another life. They maintain their energy in the astral world. Fear loses its function for growth only after the energetic reunion of the Soul Family and the transfer into the causal world of consciousness.

Why do we assert that humans need fear as part of their soul pattern, of their MATRIX? To cope with the reality of fear is part of the human condition. It is a condition which encompasses not only spirit, soul, psyche but also body. A fundamental characteristic of mankind is its mammal body which just like that of apes has to find means of survival on a planet ruled by physical dangers. Humans (primates endowed with reason and a specific soul type), are constantly afraid and must be afraid of not being able to cope; not being able to relax and feel joy; of losing the esteem of their society, of being destroyed by unpredictable events like natural catastrophes, of being hungry and thirsty, of losing their life through extreme vulnerabiliy, of missing important opportunities and making wrong decisions. All these are basic, ever present, challenging and at times life-threatening realities. But to experience them intensely all at once during the course of a single life-time would be too stressful for the human psyche and for the body that contains it. That is why the soul pattern offers the opportunity to experience in depth one of the seven basic fears—in detail and in a more sublimated form. The chief characteristic is part of each and every soul MATRIX, and constitutes the motor of your inner growth processes.

The seven Chief Characteristics of Fear are: SELF-DEPRECATION (1), SELF-SABOTAGE (2), MARTYRDOM (3), STUBBORNESS (4), GREED (5), ARROGANCE (6) and IMPATIENCE (7). Like masks they conceal the corresponding seven basic fears: fear of inadequacy (1), joyfulness (2), worthlessness (3), unpredictability (4) privation (5), vulnerability (6), or of missing an opportunity (7). Everybody is more or less familiar with these basic fears and mostly aware of them. But whoever has chosen one of these fears as his Chief Characteristic, an integral part of his soul pattern, experiences this basic fear as the dominant one. At the same time it is the least obvious and the least conscious one. This means that one will be ruled by it, that this fear has taken root in the unconscious.

Every Chief Fear has two poles. As in all other archetypes of the soul, there is a minus and a plus pole, but these poles differ from other polarizations of the MATRIX in that both poles are determined by fear. Thus the plus pole should in no way be viewed as a virtue or as positive in a moral sense. The plus pole of each Chief Characteristic is marked by a mask of strength and friendliness. As a rule it is considered a virtue by the bearer (e.g. modesty, selflessness, resoluteness, audaciousness) and will also be regarded by many others as a virtue. We would like to strongly stress, however, that herer—as an expression of the Chief Fear—the plus poles, e.g. modesty, or pride, are false virtues since virtues can never be rooted in fear. Virtue in the truest sense is an expression of love.

The minus pole, on the other hand, is easiy to recognize by an observer of the Chief Characteristic. Each of you can identify the forms of other people's fears. They hurt you and make you angry. Only in regard to yourself will you find it difficult to identify those very familiar and seemingly natural character traits, which are an expression of your basic fear, a manifestation of your Chief Characteristic. But once your attention has been drawn to your own archetype of fear and you can name it, it will be less difficult.

Before an incarnation, the soul chooses its Chief Characteristic of Fear in order to feel itself through the friction with the Chief Characteristics of all fellow-men. Fear in this respect is not at all superfluous—on the contrary, it is essential to physical condition and human life. And each observation of this root of fear and its manifestations increases your own humanity. It will fail to help you grow only if you allow it to linger completely in the darkness of the unconscious. But even if it does, that makes you human, because growth in consciousness isn't everything.

When a soul prepares for its impending incarnation, it selects one of the Chief Characteristics to deal with within the framework of its soul pattern. It chooses its parents as well as the conditions of its bodily existence as far as possible on the basis of how this fear and the tension created by it can be brought about—with the corresponding generation of growth-inducing friction.

The fixation of the Chief Characteristic is a fluid occurence. It cannot be determined chronologically. There are fixations which are already established in the early embryonic stage, traumatic experiences which the unborn child perceives and which are ulitized in the shaping of its fear. Many other fixations can only be observed in the second year of life. However, they are usually already prepared for psychologically before a severe trauma provides the final structure and strength of the Chief Characteristic.

It may take only a few or even many years before a Chief Characteristic is manifested in its definite form. But the essential development of the Chief Characteristic is concluded between the 16th and 25th year of life. Then there follows a plateau phase. The chief characteristic is perceived as character. Only in mid-life, when there's a chance of individuation and growth in the psychological sense, can one begin the descent from the plateau of the fixated fear and weaken its poles. Slowly the hardest traits of the character mask fade away. But since this kind of basic fear is needed for life-long learning and essential experience during an incarnation, it will never completely disappear.

The chosen basic fear as an indispensable part of the MATRIX can be compared to the root of a huge tree. All other »normal« little fears or worries form its branches and boughs. And just as the roots of a tree gen-erally are not visible to you, so is your basic fear to a large extent invisible and thus at first inaccessible to your consciousness. However, these basic fears with their Chief Characteristics are the decisive motors of each person's behavior and reactions, even though they are not conscious of it.

Our comments on the hidden deepest roots of your fear-structure are therefore intended to help you find access to your most secret motives and to lose the fear of fear.

Whenever you deal with the manifestations and effects of your chief fear, you take a big step forward on the path to your liberation. The Chief Characteristic is like a signal flag. It serves to provide a clue to the hidden basic fear. Or to put it another way: you can recognize the features of your basic fear in your Chief Characteristic. You'll soon see that dealing with the Chief Characteristic and the basic fear which lies beneath it will help you in a way that is beneficial not only to self-knowledge and inner clarity. It also strengthens self-love and leads you to greater love and understanding for your fellow-man. We're not telling you to love your Chief Characteristic of fear. We only recommend that you pay attention to its existence, acknowledge it and observe its consequences.

Fear forms a shell around your ability to love. If you want to gradually break through this shell, it's good to proceed cautiously in order to expose the core of the matter. We indicated that life circumstances and parents play a part in the fixation of the chief fear. But neither your parents nor life are to be blamed for presenting the necessary tension, friction and indispensable challenges the child needs for the development of its chief fear.

We avoid any judgement and you should do the same. No Chief Characteristic is worse than any other, none is better or easier to bear. Each of you carries a heavy but necessary burden in your own Chief Characteristic. But although it is comparatively easy to accept the general fact that others also have fears, the actual effects of other people's Chief Characteristics disturb you very much. This is why you often demand of others something that isn't possible for yourself: namely, that they renounce their chief fears or forgo their manifestations as a favour to you. Of course, you are just as unaware of the scope of your fellow-man's basic fear for his soul's welfare as you are of the deep and significant roots of your own false virtues. Therefore many of you will, through the spiritual or religious traditions of your society and through your own self-image, try to cast them in a pleasant aura; for none of you happily views his fear in a harsh light.

But it is no accident that a number of the chief fears which we've described resemble the seven vices or chief sins of the Christian tradition. Other religions have similar lists, although only seldom will priests mention that sins and vices are reflections of fear. They condemn the sinners and don't realize that they are thereby strengthening their fear and in such a way doing exactly what they were trying to avoid. They punish the sinner and therefore increase his misery. Recognition, understanding, observance and acceptance of the Chief Fear and its manifestations will significantly help everyone to no longer be ruled completely by fear any more than is necessary for the development of their soul.

In dealing with your Chief Characteristic, we advise you not to fight against it. Either it it will react with increased strength or retreat even deeper into the psychological underground, which is not beneficial. But experience shows that the Chief Characteristic does not like to be observed. The less you condemn the consequences of your fear, the less you despise and punish the mask of the Chief Characteristic and the fear it is hiding, the more it will gently melt like a glacier in the summer sun.

It is in no way a necessary requirement of being human or of an individual incarnation to conquer one's chief fear. Even if fear in the guise of stubbornness, vulnerability or impatience increases during the years, each life has its own worth.

If a person develops the possibility and impulse in the middle of his life to move further from his Chief Characteristic, to discard the mask and gain more authenticity by reducing his fear, this is one of many options. But certainly and truly it is not the only possibility. Each life is to the same degree meaningful and worthwhile even if this kind of individuation doesn't take place. Otherwise the life of an Infant Soul, a Child Soul or a Young Soul, most of whom never sense the desire to practice introspection, to turn inwards and think over their lives, or to test and recognize their fears, would be completely futile. This isn't the case. This can't be the case. Because it does not make sense to the AllOne to create meaninglessness.

The Chief Characteristic fixates itself, according to each individual case, as soon as possible in a young life. Then, layer by layer, events occur to secure this fixation so that to the individual mind existence appears to take shape following a definite pattern. Certain situations occur again and again. More and more, life is seen only through the eyeglasses of your Chief Characteristic.

But it can happen one day that a person drops his glasses on the floor and they break. Then he has to cope for a while until new glasses are made. To his amazement he then can often see more definitively and clearly than before, since many people are unaware that they wear glasses which don't suit their eyesight. This is also the case when viewing life through the old glasses, sometimes inheritied from the father or mother, of the Chief Characteristic. If one's fear-glasses break (this often happens because of a further traumatic event), then it is suddenly quite easy for a person with the appropriate disposition to glimpse new perspectives. One can now ask what really caused the glasses to fall and break.

But many people wear their thick glasses of fear without even noticing them. Throughout their whole life they remain undisturbed by them, although they might possibly see better and look better with thinner glasses or no glasses at all. Now remember, there's no reason to condemn them for this. Each life has its own individual meaning. And even a Mature or Old Soul has the right and the possibility to remain on the plateau of any fearful fixation.

But most Old Souls, just like late Mature Souls, are imprinted with the sense that the history of their lives is slowly coming to a conclusion. Their longing for a disembodied existence becomes ever stronger. Realization of the relativity of time and space also increases. Despite the fact that there is a certain urgency on the conscious level, it's apparent on other levels of awareness that each soul has enough time to explore bodily existence with all its aspects of fear and love and to develop as is deemed necessary—in all areas.

The Secondary Characteristics of Fear

We've said that the Chief Characteristic is the root system and trunk of your tree of fear. The many minus poles of the various other elements of the MATRIX form the smaller branches and leaves. The main branches, however, consist of the so-called Secondary Characteristic and its poles. You also choose your Secondary Characteristic from the group of seven basic fears. This secondary characteristic of your fear, which is joined to the chief characteristic, has—just as the Chief Fear—significant functions. The first and most important function of the Secondary Characteristic is to cover areas of sexual love, relationship, dealing with family members. These are areas which really only come into play in adulthood and which you will have to cope with as you advance in years.

The primary function of the Secondary Characteristic can be described as the psychological necessity to draw the few remaining fear-free areas into the domain of fear. This sounds like an absurdity or even cynical. However humans usually don't feel well when they aren't allowed to have a little fear. If in general, your attitude is impatient (with others, with yourself, with life as such), your soul can combine this with the Secondary feature of arrogance, or stubbornness, or greed etc., and the result will be very different. Or you can combine your Chief Characteristic of Self-Deprecation with Stubbornness, Greed, Arrogance, Impatience, Self-Sabotage or Martyrdom. Any combination out of seven is possible, but not twice the same.

Your fear structure as it presents itself in this life has been created during many thousands of years. You have had the same Chief Features and Secondary Features in various epochs, circumstances and combined with different MATRICES several times before during your incarnation cycle. Thus you can draw upon ample experience. And there is yet another factor perpetuating fear. We'll give you an example: Most of you grew up in family circumstances and social traditions in which worries of the parents for their child were more important than their love for this child. Instead of offering love, many parents adopt a behaviour of concern. They believe that the more concerned they are, the more they show love. But »to be concerned« about a child means to surround the child with fear. As you become adults, you assume this attitude, too, and start worrying about your own children and your aged parents. And to you this seems to be an expression of love for them. However we tell you: this is nothing but an expression of your fear.

In whatever way this Secondary Fear is expressed, whether in stubborness or greed, in arrogance or martyrdom, you'll recognize that it will especially come into play when you observe your attitude toward life as determined in your MATRIX, whether it be idealistic, realistic, spiritual or cynical. All these Mentalities will be marked by your Secondary Characteristic. For example, you can cynically dismiss your concern about your elderly mother although she obviously needs you, or you can selflessly sacrifice yourself for her even though so much selflessness is required neither by your mother nor by life itself.

What we've said can be applied to all areas of fear, to all seven Characteristics which form the composition of your personal pattern of fear or fear-tree. The Secondary Characteristic has the additional function of taking over in case you transcend your Chief Characteristic during the course of your life, for example after you are permanently enlightened. It happens, although very rarely, that you reach a certain point while observing the Chief Characteristic in which the fear bursts open like an ulcer, pours out threatening to poison your whole life, and then heals. When the Chief Characteristic is healed—and this occurs usually in connection with a clearly recognizable cause—the Secondary Characteristic takes over the original functions of the Chief Characteristic and allows you to continue living within a human society which has made fear its ruler. However, the Secondary Characteristic will never practise the tyranny which the Chief Characteristic had over you.

The Secondary Characteristic is always weaker than the Chief Characteristic. Their relationship is approximately 70 % : 30 %. It appears where there are possibilities of great intimacy, of interference, especially in matters concerning the family, partnership and friendship. When human relationships present possibilities of a special closeness and a special fear of closeness arises, the Secondary Feature comes into action. Its other function, therefore, is the regulation of closeness and distance.

Closeness is always an indicator that the Secondary Fear may exert its power, as closeness makes you vulnerable in a special way. When you feel fear coming up, you could ask yourself: who has come very close or too close to me or to whom would I like to become closer? The Chief Characteristic is valid in many aspects of life in which other people only play an indirect role. In contrast, the Secondary Fear takes effect when someone comes close to you—or as you often feel it—too close. Should you feel crowded, under pressure or vulnerable to an extent that your fear is no longer able to bear this closeness, you become anxious. You feel like destroying this closeness by becoming impatient or arrogant or stubborn or greedy for more. In general you lose the control which is so important to you if closeness becomes overwhelming. Your relationship to human nearness, to an intimacy which we view as part of true love, marks your attitude.

The Chief Characteristic, the Secondary Characteristic and the minus poles of all other MATRIX elements together provide the structure of fear of every living soul. Both characteristics are chosen between lives. The soul needs to experiment with basic fears in order to understand more what it means to have the body of an human and to create a contrast to the kind of love reigning in the astral spheres. The circumstances of the individual incarnation are planned so that the basic fears can become fixated in early childhood through various major or minor traumatic situations.

Energy I

Self-Deprecation

Fear of Inadequacy

– Self-abasing   Modest +

This is the fear of incapability and inadequacy. It is a fear which is expressed in Self-Deprecation. One can recognize it easily when someone is especially diligent and ambitious, when this person does considerably more than others at his job and yet remains modestly in the background; but also in someone who displays his self-confidence and extreme competence especially prominently and constantly must prove himself. Or it is seen in persons who cannot bear to be praised for anything good or competent they have done.

It is a fear with the characteristic of the basic energy I. It is therefore also the archetypical fear of the Helper/Healer's soul role. The Healer as an archetype represents the mild, unobtrusive Helper, always ready to be of service, never insisting on gratitude, a warmhearted modest figure in the background, always feeling the need of others, completely oblivious of his or her own need. Self-Deprecation is the fearful reverse of that good-natured selfobliviousness. It shows false modesty and tends to take pleasure in showing the world the incompetent (or over-competent) side of one's character. Another sign of Self-Deprecation is found in those who put you on a pedestal and at the same time belittle themselves.

Self-Deprecation denies one's own needs and stresses those of others. The person generally appears to be one who is widely accepted by those around him, is often considered to be very pleasant since he doesn't create any problems, and always smiles modestly. Even those who sense his fear don't suspect at the beginning anything disturbing or distancing about the person.

Self-Deprecation, namely the fear of not being able to achieve or the fear of being incapable, expresses itself in various pleasant, modest, set phrases. You all know them: »Oh, no, I don't dare attempt that.—Ah, you're so much better at this thing than I am.—That doesn't suit me, I'm not good enough. Sorry, but I better not even attempt to do that, I might make mistakes.—I know nothing about that! But you know much, much better than me.—Excuse me, may I bother you?—How did I deserve such praise, so much happiness?!«

In contrast, whoever unconsciously supresses this fear of inadequacy, often thinks: »I can do anything I want to. I'll show you. I won't make any mistake ever. When I strive for perfection, I'll be more appreciated.«

A person who hides his own needs and feelings, especially his abilities, from himself and others understands to a great degree how to inspire a feeling of competence and greatness in people around him. Since he happily stays in the background and makes himself inconspicuous, everyone around him appears greater and more significant. As long as his fear isn't realized as such, this makes him a person approved by those who feel immediately bigger, better and stronger in his company.

The person who's plagued by the fear of not being acceptable or not being competent, intelligent or capable enough makes sure that he seldom encounters situations in which he'll feel challenged. Even the slightest challenge like a school exam is enough to convey a feeling of inadequacy in him. It causes deep anxiety. Then he will diligently apply himself, sometimes to an extreme extent, but in doing so he'll consistently remain self-effacing.

But this is not true modesty. It is a false modesty, a fearful attitude of humility, a self-abasement which is intended to quell his fear. Everyone else seems always better, more courageous, stronger than him. They are healthier, they're further along on their spiritual path, more beautiful, cleverer or of a better family and educational background. And these attributes to others will be packaged in the set phrases we've already mentioned.

Those rooted in the Christian faith will have a very easy time with this Chief Characteristic of Fear. For modesty, be it true or false, is regarded as a great virtue and gives them a general framework in which they can house their fear. But also many people who move in esoteric circles or who have set out on a spiritual path happily misuse the new knowledge and meditation techniques in order to maintain a low profile and feel unimportant. There's the great cosmos, there are all those enlightened people and those who are much further along than one's self. They, therefore, have the possibility—in view of the enormous breadth and depth of the spiritual dimension—to feel very small, very new and very unknowledgeable. Or else, they can take refuge in the notion that humans are just a speck of dust compared with the universe, or that all life is Maya and their own existence of no reality and consequence at all.

The fear of inadequacy can express itself in a threatening manner if a person who doesn't have much self-confidence is placed in a position of professional rivalry or must pass a test. A person with the Chief Characteristic of Self-Deprecation will torture himself until he feels completely stupid and incapable. Because of this alone he easily comes up short since he doesn't believe in himself. And when he must take a test, he convinces himself so thoroughly that he doesn't know anything, hasn't learned enough, has forgotten everything, won't be able to open his mouth and wouldn't be taken seriously anyway, that he influences the test correspondingly. Or, if he isn't aware of his fear at all, he will, because of insecurity, study so long and so thoroughly that in the end he'll know three times more than was necessary for the test and feel completely empty and exhausted as a consequence of all this energy-consuming and unnecessary effort. And he'll be bittlery disappointed that nobody even noticed how much he knew.

False modesty usually is expressed in either perfectionism or self-debasement. A self-deprecator may want to explore the many possibilities that a person has to compare himself to others and to manoeuver himself into a position in which he can either significantly lessen or increase his competence. But since modesty and humility are highly valued in society, he happily identifies himself with these attributes He is proud of them and feels confirmed by the fact that others aren't much bothered by his fear but—quite the opposite—appear to be uplifted and made happy by it.

The person with the fear of Self-Deprecation and a constant feeling of inadequacy will need a great deal of courage in order to recognize this fear in himself and to free himself from all the pseudo-positive judgements he experiences in society. He usually delights in deprecating his attributes, his talents, his power, his ability to love, his warmth, his good looks and his greatness, but he also denies his rage at all those who appear to be greater, better, more beautiful and more intelligent than him. For of course such people do exist. There are indeed people who, according to current criteria, have more to offer. But the person with this fear of incabability uses this actual fact as evidence of his own inferior quality.

When he's sharply criticized for any mistake he often feels some-what better, and is frequently spurred on to further great efforts. He feels reaffirmed in his incompetence if someone tells him he's incapable, incompetent, not all-knowing. Then the world is in order for him since this exactly corresponds to his secret self-conception. On the other hand, if someone talks about his qualities and compliments him, he often feels unwell and uneasy, becomes unsure and thinks that he's being mocked. In his view, there must be something wrong with those who praise him.

The person with the Chief Characteristic of Self-Deprecation will not be able to receive much confirmation from other people. What he receives is, in an inexplicable way, never enough. He'll also as a rule have to work hard in order to raise himself from the place where he has demeaned himself. For every praise, every word of encouragement from others will cause new false feelings of modesty. He'll always believe that he didn't deserve the praise given him. He must become even more perfect.

People with the fear of Self-Deprecation usually have many qualities and amazing talents. But they're afraid and ashamed of putting these qualities and these talents to the judgement of their fellow-men. As a rule there are one or more experiences in early childhood in which a small child at the peak of his self-affirmation receives a rebuff either from his parents or teacher and thereby lands in great confusion between his self-perception and the negative perception of himself by others.

Already as a child he tends towards feelings of inadequacy and prefers to compare negatively with his siblings and little friends. He does not depend on his own self-perception but rather acknowledges as correct any criticism of those who are above him. Because of this he'll trust the negative judgements of the respected persons and will always feel more confirmed in his feelings of unworthiness than in his capabilty and competence.

This feeling of inadequacy, in contrast to that of those who suffer under the fear of Martyrdom and feel worthless, is based not on moral categories or inner worth, but rather on abilities. Therefore statements such as: »I can't do that. I don't know, or: I have to be capable of everything and know everything or at least pretend to« are made by people with the fear of inadequacy much more often than by people who have Martyrdom as their Chief Characteristic. The martyr will always feel ready for anything in order to prove his worth and will try to strive until the last to achieve it. The person with Self-Deprecation as his Chief Characteristic won't even make an attempt to do this. He'll have the feeling from the very beginning that he isn't capable of doing something great and that even if he attempted, his efforts wouldn't really be valued.

He happily withdraws into himself. He has the tendency to make himself invisible and seldom raise his voice. The greater his talents are, the less he wants to display them. Therefore it's especially sad for these people to go through life with this perpetual camouflage and at the end discover that they were never recognized because they never showed themselves to anyone.

The person with the Chief Characteristic of Self-Deprecation ususally has a rich and strong inner life full of fantasy. But little of this is displayed to the outside world since he fears being condemned for what he thinks of himself. The basic fear of incapability easily leads to secret fantasies of power and greatness: »One day I'll show you!« He dreams for himself everything that he doesn't consider possible in real life. Therefore he likes to sleep. He often dreams of flying. In his dreams he appears as a figure of greatness, strength or power. Or else he suffers from nightmares in which others are superior and he himself is paralyzed, incapable, impotent, standing on the street naked, acting as someone who can't save himself from the superior strength of others. The person with the Chief Characteristic of Self-Depre-cation always secretly awaits the day when somebody at last discovers what fantastic things he's capable of achieving. He waits for someone else to remove the veil from his face and in amazement and admiration praise the greatness, beauty and goodness, the cleverness and incredible maturity which has been discovered.

Many people with the Chief Characteristic of Self-Deprecation seem to ask all the world: »Please excuse me for being born at all.« It would be helpful for those who are plagued by this fear to begin in very small and slow steps to pull back the cloud of fog which separates them from their own reality. It's important that they be able to identify those statements we've mentioned which clothe the concepts of incapability, incompetence and lack of knowledge in the guise of false modesty and to single out the personal »classic« among them. Then, when you're aware of it, always add a small following phrase: »But that's only what I believe about myself.«

We'll give you an example. If such a person thinks »I can't do it«, he should add: »But that's only what I believe about myself.« If he says: »I can't be praised«, he should add: »But that's only what I believe about myself.« If he says: »You can do that much better than I can«, he might add: »But that's only what I believe about you«. If he thinks: »I can do that better than anyone else«, he should also add: »But that's only what I believe about myself.« This standard phrase doesn't have to be said aloud. It's enough that it be applied as a conscious support whenever a set phrase of Self-Deprecation is used by a person in order to debase or raise himself inadequately.

It's also important to realize that modesty which only arises from fear of being despised or respected and thereby to be punished, or to display oneself in all the natural beauty and greatness that every person possesses, is not true modesty but only a pitiful crutch, a tool this fear uses in order to continue practicing its tyranny. The wall-flower syndrome, which results from false modesty, can often be overcome by a great act of self-liberation. This self-liberation then takes the form of a burst of laughter. Humour, therefore, is of great assistance to those who suffer from a feeling of inadequacy. They can also urge people who respect and love them to help them view this perceived incapability with a little more humour. Laughter is the best way to dissolve fear.

Energy 2

Self-Sabotage

Fear of Joyfulness

– Self-destructive   Self-sacrificing +

Self-Sabotage is an expression of a strong fear of losing control over what a person regards as important, necessary and life-preserving. These are joy of life, happiness, love, security. When control cannot be exercised in such a way as a person with this fear desires, he prefers to destroy the situation, to obliterate it. In such a way he tries not to allow his own liveliness and vivacity to brim over—for that would be too threatening.

This is a fear with the the basic energy 2. It is therefore also the archetypical fear of the Artist's soul role. The Artist as an archetype represents the cosmic child filled with the sheer joy of being. This Chief Characteristic is therefore the reverse: a fear of sheer joy and of being fully alive.

A human being with this specific Chief Characteristic of fear is really a very lively and joyful person, often even obsessed with the idea of obtaining pleasure always and everywhere and enjoying himself. The potential is there. Nevertheless, he prefers to put on a grim face and ill-humored expression, and he thinks people will take him more seriously than if he smiles. What he fears most of all is that people might consider him silly or superficial. Sometimes you can make him laugh but you have to take him by surprise in order to crack the shell of his self-control. When this happens, it is like a miracle. The person's facial expression changes so radically that he doesn't seem his previous self. The smile of a self-saboteur is like the radiant sun suddenly breaking through the darkest clouds on a gloomy day.

The compulsive need to contain one's joyful vivacity can have many facets and can take as many forms as a person has days of his life. If, therefore, fear arises over not being able to control a love relationship, the person who's afraid of his own joyfulness prefers to destroy this relationship rather than trying to live and to love without this control. If he fears not having all the threads of his career in his hand he decides subconsciously to do something to end this career, such as embezzling money or making a serious investment error. He prevents his own success even if he blames others for this action. If he has the impression that his body no longer does what he wants it to do, he'll decide to suddenly become ill and to infect himself or to cripple his immune system in order to destroy his body instead of correcting his rigid behavior and allowing the body a differing, changing state.

Should a person with the fear of joyfulness feel threatened by economic collapse, he'll prefer to spend his last cent and lose it in a casino rather than admit that he can't influence all the states of the economy and stock market.

As is already apparent from these examples, there are endless possibilities for a person to sabotage himself, to destroy what he has created and question what is important to him. Many other measures help to shatter an individual's joy of life. These can be medicinal or drug abuse, an excessive consumption of alcohol, the alleged freedom to put one's life at risk in sports like mountain-climbing, deep-sea diving or in acrobatic activities or through an intensive life-style where pursuit of pleasure doesn't allow a moment's peace It pursues enjoyment and then ends in a heart attack or a serious accident.

The fear of not having tight control of one's existence in all or only certain areas leads a person with the Chief Characteristic of Self-Sabotage to all sorts of passive measures as well as activities. They don't have the outer appearance of destructiveness but result, in their use and frequency, in destroying a spirit, a body, a job, a love, one's security.

If a person with the Chief Characteristic of Self-Sabotage doesn't aim his auto-aggressive powers against himself, he can choose the possibility of acting destructively against others. He can ruin others' enjoyment of life. A spoilsport and eternal pessimist, he can lower the energy level of his surroundings and make intrigues in order to destroy what others consider precious, joyful or holy. He believes that in such a way he is directing his powers outward. But the end result is that everything that he undertook against others comes back to himself and makes certain that neither friendship or professional relationships, nor satisfactory parental or sexual relationships can play a long-lasting role in his life. He is unconsciously caught in constant efforts not to allow any permanent source of joy in his life for his entire behavior is aimed through Self-Sabotage at always robbing him of what could provide happiness and security. If he then sees that nothing in his life is permanent, that his marriage has fallen apart, his work is unsatisfying, unsuccessful or that he has been fired, his health is ruined, his financial situation hopeless, he sometimes decides to end his life.

However, this step—actually committing suicide—is the very last which will be considered. It happens much more often that so many self-destructive measures mark the existence of a person with the fear of joyfulness that he chooses suicide by instalments as being more effective in destroying his joy of life. But this is something he isn't consciously aware of and will constantly blame others for.

It seldom happens that a person with this fear actively ends his life. If it happens, then that's because this life was the last thing that remained under his control: deciding himself when and how to end his own life, for the thought of not even being able to control this anymore becomes unbearable to him.

But self-destruction as a fear of joyfulness and aliveness can first be observed on a daily basis as an almost unnoticeable self-sabotage. Let's take an example which shows very succinctly the banality of daily self-destruction: a woman wants a beautiful dress which she has seen in an expensive shop. She decides to buy it but must either overdraw her bank account or sacrifice something important, such as an annual vacation, in order to pay for the dress. She buys the dress and puts it on immediately. In great delight over her finally reached decision, she goes to the next coffee shop to celebrate the occassion and spills a cup of coffee on the new dress, thereby ruining it so completely that she'll never be able to wear it again. This is a typical example of unconscious self-sabotage. The woman we've mentioned isn't capable of enduring so much happiness and joy; unconsciously and instinctively, she has to destroy immediately something intended to create a feeling of well-being and joie de vivre.

Another example: a man makes a first date with a woman he likes very much. He's confronted with a situation that makes him uncertain since he doesn't know how she'll react to this first meeting or whether he'll be attractive to her. So his psyche makes sure he creates a pseudo-control over the event in which he expects the worst. Through gloomy projections and bad premonitions he falls into a very negative mood. On top of that, because of his repressed joyfulness and negative excitement, he develops such bad breath and some blemishes on his face that the woman who had happily awaited this desired rendezvous is visibly repulsed. All her inner reservations which activate her own insecurity and fear of the date come to the foreground.

This fear of not being able to control this important first meeting leads to the man being unable to enjoy the situation and thereby exactly what was feared happens.

We describe all these developments and factors as »Self-Sabotage«. Each person who has this as his Chief Characteristic will recognize a multitude of similar occurances and unconscious measures in his life which destroy whatever he desires. Seldom, however, he realizes that it is he himself who causes this simply through his fear of not being able to control the situation.

Self-Sabotage has self-sacrifice as its pole of false virtue. This means that a person with the Chief Characteristic of Self-Sabotage very much tends to sacrifice himself for a thing, an idea, for a person or a project. It describes a behavior which neglects one's own needs of security, one's own ideas of happiness, or wishes for satisfaction as unimportant and to put them so far in the hidden dungeon of the false personality that they're no longer visible.

The person with the Chief Characteristic of Self-Sabotage sacrifices himself on the altar of his fear. In contrast to the Martyr, he does this silently and without complaining. He doesn't dare to feel or say what would do him good or make him happy. He can't escape from believing that no one will fulfill his wishes anyway, no one will console him in his need, no one could give him anything like a gift with no strings attached. He antici-pates this, and it will come true. Or he refrains from expressing his needs to others because of the belief that they'll only react negatively to these needs, will mock him, punish him and could destroy him. The desire to control the reactions of others leads to the anticipation of these reactions, which are mostly negatively imagined. So it often happens that the partner, colleague, friend or family member doesn't ever learn about the person's secret wishes, but constantly wonders why they meet rejection and distrust despite the fact they were prepared to do much in order to make the self-saboteur happy after all.

The person with the fear of his own joyfulness, however, doesn't really want to be happy. He believes he does, however, and always imagines it in his mind, but doesn't really take it into consideration. He therefore decides, without realizing, not even to give happiness a chance since it could develop its own dynamic which he would no longer be able to control. Consequently, he's often a lonely person, a lone wolf who isolates himself because he doesn't believe he's capable of being loved by others. And, of course, they react to his constant ill-humour and distrust.

The false virtue of self-sacrifice can also be seen in the case of a person who cares for a sick relative and does it in such a self-sacrificing way that he no longer sets boundaries or gives thought to himself. He goes for years without taking a day off, administers all medicine personally although the ill person is in no way crippled or physically hindered. He doesn't allow a doctor or a nurse direct access to the patient, does everything himself and won't follow the doctor's guidance in the administering of medication because he knows better.

It's soon clear that such behavior is aimed at not losing control over the helplessness of the patient. This kind of self-sacrifice destroys relationships. The patient will find it very difficult to become well again for his care-giver will slowly take the power of recovery from him and put it in a closet. The joy of both will be destroyed. This care has the appearance of great love but often there's a background of an old, unlived desire for revenge which in this way can be lived as a selfless sacrifice.

Such self-destructive behavior is displayed in many forms and assures that everything a person begins ends badly, that all people misuse him, fate is cruel to him, the court never rules in his favour and every partner abandons him. This crass form of Self-Sabotage is in many ways suicidal since the frequency of the disturbing events leads gradually to the individual losing complete control and then actively destroying himself physically in order to preserve his last bit of self-determination and dignity. This suicide by instalments—the unconscious, passive self-destruction by wiping oneself out or »making oneself kaputt«—occurs often but shows inconspicuous and pity-evoking features.

Whoever hears the word »self-destruction« thinks immediately of a final and irrevocable measure which describes the destruction of a human body by one's own hand. What we understand as self-destruction is something else but it includes suicide as one of many possibilities.

It can often be observed that a person with the Chief Characteristic of Self-Sabotage had a family environment in which his little happinesses and pleasures (a game, a gift or a sweet) were begrudged or even destroyed. Maybe a sibling enjoyed breaking one's favorite toys or parents, because of their own fear of joy, couldn't endure the naive, child-like happiness or anticipation of their offspring. They act in the belief that they must warn the child of too much thoughtless anticipation, or they want to prepare him realistically for the adversities of life when they tell him: »Don't be happy too soon! It probably won't work out! It will end badly! The bird which sings in the morning is caught by the cat at night« and so on.

The destructiveness hidden in such an attitude is not readily apparent but has a lasting effect. Of course, also a traumatic loss at an early age can be a cause of the fixation of Self-Sabotage: the death of father or mother, being placed in the care of unloving relatives or brought up in a rigid orphanage; ways of upbringing which include many beatings and punishments whose purpose is to destroy what the child considers its most beautiful and favorite things, all that makes him happy. To avoid enduring the pain any longer, the child unconsciously develops the wish not to be happy about anything at all anymore and prefers to destroy his own toy, his fantasies and happiness himself rather than let others destroy these possibilities of satisfaction.

Consequently, such adults later develop the unconsicous impression that there's really nothing in life to be happy about. The fear of happiness, joy and liveliness is so great that they're blind to the natural, given possibilities of experiencing it and enjoying themselves. If a person begins to realize that in many ways he practices Self-Sabotage, it's adviseable for him to start schooling himself again in his capacity to recognize the potential for happiness which is available to him as a human right. This is brought about in the most lasting manner when one concentrates on the small and greater moments of joyfulness which, because of this Chief Characteristic, all too often have been lost or forgotten. A happiness-diary, which can become a helpful companion on all paths and in which all events and joyful, lively feelings, even the apparently insignificant ones, are noted down, will within a short time change one's life-view to a positive one and will help a person with the Chief Characteristic of Self-Sabotage to relate to his joyfulness in a new way.

The sheer joy at being alive is synonymous with physical vitality. Even pain can contain a certain amount of happiness. Self-saboteurs must rediscover these dimensions and integrate them confidantly in the memory of earlier experiences.

Energy 3

Martyrdom

Fear of Worthlessness

– Victimizing   Selfless +

The fear of being worthless, which can sometimes grow to a painful pseudo-certainty, leads a person to become a Martyr. He becomes a Martyr because his false virtue of selflessness, or his ability to let himself be victimized. He believes he has to endure pain and adversity to be of value to his family or society. He is extremely active, tiring himself with works that are often unnecessary and unwanted, but he wants to earn the gratitude and esteem that he can't imagine would be granted to him if he just enjoyed being alive.

It is a fear with the characteristics of the basic energy 3. It is therefore also the archetypical fear of the Warrior's soul role. The warrior as an archetype represents the belligerent, active, enterprising and protective individual who feels that he can achieve anything, especially for others, if only he wants to. This Chief Characteristic of martyrdom is therefore the reverse: it is a fear of success, a constant feeling of having to prove oneself, of being basically a loser and victim and a desire to be an obsessive do-gooder in order to be respected and loved.

The person with the Chief Characteristic of Martyrdom is so deeply convinced of his worthlessness that, understandably, he can't deal with this conviction. It would deny his reason for existence. Often this person was an unwanted or abused child. And since he can't live with the feeling of being unlovable, he spends his life trying to prove his worth. His method is best described by the sentence: »I want to please everybody always.«

He proves his worth to himself and to others at every opportunity, day and night. He is unceasing in his efforts to please precisely because the inner certainty of worth which he strives for never comes about. Therefore, martyrs, in spite of their Warrior-like vitality, often look exhausted. It is in fact tiring to prove something that cannot be proved—existential worth! Moreover, his fears increase as the years go by and, like an addict, he does more and more to present himself selflessly even as a target of accusations and blame in order to maintain his delicate balance of worth. His trademark is a constant guilt-feeling in him and around him.

The person plagued by this sense of worthlessness really deserves compassion, for it is hard to live with this painful illusion of having to be a paragon of goodness and nobleness so that one can be tolerated by existence. But one also needs to be a little severe with his or her emotional habits, for this Warrior-like fear demands some confrontation so it can be softened.

Blame and guilt play a central role in the life of a martyr. Since he blames himself for everything which happens to him and others in order to increase his worth, he quickly reaches the point where he can't bear the burden anymore and then must begin to blame others, in order to lift the weight from his shoulders. Then he again feels guilty, and because he's done this, he can again view himself in a bad light. Then it's confirmed that he isn't worth anything and, as a next step, he'll become even more selfless, will offer himself as a scapegoat for the guilt of others and as someone willing to suffer in order to lift the suffering from others. If someone hurts him, he'll excuse himself and ask to be forgiven.

As children, martyrs are extremely sweet, always helping mother, giving away their favourite toys and being real sunshines. And even as adults they are generous and good, lend their money to unreliable people, never ask it back and always pay the check if someone takes them out for dinner in a restaurant. He is great in giving but refuses to accept favours or gifts, because that makes him feel guilty. If you give him a present, he'll give you three.

But it isn't worth it to the martyr to really become worthy. He fears that a healthy feeling of self-worth will draw the rage of people around him. In order to avoid this, he'll move into a morally indefensible position, in which he can always say that whoever attacks and accuses him of something just doesn't realize his true value. He takes the greatest satisfaction in not defending himself but rather offering himself in sacrifice. He believes that any attempt at defense is beneath his dignity because only God knows how deeply noble his attitude has been. He even likes to be offended in order to withdraw to his last bastion. Here he raises himself and his own worth so as to look down at those poor fellows who feel it necessary to criticize their fellow-men and to openly show their lack of loving understanding.

He likes to put people around him under moral pressure in the hope that under this pressure they'll realize his worth. In order to apply this pressure without actually doing so directly, the martyr falls back happily on physical illnesses, which, in his value system, fulfill dual functions. First, he believes that a person is only allowed to become ill when he has sacrificed himself for others and then breaks down in justified exhaustion. Secondly, he's convinced that his illness creates the opportunity of finally receiving from others the attention and concern which he wasn't capable of getting before in spite of being so selfless. When serious illness no longer permits him quietly and reproachfully to sacrifice himself and his activities cease, he believes that his fellow-men will finally realize all he did, all he overcame and achieved. Then he hopes they are plagued with remorse.

The poor Martyr feels happy when he can finally achieve through his illness what he had hoped to get through his selflessness: gratitude, attention, admiration and love, although he doesn't realize that he had to forfeit his health for this. He tends toward chronic illnesses, long bitter suffering, complaints that draw the pity of others and grant him the opportunity of being brave and uncomplaining. He will, as a rule, suffer quietly and heroically, won't dramatize his pains or difficulties (but sighs deeply and reproachfully from time to time), in order to again force others to care for him and take his situation seriously without having to say anything to achieve this. They should at best admire him for his capacity for suffering or at least develop feelings of guilt in the face of their lack of compassion.

He demands consideration not with words but through his behaviour and in the meantime tyrannizes those around him by his silent suffering. Then everyone does what he wants and needs without him demanding it and having to face the prospect of being rejected or hurt. The matryr in his fear and despair is a subtle manipulator.

The Martyr would rather not make any demands for himself but always be there for others so he can accuse them of exploiting him and not recognizing his valid needs. He doesn't like to care for himself but exhausts himself in the care of others. All this is almost completely unconsciously done, because he believes in his own incessant goodness.

He's often not in a position to create life conditions which would give him security. He relinquishes his rights in the hope that others will voluntarily grant or promise them to him. His ultimate hope for recognition is half-consciously aimed at the time after his death. He believes that then finally everyone will miss him and will realize what he meant to them and how much he was worth. And if he's deeply religious he'll believe that he'll at last be rewarded in heaven for his sufferings and illnesses, his victimizing and selflessness.

Unfortunately, the Martyr is a walking accusation for the people around him. They have more feelings of guilt in his presence than they can bear. What a Martyr wants to avoid, namely to be abandoned or rejected and to be ignored as worthless, happens that much easier and confirms his illusionary unworthiness. For one can only free oneself from the moral pressure of a Martyr by retreating from him or her or through a severe clash. This is an act of love from those who are close to him. A row, however, must result in the determination that the worth of the Martyr is basically unquestioned. This will calm and reaffirm him for a short time but the assurance doesn't keep the promise it made. The Martyr finds new reasons to feel unworthy and to fight for his worth, for this is what his fear structure needs.

A person with the Chief Characteristic of Martyrdom, who's prepared to stake his life on defining his worth, is easily blackmailed. He's ready to give up everything in order to have final proof of his right to exist, so that he can maintain his self-worth. Without realizing it, he sells and betrays himself in the incessant hope that one day he will no longer be dependent on the value judgement of those around him but be able to establish his worth firmly in himself since he has gathered enough proof. He ingratiates himself with anyone who even gives him just an ounce of esteem. And he's convinced that a quantitative collection of small confirmations of worth will be enough in the end to prove his quality.

The Martyr doesn't like to beg for that would reveal his need. He wants others intuitively to sense his needs. Since the Martyr is, in his own way, proud and since he helplessly waits for his worth to be confirmed, he doesn't dare demand a positive, active gesture. For he has too great a fear that this will be denied him, that he'll be rejected and he will again be given confirmation that his secret wishes are not worth discovering by anyone around him, even though it might be just a small favor!

When a Martyr asks for something and his request is finally fulfilled, he finds it difficult to be happy about what has been granted him. He only feels that his powerlessness is confirmed and reacts bitterly that he had to ask for something rather than being given it. He would prefer to resign himself to the fact that he isn't seen and isn't loved, rather than to fight for his rights which, in his fantasies, no one grants him anyway.

The Martyr nurtures the false virtue of selflessness to an extreme. He takes care to always be magnanimous to the utmost of his powers and tries in such a way to hold up a distorting mirror to others, for when those around him seem less magnanimous and less selfless than himself, they must needs be less worthy, and so his own worth increases by comparison. But if he senses that his selflessness isn't accepted, that no one really values his sacrifice, he would like to blame and punish them. However, this would again be an act in which he would reveal himself as needy and since this is his greatest difficulty, he much prefers self-punishment, doing to himself what he would like to do to others for their alleged unkindness.

The tendency toward self-punishment is displayed in the chronic and psychosomatic illnesses we've already mentioned, and also in external events, in catastrophes and tragedies which the martyr almost necessarily encounters since he is, in his own eyes, the personification of innocence and goodness. Unconsciously, he causes events that would never happen to others. It's difficult for him to view the catastrophies and tragedies of his life as a result of his own fear that is actually attracting evil because he is so exceptionally good himself. He is convinced that life is unkind to him and that he's subjected helplessly to the adversities of an evil fate: »My whole life I was always there for everybody and now I'm alone: People are ungrateful, I've lost my money, no one takes care of me. Life is really unfair.«

His fearful concern is always aimed at those he loves and whom he feels dependent upon because of this love. He tries in turn to make them dependent on him in order to ease the burden of fear. He expresses this by placing himself in the background, making his own interests subordinate to others and doing it in a way that creates a guilty conscience and feelings of guilt around him. The Martyr renounces his own natural rights to live. He conscientiously fulfills all duties without complaining and in addition takes on as many responsibilities as he can bear. If he doesn't have any relatives he can make dependent on himself, he'll take on the suffering of the world and the responsibility for all possible political, ecological or psychological connections which assures that his fearful psychological state doesn't get out of balance.

The person with the Chief Characteristic of Martyrdom renounces true love in a relationship. He renounces recognition and normal demands that others would make, for instance an old age pension or a healthy place to sleep, a workplace which doesn't have a draft. »Oh, it's all right, I can cope somehow...« The words: »It will serve my mother right if my hands freeze. Why doesn't she buy me any gloves?« is in many ways the classic statement of a Martyr.

He wants to be praised for the fact that he places his health and life at risk because of his convictions. And he views these convictions as his most precious possession. No matter how he defines his ideals, they can be reduced to the thought: »If I renounce everything, I'll someday be richly rewarded.« And since this possibility only presents itself when the martyr has sacrificed himself, it's very difficult for him to rid himself of his fear and then begin to affirm his right to air, light, life and love.

A Martyr doesn't like to be helped since he finds help a confirmation of his unworthiness. It's painful to him that he might need to accept the help of another person, whether it be practical or therapeutic. He can't reconcile the thought that he's so efficient and at the same time so helpless. Needing protection and help makes him feel worthless. Therefore, it is especially difficult for a person with the Chief Characteristic of martyrdom to admit his fears and weaknesses, for his selflessness causes him to never trust someone to such a degree that he would be able to accept something from them.

If a person with the fear of worthlessness lets another help him, whether it be in hanging up curtains or overcoming his fears, he soon feels plummeted into the abyss of new fears simply because of the fact that this assistance can make his helplessness visible. Therefore, for the Martyr there can only be an easing of the situation if he's prepared to question his idea of worth. If he can risk checking to see if it's really so desirable to do everything himself, to keep others away, to always give and never to receive and to take the possibility away from others of doing something good to him. He must consider whether the pride which stems from selflessness really provides what it promises.

In his own way, the Martyr is just as isolated because of his fear of unworthiness as is the arrogant person, who out fear of being hurt keeps everyone away from himself. The martyr cannot take criticism, because any kind of criticism seems to destroy him on the spot. He will then defend himself as if he had been threatened with a sword. Also he is mortally afraid of conflicts and arguments, because he feels that all fault must necessarily be on his side and he's to blame for everything that went wrong. He continually needs others to confirm his worth or unworth, but he can't really be close to them because he doesn't concede that they have their own ideas of worth and that they can decide themselves whether a person deserves their esteem or not. Without realizing, he withdraws from the love which is constantly being offered to him because he thinks he isn't worthy of this affection. Thus, if friends of a martyr or members of his family want to help reduce his fear, great caution is necessary. One has to assure him—as best as possible—that he's loved even when he's a little egotistic or selfish, when he takes a break or a holiday, when he is in good health and spirits insted of being exhausted. But one must realize in so doing that the martyr's definition of egotism is completely different from those of other people. For him it's already a selfish act to use the bathroom ahead of other family members or to take an extra spoonful of pudding.

He always hopes to be rewarded and loved for his sacrificial behavior. If one begins a loving little game with him in which one tries to make his martyr role within the family or at work a matter of attention, if one exaggerates a little without offending him and at the same time assures him that one recognizes his services but won't allow him to assume a stance of selflessness for himself alone, one will be able to break through his fearful isolation. You'll be able to convince him that his worth is completely independent from his actions. Moreover, that he doesn't have to work so hard to be recognized as he believes. On the contrary, he'll find more affection if he is more assertive and allows himself to cut a large slice from the cake of life and consume it with pleasure instead of renouncing selflessly and therefore denying others the pleasure of seeing him enjoying himself.

A person with the fear of unworthiness will often complain that others exploit him. He has few possibilities of seeing that he causes this himself and of understanding how much his self-confidence depends on other people exploiting him or sucking him dry. The key to a change in this fearful behaviour is for those who love him to gently but emphatically and relentlessly reject his offers to be exploited. They need to make it clear to the martyr just as emphatically and relentlessly that they feel offended when they are never permitted to do him favours, to spoil or help him or to affirm their own ability or goodness.

The person with the basic fear of unworthiness longs to be a worthy person. He believes, however, that worthiness can only be attained through selfless acts or won through sacrifice. If he can realize that a worthy person is someone who just believes in his own existential worth without needing constant reassurance by his fellow men, he is saved. There is no worth that can be achieved through work. The existential worth of a human being is always present, it results from the worth of his soul. There are no possibilities of denying this. The worth of a person consists of the eternal beauty of his soul. It can neither be given nor taken. It is his property, his indisputable possession. It is this which the martyr can't believe. He is convinced that »good« or »bad« deeds can alter the specific balance of his soul. Therefore, a person with this Chief Characteristic can help himself best when he develops trust in the worth of his soul, which is unique and incomparable.

Energy 4

Stubbornness

Fear of Unpredictability

— Obstinate   Resolute +

None of the basic fears is more widespread than the fear of change and unpredictability. You all believe that you're interested in something new, in experiencing something different and exciting, in changing your situation, making progress and not stagnating. But this is only a sanctimonious wish. Most souls who inhabit a human body would prefer to make sure that everything remains unchanged, if only they could. They feel secure in what they know. They want what makes them feel secure to remain the way it is — forever.

Only a few of you are ready, even if only in a philosophical sense, to realize that life and change are indivisibly inter-connected and that life is synonymous with change. Your body changes with every breath you take, the planet changes with each micro-second of your life. Existence is and remains unpredictable. The only thing that remains constant is the principle of change itself. To negate this principle means to deny life. But people who have the fear of unpredictable changes try to do this anyway, and that makes them obstinate.

It is a fear with the characteristic of the basic energy 4. It is therefore also the archetypical fear of the Scholar's Soul Role. The Scholar as an archetype represents the meticulous, conservative, calculating, distant, lonely, just, orderly, practical and highly responsible person. This Chief Characteristic is the reverse: it is a fear of losing control over the traditional order of life and of being exposed to the unpredictable, sudden, unexpected machinations of existence. Stubbornness as an aspect of the neutral level 4 of assimilation cannot really be felt as an emotion, but can be identified by its symptoms: a general contraction of the body, pains in the shoulders and a stiff neck, often also the tendency to grind one's teeth or hold one's jaw tightly during the night. Stubborn people may also accumulate tissue liquids or suffer from constipation, because letting go is difficult for them.

If a person with this fear is happy for a while, he wants more than anything to hold on to this happiness, to fixate it, and will do everything to hold on to it. But in so doing he fails to realize that he is endangering precisely what he wanted to preserve. If a person with the fear of unpredictability is unhappy for awhile, he becomes accustomed very quickly to the conditions of that state of mind. Even though he always says that he wants things one day to be different and even though he believes himself that he would like to change the situation, his fear produces an unbelievable number of arguments that can show him that what he has is still better than the unpredictable which could evolve from change.

The fear of change is the fear of the unknown. A person knows what is. What he doesn't know makes him fearful. For he no longer has this under control. He doesn't know what's going to happen. And he very much desires to move from one state of security to the next since insecurity plunges him into a deeper state of fear. If changes are unavoidable, the person with the Chief Characteristic of Stubbornness reacts with an intelligent trick. He will quickly, obstinately and resolutely decide in favor of the new stiuation and will frantically adjust to the changed circumstance as fast as possible. He likes to be admired for having made the best of any situation. This resoluteness and determination is his false virtue.

The unknown, the new frightens him; therefore he tends to explore the new situation as quickly as possible. He'll face it determinedly, tries to sound out all the facets and become acquainted with everything that's strange in order to adjust himself to it and again reduce his fear. This can concern new colleagues, changes in a profession, changes in social status like marriage or divorce, birth of children, changes in health or location, losses in the stock market—simply everything which makes up the normal aspects of life.

The iron determination which a stubborn person displays when changes are unavoidable and at the same time unpredictable gives him a feeling of strength. The obstinate person blossoms following a decision which was long overdue and which changed a situation which had lasted so long that it had become unbearable. The possibility of letting go of the old and the suspicion that he isn't yet in control of the new provides him a short moment of clarity between two phases of fear. His eyes shine and even though he's ruled by fear, he must temporarily give up the thought of being in control of the situation.

Not knowing what is going to happen next is both terrible and won-derful at the same time. To be open again, to be freed from stubbornness is like being freed from a prison. But the stubborn, obstinate person, because of the fear of not being able to cope with the insecure situation, will quickly build new prison walls. Then he's surprised that everything is again almost the way it was. And if another person wants to change him, if the troublesome changes made by others are carried over to him, then he tends to take a rigid and dogged stance, refusing to comply, determined to insist on his usual opinions and habits and thereby to prevent something new and positive from occurring. It's very difficult for a stubborn, obstinate person to be convinced that change might bring something positive, even happiness.

This rigid person has a problem with flexibility. He believes he is the most flexible person in the world, because he adapts so quickly. But that's only out of fear and because he can't bear unclear, insecure states of mind.

He arranges everything in such a way as appears right, that's flexibility to him. But what seems right to him usually has the opposite effect: it can actually make him unhappy. But he doesn't want to see this. He has great difficulty recognizing what will really help him to advance and grow. For to become involved in advancement and growth always means change. Moreover, spiritual growth is completely unpredictable since it follows its own laws.

Without realizing it, all stubborn people suffer from the impression that they must shape their lives all by themselves. Their highest value is autonomy. Whoever fears changes, fears something new and above all fears the unpredictable aspects of the unknown. He wants to be independent, to make all important decisions alone. He tries to arrange life with his own stubborn self-dynamic powers through being responsible for everything and everyone. This means affording little room, little time and little possibililty for the interplay with other people's needs and decisions and especially for the individual's higher powers to take part in shaping and forming that life which is being created not by him alone.

A stubborn person is caught between his desire for the old and his longing for the new. For he is certainly not someone who never wants to change anything. He only wants to decide absolutely for himself when, how and which way changes are going to take place. Obstinacy is confused with will-power. Anyone who wants to change a stubborn person faces an almost impossible task. They must rely on the fact that movement will happen in the situation only if they allow the stubborn person the illusion of making a lonely decision.

Stubbornness is an expression of a deep need of closeness and a deep fear of it at the same time. It is a rocky path of not admitting to oneself forlornness and feelings of sadness and loneliness. The stubborn person is always determined to take the steep, hard and difficult path, In so doing he often stumbles since the necessity of overcoming great difficulties in loneliness and, despite all adversities, to survive, becomes an early habit and creates an illusion of strength, endurance and a life-preserving power of resistance. The stubborn person easily fears that all of the proven powers which form his self-perception could turn out to be superfluous and could then rob him of a large part of his identity and life purpose.

Stubbornness often has difficulties with self-abandon, subordination or with admitting and giving in. This is because as a child he wasn't able to gather enough experience with defiance and saying no to his elders, so that the development of his own will-power was prevented and that now he has to stomp stubbornly through life and to insist: »I'm determined to do it exactly the way I want even if it harms me. It's all the same to me.« Stubbornness says no to change and thus no to life itself.

The fear of change, which leads to the desire that everything remain the way it is or return to the way it was, is often rooted in early childhood experiences which caused great insecurity. As a rule a child who later, as an adult, fears changes, had tender, loving parents or at least a tender, warmhearted mother. Therefore, he experienced in the first months of his life great security which he thought he would never lose. Then the day or hour comes — much too soon! — in which the mother or both parents have other worries, are distracted, or decide that the child must become more independent. Perhaps they're overburdened or sick, perhaps they've reached the limits of their abilities and possibilities. Maybe the child or the mother must spend some time in a hospital or the parents go for a holiday, leaving the baby to an aunt, babysitter or grandmother he's never seen before.

This may often only be a temporary state of affairs and is not illmeant, but for a infant with a Chief Characteristic of Stubbornness who's only a few months old, to be suddenly put in the care of unknown people, this condition seems forever and is frightening in a way it wouldn't be for a baby who, right from the beginning, was never much cared for or held. The sudden change from a blessed state of security to the fearful feeling of abandonment, to a loss of orientation in which a plunge into nothingness compares to a near-death experience, plants in the child a seed of panic-stricken fear of every violent, unexpected change. It's not the gradual changes from one day to the next which plague a person with the Chief Characteristic of stubbornness — it's the unexpected, the unpredictable, the severe and suprising events which cause him trouble in maintaining his balance. All his life he'll be afraid of being abandoned. He'll often be extremely jealous, appear needy and emotionally insecure, almost stifling those who love him. At the same time he creates around himself an aura of complete independence: »I don't need anybody to get along!«

Something unpredictable, incalculable, unforseen could happen to his relationship. That is his greatest fear, a repetition of what happened in his earliest days. If the partner (often a surrogate for the loving mother) threatens to leave, the stubborn person, with great determination, will pack his bags immediately or go to see a divorce lawyer the next morning. For it seems much safer to decide for himself that the marriage is at an end than to be forsaken. An unexpected event which is severe can plunge him into the depths of a depression which can last a long time before he recovers. He's afraid of situations which he can't control well and with which he isn't already somewhat familiar. Therefore he has trained himself to be extremely reliable. He keeps all his promises, is loyal and true in relationships, is punctual and dutiful. But at night he's a bad sleeper, for going to sleep means giving up control And who knows what might happen while he's not paying attention? He finds it difficult to relax, takes sleeping pills to forget his worries about the insecure future and then wakes up to another day in his life where he feels alone, compelled to take solitary decisions and to master his life without the assistance of the many people who love him and would like to be of help, but he doesn't let them.

Whoever has chosen Stubbornness as a Chief Characteristic should remember and take time to relive anew some of the traumatic events of his childhood. Then he'll notice that in the wealth of his memories some events can be identified where he had to overcome very sudden, severe changes. These could be: an early illness causing separation, an unexpected revelation (we are not your real parents), a severe disappointment, a loss (mother died or married again), an abandonment (father leaves, sibling dies)—anything which wasn't predictable and calculable.

As you all know, the unpredictable is a law of existence. But the stubborn person would prefer to neutralize it, because he fears that he could again be seized by the same deadly panic as he was by his first loss of security. Thus, he projects an endless series of similar, even if lesser, events into the future. Of course, he finds confirmation of this fear in every moment of life, and he buries himself more and more in the impression that he is someone who—as best as he can—must protect himself against sudden changes with all his powers and energy. Being independent and financially autonomous seems a safe way out of this trouble. He'll do everything possible to anticipate the uncontrolled and the unpredictable. Or, if this isn't possible, he'll try to deal with it as bravely as possible and absolutely fearlessly, or this is his illusion. If change is inevitable, then he'll live up to it in courageous determination. Since indeed unpredictable change is a fundamental, existential threat to him, he mobilizes powers which would be worthy of a life-threatening situation in the case of even small new events. He always applies all his powers and seems to increase in strength when such a threat arises. What comes easy is of no interest to him.

This kind of obstinate overcoming of difficulties is called determination or resoluteness, the seemingly positive pole of this Chief Characteristic. Resoluteness to survive was certainly appropriate when the character of a stubborn person was first being formed. For at that time it was indeed a matter of life and death for the infant during the first traumatic experience of loss, and the contraction of will-power and muscles was needed for survival. But later, in adult years, it's no longer a question of life or death. However, all powers will be brought into play as if it were. The body contracts, becomes stiff and rigid, especially in the neck and shoulders, and the psyche, becoming chronically stiff with the fear of the unknown, is afraid even of nice surprises.

Obstinacy, defiance, stubbornness, obdurateness and doggedness are internal processes. Externally, however, the stubborn person often appears as if no one else desires or seeks change as much or as often as he does. His life is in constant movement, he incessantly seeks new opportunities to prove to himself and the world that he's flexible and strong, a survivor constantly keen on change.

But this is only a helpless way of battling his fear. For as long as the stubborn person constantly and actively keeps things around him in motion, he won't sense his fear. Those who are stubborn have, more than others, the fear of standing still and languishing in the prison of unalterability. Wild and often harmful determination helps him recover all too quickly from unwanted phases of stagnation. He's disgusted by stagnation which he notices with regard to himself and others. The stubborn person appears courageous, strong-willed and dependable. His will-power masked by obstinacy is sacred to him. If someone tries to break his will, they won't have any success. If a stubborn person becomes very fearful and falls into the negative pole of hardening, inflexibility, doggedness and obstinacy, there will be nothing in the world that can move him from his position or stop him from persevering in a situation, be it ever so negative.

We've said that Stubbornness is the most frequently occuring Chief Characteristic of fear. If it was really true, as humans believe, that everyone wants changes and seeks new things, there would be a more positive trend for change in your world. But as soon as a major change takes place, the many stubborn individuals among you assure that everything will soon return the way it was. The conservatives, the traditionalists who, in institutions, often represent stubbornness, also want to return to the old and to what they know because they feel secure there. The viewpoint here depends on their Chief Chararcertistic, as to whether they regard the old times as a fantastic, beautiful era, or whether they long to bury the past as fast as possible. The impatient among you can hardly await the dawn of a new age because they fear missing possibilities in the present.

From our causal viewpoint, the new is no better than the old. But from your human perspective of the physical world, living under the law of duality, you must constantly fluctuate between the poles. Change is neither good nor bad. It's a natural law. But stubborn humans constantly fear being cast out from the security of the old and of standing completely abandoned, lost and lonely. People with the Chief Characteristic of Stubborness suffer from the fear of being abandoned and cast aside. Whoever wants to overcome this fear would be helped best by physical contact in order to become aware once again of their fellow men's solidarity and their protecting existence.

If you love a stubborn person and realize that he is caught in a compulsive web of fear and can't escape by himself, it's often enough to touch his hand, put your arm around his shoulder or your hand on his cheek. If the fear is overwhelming take the stubborn person in your arms, let your body warmth flow into him or even take him on your lap like a small child. For it's the lack of security and the fear of physical abandonment which long ago has anchored his Chief Characteristic.

If contact with other people doesn't appear possible, the stubborn person can make the wonderful discovery that his fear will lessen if he takes a warm, relaxing bath, makes himself a hot water bottle, takes a teddy bear or a special pillow to bed or something else that gives him primeval comfort. It would be a shame if he renounced this possibility of providing himself a little security. Warmth, comfort, contact, touching and being touched are the medicines which dissolve the tension, the fearful rigidity and the defiant doggedness and which can protect the stubborn person from his fearful wild determination which all too often causes behavior that does him no good.

Energy 5

Greed

Fear of Privation

– Insatiable   Demanding +

The fear of privation leads to the Chief Characteristic of Greed. This is the fear of never getting enough, of coming up too short. It is the fear of starving, of having to do without nourishment, regardless of which kind. Different people need to be fed in different ways, and for some amassing money, fame or power, or even knowledge or sex partners, is as indispensable as food.

It is a fear with the characteristic of the basic energy 5. It is therefore also the archetypical fear of the Sage's soul role. The Sage as an archetype represents the sociable, jovial, communicative, magnanimous person who basically feels that he himself, life and nature and the gods are generous, that there is enough for everyone. He has an overflowing, outgoing personality. Greed as a Chief Characteristic is therefore the reverse: a fear of never getting enough, of hollowness and emptiness, of not being able to participate in the fullness of existence.

Whoever is afflicted with the Chief Characteristic of Greed senses that he wants more and more, that he cannot do without this or that and is seized with panic when he doesn't get enough of it.

And what is he greedy for? The objects of his desire are as varied as life itself. The greedy person wants more of what, in his view, he still lacks: more temperament, more happiness, more success, more money, more attention, more peace, more relaxation and rest, more rights, more good health, more clarity, more growth, more beauty, more substance. The list can be extended in any direction. The older a soul with the Chief Characteristic of Greed becomes, the more refined the objects of his desire will be. He'll concentrate on things other than those of a Young Soul. It's no longer career, success, recognition, beauty or material goods which are in the foreground; fear will be directed ever more toward not getting enough friendship, enough love, enough intensity, enough insight or clarity. A person with the Chief Characteristic of greed has a life-long empty feeling, a hole in the stomach that cannot be filled.

Greed leads a person to invest all his energy to get that which he seemingly lacks. He'll be demanding and discontent. His friends, family and partners will feel that he is insatiable, that they give and give and give, and it will never be enough. In the end they prefer to turn away from him, because their love and generosity are not really being appreciated. He'll put all apparently unimportant things last in order to acquire in sufficient quantity what his fear of lack causes him to view as indispensable. And the greedy person will always place his goal somewhere far away or even unreachable for only then can his greed be maintained and can live from the energy which is projected into it. If a person is greedy for money, he'll fail to achieve the satisfaction that others have when they accumulate a certain sum of money. It will never be enough for him, and he'll not be able to enjoy it either. His fear will tell him: »Only when you have achieved such and such a sum will you be secure, but not yet.«

And if a person is greedy for success, this success will never be sufficient. He'll want more and more of it. The same applies to a greed for fame or recognition, for spiritual awareness and for intensity of experience. Unfortunately, the greedy person through his fear makes certain that he will never receive enough of what he desires. His fear of privation ensures that he will never be truly content within that particular area of his existence on which his greed is focused.

Since in your society greed is viewed as a serious vice, one of the seven deadly sins, the greedy person feels compelled to focus his fear of privation either on areas which are socially acceptable (such as success, beauty or material goods), or he decides not to reveal his greed to anyone. Then he'll escape into a behaviour full of self-denial and shame which sickens him, especially when he tries to convince others that he can exist very well without love, attention, success and material goods. Often those who follow a voluntary path of asceticism can't come to terms with their fear of lack and therefore bring about this condition of poverty voluntarily. This seems less frightening than to confront their greed for »more« and the subsequent need to rebuke themselves because of their strict inner code. A person with the false virtue of asceticism can easily be recognized, because he'll accuse others of being greedy. Someone, however, who really needs little and does not renounce out of fear, will never reproach others for enjoying what they want and need.

The Chief Characteristic of Greed is subject, therefore, to a great degree on the ideological or ethical norms of a particular culture, society or group. As you know, it's not offensive in certain social circles to be greedy for refined dishes or unusual adventurous experiences or sex, while it is acceptable in other circles to be greedy for enlightenment or self-discovery without the fear of rejection. In other sectors, it's acceptable to strive hard for money and success. It often happens that what is regarded as taboo in one group is valued and considered highly desirable in another.

Those who are greedy will have to keep in mind these standards. A person who, for example, is greedy for communication, in a family or social environment in which straight communication is viewed as a threat to the social order, becomes a worrisome, troublesome outsider. He will quickly find that he'll be chastized for what he considers indispensable. Then he has the choice of distancing himself from views which don't appeal to him or join some other group. It often happens that he may suppress his greed, internalize it and turn it into the opposite of the thing he lusted after. For instance, he may withdraw from life, become some kind of hermit, flee into a dream-world and thus appear more uncommunicative than his environment would demand.

Obvious greed is always embarrassing or even distressing for those who suffer from it and also for those who observe it. People in the vicinity of those who openly express their greed quickly feel threatened and are tempted to put them in their place. A greedy person tends to encroach upon others. He is intent on grabbing as much as possible of what he wants and his fear doesn't allow him to take into consideration the results of his greed which is often the hostility and rejection by his fellow men. However, sometimes certain forms of greed don't violently contradict the norms of society as, for example, greed for justice or greed for food. They become so apparent—as an addiction to judicial proceedings or extreme overweight. In this instance, the greedy person suffers more than those around him. He can't control his addiction, he can't stop it. He feels that he'll die if he doesn't get what he wants—whether it be justice or nourishment.

The greedy person sometimes hears from others that he expects too much or takes too much. Frequently, however, he makes clear to those around him or to members of social groups that they are blatantly enriching themselves, that they are violating religious or socially acceptable forms of restraint and asceticism. In general, the greedy person is much more sensitive to the greed of others than to his own greed and enjoys reproaching them.

Deep down, the greedy fear starvation. Therefore, it's understandable when we tell you that this Chief Characteristic of Greed, the fear of privation, is mainly caused in a child if sustenance is given in such a way that the child feels it is actually being denied. Mothers, who believe that they should nurse or feed their child only at a certain time of day because the child will otherwise be spoiled, or who forget to feed their child at the right time, produce in their infant the constant fear of not getting enough. At a very early age this leads to the child eating and storing more than it can digest at the time. Soon it believes that »Eating is love. I have to make sure that I get enough, I have to take what I can when I can because you never know if I will be offered it again.« Of course, this is not the mother's fault. The child's soul has a need and predisposition to develop his Chief Characteristic of Greed, and chooses his mother accordingly.

When a child becomes a little plump because he eats too much out of fear of not getting enough later, his mother will often feed him less, thereby reinforcing his fear of lack. In later years this fear manifests itself either in a person whose hunger instinct is disturbed, being noticeably underweight since one forgets to eat, or because of bulimia or anorexia nervosa, or in being significantly overweight in an attempt to store up for bad times, as a precaution against weeks and months of lack. Only when the fear of not getting enough food is sufficiently sublimated in an adult can it be expressed in less obvious ways.

We've already said that greed for spiritual knowledge and growth is also an expression of fear, a fear of not achieving in time that for which one's soul strives, a fear of wasting one's life, a fear of ending up in hell or being punished for karmic reasons. All this can lead to aspects of Greed which are apparent to a loving observer but which provide the affected person with plenty of opportunity to justify his fear of lack. This also applies to Greed for perpetual good health, for an ever peaceful relationship, for continuous sexual satisfaction or for eternal happiness and diversion.

As one can easily imagine, greed leads imperceptibly to a structure of addiction. Therefore, among addicts of any kind you'll find many who have succumbed helplessly to their greed. Fear of a lack of relaxation often leads to dependency on sleeping pills or painkillers, fear of a lack of intensity often leads to addiction to psychedelic drugs, alcoholism is often a reflection of greed for security and oblivion. The same is true for addiction to success, sex or wealth. Those addicted to beauty and attractiveness will see their beauty surgeon every few months. Whenever the fear of lack gets the upper hand, it will rule the greedy individual in such a way that he or she will no longer be their own master.

If a greedy person decides to ease his fear of not getting enough of whatsoever, if he really wants to gradually escape the yoke of his fear, he would be well advised at first to explore the special area in which he imposes a voluntary asceticism on himself. For this asceticism is a hidden and there-fore dangerous side of Greed. Then he can consider what appears most im-portant in his life and at the same time the most difficult to achieve. It's especially important for a greedy person to clearly define the focus of his Greed. Then he is in a position to ask: »Can I obtain more of this? May I allow myself to take more? And can I do this openly?« The fear of punish-ment for openly expessing Greed and want and need is very deeply rooted and widespread. He feels shame and fears that what he wants will be snatched away from him and that someone will slap him on the finger if he stretches out his hand for it.

A greedy person can cope much more easily with his Greed if he acknowledges it. Because he'll then see he already possesses more and has received more than he even realized. The greedy person always feels poor in the area where he senses a lack. He believes he is a pitiful beggar in this respect. Only upon closer observation, will he realize that he isn't poor in the area where he perceived a lack, that he's not as helpless a victim of cir-cumstances as he believed and that nobody is trying to deprive him of what he wants most. He'll also realize that now that he's an adult, there's no longer anyone who can deny him food and therefore threaten his life. He can realize that he's in a position to feed himself, that he's no longer dependent on being fed and cared for, that he's capable of providing himself all the attention and love which he failed to receive at an earlier time at the right moment. Then he can relax, and he'll suddenly realize that his Greed is no longer clothed in the belief that he'll never receive enough of what he needs.

The more often a person with the Chief Characteristic of Greed and the fear of lack allows himself to consciously satisfy his greed in the small things of daily life, whether it be twelve pieces of cake or an uninhibited night of love, whether he consciously allows himself for a whole day to buy everything he always wanted, even if this temporarily puts him a little into debt, the better will he be able to deal with, and to lessen, his fear of not getting enough. In relationships, it is healing to admit that one's always hungry for more love, tenderness and attention. Then both partners can agree to satisfy the need or to laugh together at this insatiabilty. Every conscious exercise of this type will help him realize that his state of lack is not as threatening as he feared. He will learn to accept the hollow feeling and by so doing, will experience more satisfaction and contentment than he ever knew.

Energy 6

Arrogance

Fear of Vulnerability

− Vain   Proud +

Arrogance is a mask of fear worn by those who are extremely afraid of being hurt. This hurting is brought about through being either ignored and not taken seriously, or by being sneered at or ridiculed. It is the fear of being overlooked, of not being noticed. Arrogance is the Chief Characteristic of those who react to being passed over and ignored by sneering at the wrong-doers. This special vulnerability arises within those who don't dare show themselves but wait around for people to discover their qualities. And if they don't do this, they're viewed as unloving and stupid.

It is a fear with the typical aspects of the basic energy 6. In its negative aspects, it is therefore the archetypical fear of the Priest's Soul Role. The Priest as an Archetype represents the serious, initiated person who by office is nearer to God, to eternal truth and the secrets of existence. That segregates him from all those who don't have access to higher knowledge, and traditionally he is revered as someone on a higher plane of divine cho-senness. Arrogance as a Chief Characteristic is therefore the fear of getting emotionally close to people because of »natural« superiority and sensitivity. A Priest-like inaccessability arises from the idea of being special. Arrogant persons feel (and often are) able to see secret truths hidden to others and therefore believe to be in constant danger of being persecuted. Persons with this Chief Characteristic are, in fact, highly sensitive; their senses are unusu-ally refined and they suffer from being invaded by all kinds of hostile influences like noise, bad smells, negative thoughts, unpleasant »vibes«. Their nervous system is high-strung, their nerves feel as if they were bared of protection. They feel constantly exposed to the banal, dirty or disturbing vicissitudes of life. This incessant experience hurts them and conveys the life-long impression that their whole being is like an open wound, and that every-body around them amuses themselves by rubbing salt into it. Thus, making themselves believe that all other people are boorish blockheads, insensitive brutes or vulgar ignorants helps them in a way to cope with their habitual vulnerability.

We're referring here exclusively to an Arrogance which feeds on the source of fear. Other forms of arrogance may arise from class conciousness, excep-tional physical beauty or an outstanding intellect. These manifestations don't arise from the fear of being overlooked.

This Arrogance, with the poles of vanity and pride, is a Chief Charact-eristic which, more than other basic fears, separates people from one another. And that is exactly what the haughty, arrogant person desires to happen: He wants to be differentiated from other people, he wants to be contrasted to others, he wants to be admired for his uniqueness, but especially for his »natural« superiority. That is his kind of vanity. As is so often the case, a mis-taken preconception of loving and being loved is the reason for this form of expression of fear. For the arrogant person is more isolated than others and, without noticing it, he enforces this painful isolation incessantly so that it becomes almost natural to him. Ironically, because he wants to be loved, he drives people away from him by disparaging them. He believes he can gain love only by being superior—by presenting himself as someone who always knows better, can do everything better and basically has access to secrets that must remain concealed from others. One of the best hidden secrets is his own needy self. The vain idea that he can only be loved and admired because of his uniqueness is deeply rooted within him. No failure can convince him that his superiority is not the only way to gain affection.

A person with the Chief Characteristic of Arrogance is more deeply separated from his fellow-men than are people with other Chief Characteristics. The thick glass wall he builds between himself and those by whom he would like to be loved is a protective one. The arrogant person is so vulnerable, so sensitive, his feelings of self-worth are so easily injured, that he believes he can only survive when he constantly protects himself from the nearness of others. He is in great need, but doesn't know why and doesn't show it. He's vulnerable above all because his feelings of self-worth are very delicate and require costly energetic measures to maintain them. He's sincerely convinced of his outstanding worth, a worth nobody else seems to notice. He differs in this from people with the Chief Characteristic of Self-Deprecation and also from those who use Martyrdom as an expression of their fear. They don't believe themselves to be worthy, he does to an extreme.

As a rule the arrogant person thinks much more highly of himself than he even dares show to the outside world. He finds it unbearable to have to place his worth under discussion. His outstanding value is his place of protection and refuge. Even if no one around him will realize it, he's convinced of it .But it's apparent that he assesses his worth much too highly out of pure fear that it could be questioned.

A person with this Chief Characteristic is always plagued by the fear that someone could appear in his life who would be greater, cleverer, more capable, more good-looking, more intelligent or even more sensitive than he is and would thereby place his too-highly assessed worth in question. Therefore, in order to protect himself he must disparage all those around him who might present even a remote danger. And he behaves all the more generously and condescendingly toward those who, in his opinion, couldn't even compare to him. For them he has great empathy, he feels some kind of affection and sympathy for them. But he easily becomes competitive with those who could be equal to him, but who of course never will be, and tries to outdo them or put them in their place.

The haughty person tries to master his fear by withdrawing in order not to sense the isolation that he causes in so doing. He is happy being alone since then no one can attack him or make him feel insecure. He is often a great individualist, for to do something which no one else does, to think something that no one else thinks assures him of his great and unique qualities. He choses to be a loner in order not to sense his loneliness. He often has difficulties with the states of tension which rule his body because he's always highly tensed so he can maintain the walls of his defense. He doesn't want to let anyone become close to him, because he could reveal himself as an enemy and inflict the ultimate deadly wound to his delicate psyche. That's his main worry. At the same time he longs very much for a true, deep contact, that would embrace him and make clear to him that he'll be accepted and loved if he dares to leave his refuge and presents himself unprotected to his fellow-men, even at times when, in a weak moment, he really shows himself the way he is: extremely vulnerable, very shy, insecure and unbelievably in need of love.

There are two different groups among people with the Chief Characteristic of Arrogance. You can quickly recognize those who project their haughtiness outwards for they're easy to recognize. They're still brave and capable enough of contact so that they openly disparage others, dress them down or cruelly show them their stupidity and incapability. The other group buries their haughtiness beneath thick layers of silence. These are people who are so inhibited, so shy and so vulnerable that they protect the idea of their own greatness and incomparable worth as a dangerous secret. They don't trust anyone to ever recognize their qualities, they fall deeper and deeper into isolation and freeze at the thought that someone might come close enough to discover their precious secret, for then everything would be lost, there would be no more protection for their bleeding ego. Since they don't even sneer at people any more but bury all their feelings of superiority inside, one doesn't have a chance of becoming friends with them; only those who are just as sensitive as them, but maybe less fearful and thus more loving, can be as clearsighted as to look through their protection wall.

The person with the Chief Characteristic of Arrogance is always shy. But the first group covers up this shyness with unpleasant superciliousness while the second group no longer sees any possibility of breaking through the divisive glass wall with arrogant words or boastful remarks. People who only live their arrogance within themselves are those who never say anything but who are secretly disparaging of others. They are those who would never dare let others notice that they could be better than them. Quite the contrary, they carefully hide this certainty since they fear they can't expect understanding. They withhold their perceived superiority from those around them so as not to burden their poor fellow-men, or frighten them, or give them the dreadful feeling that they're small and insignificant.

The arrogant person is more sensitive than others when it comes to sensing hypocrisy, false tones and general untruths. Therefore, no one will come close to him through flattery, false feelings or through false admiration and respect. His fears of being hurt and being exposed have so sharpened his sensibilities that he likes to expose the life lies of his fellow men and does so with great success. Derision is his tool. He doesn't realize that his strategy of exposure chases away the people who in their own awkward and fearful way try to come close to him. Therefore, those who want to love an arrogant person must always take care to show him only authentic and sincere feelings. The person with the Chief Characteristic of Arrogance can bear it more easily if his partner or member of his family withdraws from him and lets him know that they are hurt or don't agree with his behavior or ways of expressing himself. He finds this a clearer proof of love than flattery or sweet promises and vows of love which he would view from the outset as untrue. How can he trust them? If he believes sweet words, he might soon be hurt.

Since he insists and must insist absolutely on his moral, spiritual, practical or theoretical superiority, he wants to have people around him who would acknowledge this superiority without being repulsed by it. This would give him the possibility, at least in his private life, of taking off his armor and being the vulnerable person whom he represses in his youth, but in later years he intimately perceives: a person who has a more tender, thinner and more sensitive membrane than others. This memrane is truly more vulnerable than those of people who don't know the fear of a devastating wound as well as he does.

In his childhood he has often been ridiculed by his elders and peers. A child with a natural heightened sensitivity is often not understood or is denigrated by those around him—fathers, siblings, school-mates, sports-trainers. But an arrogant child or adult will be hurt by remarks, gestures or omissions other people wouldn't even notice and would certainly not be offended by. And someone with this kind of fear will not easily forgive or forget. He has an elephant's memory. His strategy is: I never want to see you again. Get out of my sight, disappear from my life—forever!

A person with the Chief Characteristic of Arrogance constantly fears being hurt but can't easily admit to this possibility for he wishes to be, and to remain, invulnerable. He would preferably remain separate from others and continue to feel misunderstood, rejecting offers of nearness rather than being disappointed by a friendly or loving contact because he allowed someone to come close who could penetrate his defense and wound him.

Therefore, it's important for those who want to love an arrogant, proud man or woman to display a great deal of patience and careful distance in order to lessen the fearful defense of the arrogant person. Too great an advance will strengthen the walls of defense while a cautious, undemanding, patient, waiting behavior will give the arrogant person the chance of slowly emerging from his unconscious isolation chamber and realize that the doors which he closed from inside can be easily opened; but he can also close them again at any time if his fear demands it.

Constancy, loyalty and repeated but unobtrusive offers of love—even after one has been pushed away—are the most effective keys to liberate from the prison of fear the person with this Chief Characteristic has erected around his intrinsic core. If he can recognize and accept that his arrogance and helpless boasting are first of all an expression of his fear of being hurt, it will even be easier for him than for many others who are tortured by their basic fears to come out of his refuge. He'll then quickly sense the unbelievable relief and the glowing warmth that his body and his psyche experience if he can only, despite his fear, admit the closeness and love of his partner. The unapproachability which surrounded him like an invisible shell will disappear. He'll allow himself to relax only when he's convinced of the faithfulness of his partner and the loyalty of his friends.

Energy 7

Impatience

Fear of Omission

– Intolerant   Audacious +

Impatience is an expression of the fear of missing out on opportunites. Life is too short, and the burden of constant choice weighs heavily. The impatient person knows many ways of justifying his overefficient and hectic behavior since his temperamental eagerness, his desire to speed everything up and to move quickly toward his goal will generally be regarded as very positive. His haste is seldom viewed as offensive within the social context of his life. His turbo-personality appears to be stimulating and enlivening until you realize the pressure under which he constantly finds himself, the pressure he exerts on others and the feeling he gives you to be slow and inefficient. You can recognise this Chief Characteristic of impatience in anyone who hates to wait or waste time and views boredom as tantamount to purgatory.

It is a fear with the classic features of the basic energy 7. It is therefore also the archetypical fear of the King's Soul Role. The King as an archetype represents the omnipotent leader who can order his subjects about, bears great responsibility, wants things to be done immediately, cannot bear to wait or to be contradicted, someone who commands as a birth right, possesses great will power, a tendency towards tyranny and can bring about the events he desires immediately, because his subjects must obey his wishes. But a King's throne may be usurped, and he may be killed in a revolution. Impatience as a Chief Characteristic is therefore the mask of a fear to die prematurely, of not being able to achieve all those important deeds one has set as one's goal before death. An impatient person carries a heavy burden of trying to achieve what he views as vital in too short a life-span, and that is at least three times as much as other people would want to do.

However, during the course of his life the impatient person will, and must, realize, that if he really desires to grow, his efforts to do everything as quickly and efficiently as possible hinder him to achieve and are an expression of his fear. He will recognize that this need in more ways than one separates him from what he wants: namely to be exactly the right person at the right place at the right time.

The impatient person can't really believe in the value of the moment. It's difficult for him to perceive the here-and-now as complete. The future with all its possiblities and opportunities seems much more attractive than the dull present. He's always in a hurry and always tense, and he always yearns for something different, something new, something better to happen. And he fears falling into lethargy because he's afraid of missing out on what is newer, better and time-saving. Therefore, he's separated from what could fulfill him: an inner peace which derives from the knowledge that everything that is, is always right at this very moment. No one has as little understanding of this as the impatient person.

The person with the Chief Characteristic of Impatience puts a great deal of pressure on himself and on his fellow-men. Since he always wants everything to be different from what it now is, he denies himself the chance of personal satisifaction. He's always in danger of confusing satisfaction with boredom. Satisfaction appears to him as an expression of empty stagnation. He only feels happy when he has a goal which he can pursue tirelessly and which he can follow with impatient drive. If he at last achieves that goal, an unpleasant emptiness fills him which prevents him from enjoying the fruits of his pursuit.

The impatient person can achieve a great deal in life. But it will always be difficult for him to enjoy what he's achieved, for each step of his long trip from one missed opportunity to the next will fill him with a feeling of a half-measure, and he'll always view what is achieved as a small step on the endless ladder to his supposed happiness in the future.

Impatience produces unease. The impatient person suffers from the fact that he can't linger. He drives himself and, even more than himself, he drives others, whom he harnesses as helpers toward his restless goals. A person with the Chief Characteristic of Impatience has a problem with time and time management. The fear which motivates this behavior has as its source the half-conscious terror of dying prematurely. At the same time there is a deep longing to die, because then, at last, the pressure would ease and it would all be over, he could finally relax, because there is nothing more to miss or lose.

Impatience as a Chief Characteristic of fear often ensues when a child's life becomes endangered during pregnancy, during birth or during its first year of life, or if it's soul is really not certain whether or not he really wants to live the chosen incarnation with all of its consequences or not. Because of these vacillations, because of this fear of life, the soul of the child would prefer to return where it came from—the bodyless Astral World. Or it would like to return to the womb where it had been resting until the pressure of having to chose between this and that began. On that astral level, however, it was certain that it wanted to incarnate again in order to devote itself to the self-chosen duties and tasks. The desire for timeless peace which, through the agitation of being born and the first months of life—especially if the infant suffers from an illness or affliction—determines his later life, causes a desire to return to the bodyless state. But now he's alive and he doesn't want to destroy this life either which he brought about with a great deal of difficulty. However, he would certainly prefer to be in another place in another condition.

If he finally realizes that both states aren't possible at the same time, he sees no other solution than to lead his life as hurriedly, efficiently and goal-oriented as possible. And this he can do with tremendous patience! Whenever his determination lessens and from his viewpoint, real life quality, centeredness and peace could emerge, the person with the Chief Characteristic of Impatience feels unwell, begins to doubt his reasons to be alive and would like to end his days as fast as possible since he views the actual period of peace as a boring time in which nothing is happening. He feels that if hectic activity isn't possible his existence has lost its purpose.

We've already said that the Chief Characteristic of Impatience stems from the fear of dying too soon. A person who can't trust with absolute certainty that his life will last just as long as his soul needs in order to fulfill its duties will always fear that he doesn't have enough time and might leave his body before he's achieved the supposed satisfaction. The fear of dying at the wrong time results from the already mentioned unease. This is an existential unease which leads a person with the Chief Characteristic of Impatience to search tirelessly and often despairingly for the purpose of his life and prevents him from seeing that the purpose of his life is contained in being alive, that there's no purpose beyond that, no purpose in being in another place, in another condition, in another activity, in another satisfaction other than the fact alone that he's alive. It is thereby he gives his soul the possibility of following its needs, of pursuing the path that it chose with intention without ever questioning the purpose of this choice. But now there is the fear of omission.

The person, who makes the Chief Characteristic of Impatience the ruler of his life, always tends to put his life and health at danger through death-defying challenges, through foolhardy spiritual or audacious physical activities which put his physical existence at stake. He does this in order, so to speak, to force a clear statement from God that no matter what he does or how he puts his body at danger, death flees from him and that the hereafter, which, on one hand, he longs for and, on the other, is mortally afraid of, will spare him. He hopes in such a way of being freed from his perpetual doubt whether it would be better not to live at all or at least as intensely, restlessly and hastily as possible so it might soon be over.

The impatient person wants life to definitively and permanently prove to him that it's worth living, that he's needed, and that he's loved the way he is and where he is. The bold challenges, the foolhardy deeds and the habit of overexposing himself in some way, to make himself open to attack—whether it be on a human level or through the powers of nature—gives to a person with the Chief Characteristic of Impatience an intense feeling of being alive. He can incessantly hope in times like these that that he'll soon arrive at his goal and bring purpose, clarity and unambiguity into his life.

Since satisfaction and fulfillment are always in the future, the impatient person spends his life waiting for never-never. If his fear forces him to waste his life with the illusion of meaninglessness—we express it this way but for the impatient person this is not an illusion—he despises himself so much for allegedly not being able to bring any purpose to his life that he becomes even more despairing and plunges into a nebulous, disoriented, fatalistic state.

Then he'll become impatient and intolerant with himself. And in order not to excessively paralyze himself, he projects his impatience and the dislike he has for himself and his fear of meaninglessness on others. He'll excommunicate all those who in his opinion don't do enough to give their life meaning and all those who don't share the goals he has set for himself in a way that almost denies their right to exist. This makes him intolerant toward those who are completely different from him, especially those who are slow and less efficient, those who don't share his views of a meaningful intensity, but above all those who, through their own life goals and their own existence, threaten or endanger him and his delicate security by wasting time.

The impatient person can appear very exciting, charming, temperamental and motivated as long as he's not too intolerant. If things are going well for him and he's not too impatient with himself or others in a crisis, he's a person who can use the characteristics of his fear excellently in focusing on an object, a project or a structure which seems meaningful to him. Since he appears to be so exciting, he has the qualities of a leader and will be accepted as a superior or project leader as long as his fear of not being able to complete the project perfectly in the record time makes him intolerant and too demanding. Then he has the tendency to put his colleagues under severe and sometimes unbearable pressure and to dictate that they must—as he does—concentrate all their strength every minute of their lives on realizing their purpose and content in the goals set by the project. But since not everyone shares his Chief Characteristic of Impatience, others feel abused, although this feeling can't be objectively confirmed, since in the beginning they accepted and helped create the conditions of the work.

The key lies in the fact that the impatient person subconsciously recruited them to fight his life and death fears. Since, however, this threatening feeling is buried so deeply within the impatient person that even he doesn't realize it, the people he works with are, in just as hidden a way, estranged from their own totally different goals without being aware of the situation. That makes them angry and they blame him for his restlessness and intolerance.

The impatient person is torn between efforts to do everything with an almost angelic patience and his inner bustle. He swings between an efficient ability to make decisions and a lethargic laming of this ability, depending on how much fear he has of missing something important. He sways between boldness and foolhardiness on the one hand, which gains the admiration of many of his fellow-men, and a fierce impatience, which causes severe repulsion among them. The urgent manner which so clearly characterizes the impatient person and also his efforts never to stagnate or to be bored, makes him an individual in private and social life who is interesting, dynamic, lively and often, because of his daring ways, a charming person—if his Chief Characteristic isn't transformed all too often by fear or desire for death into depression. That will lead him into lethargy. Instead of doing a hundred different things at once, he will then stop completely being active, watch television all day, become passive and ill-humoured; he will hate getting up in the morning and avoiding all decision out of the fear of missing the right one.

Those who love an impatient man or woman must be patient with them, even though they feel stressed by the constant turbulences and outbreaks of energy. If they are pressured too much, they must put a momentary stop to all this hustle and bustle. But they must not expect someone with this Chief Characteristic to become meek and mild and calm and slow, just to please them. If one understands the fascination time and death have for an impatient person, it will be easy to forgive and apease him. It is good to reassure him from time to time that life is enjoyable even without incessant activity and will even last longer if one doesn't burn one's candle at both ends.

If he could only be convinced that one can exist without expending all this unbelievable energy in order to give a meaningful life more meaning; if he understood that his existence and right to exist can be nurtured on sources other than his fear; that his terror of not being at the right place or in the right body and not doing the right thing at the right time is completely un-justified, then the impatient person could lead a relaxed, satisfied life, a life that finds its purpose within itself. He could mobilize all his creative pow-ers and advance without the severe challenges which until now he has posed for himself because of his restlessness, foolhardy daring, intolerance or im-patience. He could fulfill his goals, his duties, his agreements with himself and others if he didn't hurry so much but allowed himself the peace to enjoy the moment. A impatient person can appease his fear by repeating the mantra: »I have all the time in the world« or »Time is not limited. There is enough for everybody.«

Development Goals

⑤ Acceptance   ② Rejection

− ingratiating   + kindhearted   − prejudiced   + discerning

Expression Level

⑥ Acceleration   ① Delay

− confused   + comprehending   − withdrawing   + reviewing

Inspiration Level

⑦ Dominance   ③ Submission

− dictatorial   + leading   − subjugated   + devoted

Action Level

④ Standstill

− immobilized   + pausing

Assimilation Level

III The Seven Goals of Development

Whenever a soul, in the relaxed atmosphere of the Astral World, relieved of time and space between incarnations, decides on a new incarnation, its first focus will be on a new Development Goal. For the choice of the goal of a particular life determines most other factors; they are subordinated to the Development Goal.

For example, the decision to chose a particular race or certain cultural environments depends on which Goal a soul has selected for its incarnation. The Goal of the soul determines to a great degree the experiences that a living person is intended and intends to have, and, conversely, the experiences that a person has in life depend to a great degree on the Goal his soul has set.

Humans don't have to worry about chosing their essential Soul Role which, as you know, stays the same always, in all spheres of existence. Their choice of a basic fear or Chief Characteristic also deserves little concern. They will happily and almost automatically turn to the next best or nearest fear in order to make it their own. But the selection of a Development Goal, which is valid for an entire earthly life, demands a great deal of care, a concentration and consideration.

The choice of the Goal will, as a rule, also be agreed on with other souls close to the one making the choice, for other incarnated souls from the same soul family often have to be brought in to support the Development Goal during a specific life time. Achieving an incarnation goal requires the active cooperation of several soul companions who are prepared—after consultation and agreement—to act and make important decisions which will sometimes seem adverse or hostile, but also to help and support. In any case this serves to make the growth easier for the soul sibling or to demand certain deeds from him, even to put barriers on his path, so that he must pluck up his courage or make efforts to overcome them.

Each Development Goal requires tension and friction. Just as a child often makes great progress in his physical and psychological growth if he encounters difficulties or if an illness requires him to rest for a while, so will the soul make considerable progress in its development if everyday life, fate or other people present it with certain adversities with which it can measure itself.

The Goal also has a certain easy aspect. Once your soul has chosen and set your Goal, it remains unalterable and independent in the sense that like a lighthouse it illuminates your whole life, everything that you do or don't do and experience. Whether you know it or not, whether you realize it consciously or only subconsciously, it always provides a guideline and an orientation aide on your path without requiring great or tiring efforts.

It's not you in your embodied state who has laboriously to find your way with a compass in the darkness; your Goal is always there to lighten your path. Whatever you do or don't do serves your Development Goal. Every omission just leads sooner or later to the insight that you've made a little detour. But you'll always find your way back to the main path.

You'll feel it when you've come a little closer to your personal Goal, your personal lighthouse. Your perception, whether it be conscious or unconscious, is always watchful for the needs of your Development Goal. Just as with other elements of your soul pattern, you can test with a certain clarity and ease whether you are nearing your goal or have chosen a detour. But even by trying hard you can't really distance yourself from your Goal. Sooner or later you'll reach it. That is certain.

The Development Goal is like a life theme that you keep studying from all sides. By living your life you experience it actively or passively all the time.

And even if at the end of your life you haven't quite reached the inner place where your lighthouse shines, you will have come close enough to recognize its contours and its consoling rays.

The Goal which your soul has set for itself in one life can be repeated in your next life or at another time. If your soul senses that the direction you followed in this life did you good, you can choose it a second or third time. But you can just as well set a new Goal for yourself in each of your lifetimes and, in so doing, explore in a beautiful and continuous progression all seven Goals. In the end you'll see that all seven lighthouses are located on the same great island.

Energy I

Delay

— Withdrawing   Reviewing +

The social and cultural conditions under which each of you live, enjoy and suffer are there for your growth and inner learning. At the time we are speaking to you, in the western world they are characterized by rapid advancement and acceleration in all sectors of life. The natural opposite pole of this acceleration, namely delaying or slowing down, is neglected in the name of progress. Delay is viewed as something wrong, like a stigma, a fault or mistake that must not be allowed. It's very important to us to free you from this culturally-induced misunderstanding and to show you that your belief in progress will sooner or later lead you to discover the eminent worth that lies in delay.

Slowing down is, in all of its expressions, just as worthwhile as acceleration, not only as a Development Goal but also basically. What would a car be without brakes? If you always only wanted to accelerate, you wouldn't be able to stop at the place where you were to go.

The art of braking, the art of slowing-down has a broad range of significance in many aspects of your earthly existence. Those who master the art of delaying, whether it be in a sexual act or during the recitation of a poem, will learn other things from a situation and will profit from it in a different way from those who approach what they want to achieve in a stormy tempo.

Souls who have set the goal of Delay for themselves should not be pitied by fervent believers in fast progress or be regarded arrogantly as people who, unfortunately, take a little longer than others. They should rather be viewed as showing, under the conditions of their actual incarnation, a special readiness to swim against the current. Especially because they are surrounded by a great majority of people for whom nothing goes fast enough and who find ego-fulfillment in constant change, hurry, in unstoppable advances in all developments, those humans with a Goal of Delay keep looking for places of rest in life without easily being able to find them.

Persons who achieve growth and advancement through delaying have a problem gaining acceptance in your societies when they persevere in slowing-down and insist that this be granted to them without blame. Their life-motto is: »Stop, don't go so fast! I need to take a good look at everything once more! I need time to feel what it is all about!« This doesn't mean at all that there is a lack of intelligence or grasp; a person with the goal of Delay is rarely mentally or physically handicapped, although this can be a path sometimes chosen by the soul in order to guarantee a slowing down.

Delay means winning time for introspection and reflection. Slowing-down intends to thoroughly consider intellectually and emotionally every-thing that might matter before making the next move. Slowing-down means not overlooking the tiny important details. In order to view the beauty of the whole, it is sometimes necessary to break it down into its parts and allow one-self the leisure to observe everything under a magnifying glass and to have the patience to take it apart and put it back together again.

The soul with Delay as a Development Goal is, in most cases, looking back at long periods of hurried growth in past lives. Now its desire is to grow in a new way. This soul is »out of breath« and it now needs a lifetime of peace, poor in challenges and painstaking adventures. He won't let things come to a halt, but can allow himself a delay, withdrawal, review and retreat, all providing an advancement in small steps but leading to an equal amount of soul growth as before. Only the method of advancement is now different. The person doesn't have to come to a complete stop, but can now find the time to walk slowly, to browse, to turn around, to look back into the past, to recognize the worth of what has happened before, especially in previous lives, even if he doesn't really remember them clearly. He loves the past instead of overlooking it or even rejecting it in great haste as people do who are oriented towards the future only. He can take the time to stroll along his life path and thereby have experiences which would never be possible for one who runs.

Hurry is no better or worse, it's just a different kind of advancement, and those humans who slow down are not better or worse than all the oth-ers seeking their Goal. They advance the growth of their souls in their own unique way.

We've said that it's important for all those who slow their steps to look back and take a good look at their past. This implies a temporary renuncia-tion of activity and company. Review is the positive pole. It allows time for recall, that means to look again and again at everything that has been felt and experienced or passed by on one's path in this life and in previous ones. For a Goal of Delay it is of utmost importance to look at the significance, the contents and worth of former relationships and situations in order to realize that much of the past experience is still useful and hasn't lost its beauty or terror even though it's not happening right now. To repeat the emotions that were felt long ago, to withdraw again and again in order to reexperience all the possible aspects of emotional truth is an essential part of the Goal of Delay.

Someone who has chosen Delay as their Goal will as a rule also find happiness in the structures, the myths and the arts of the past. They like to study their personal history, familiy history and social history, the past of their nation and other nations, their legends and fairy tales. But they prefer most of all to delve into primeval times which seem to awaken memories hardly anyone else can share. This reminiscence, review and reflection gives them strength, it links them to a continuity that possesses its own truth and which gives them a personal reassurance of immortality.

The person with a Development Goal of Delay also possesses a key which opens doors to the deep and dark chasms of his own soul and that of all mankind. He never scorns that which is dark, unexplainable or cruel and which is for many morally reprehensible. But he knows that it is essentially human to possess a shadow. Nothing moves him so much as the raw, the uneven, the archaic, the wild. He senses a strange desire within himself to assimilate and integrate those uneven regions. And therefore he is fascinated by figures, whether real, historic or literary, which display these sombre traits. He »knows« that he himself has not eternally been noble and good in past existences, and he understands.

At his best, someone who devotes himself to the exploration of the past by withdrawing and reviewing, in accordance with his Goal of Delay, feels connected in a very special way to all nature, not just to the vegetable or animal kingdom but also to human nature. No one needs as much direct contact with the earth and the water, with the trees and clouds. This person has a unique way of transcending his ego for a moment or an hour while becoming one with all that is and everything that once was.

However, the same person has a tendency to hide and withdraw from life if he's overcome with fear. He often flees to inner or outer regions where others can no longer reach him. If someone with the Goal of Delay doesn't feel well, is depressed, feels crowded or fearful, he has a strong tendency to regress. Since this is the archetypical goal of the Helper/Healer, he'll suddeenly feel very small and helpless and want to withdraw to a place where he's safe and alone. In this case he feels unable to ask for help, a typical trait of all Helpers. If he had a dark, warm cave, this would be his favourite hiding place but a cosy bed does just as well. As often as possible his mother's womb will be simulated as the only place promising security at a time of fear.

His psyche also creates areas to which he can withdraw in times of need. Delay produces a typical childlikeness, a naivety promising a protection which isn't real. A veil of innocence must often serve to avert all the threats of a modern world which go under the banner of acceleration and continuous challenge. Abrupt, quick changes and unexpected demands or situations are a torture for the person with the Goal of Delay. This is especially true when they hinder him in his slow tranquility or rob him of the chance to slow his life style in areas which he wants to understand better, or where he needs protection, or where he fears to overlook something which appears important and worthwhile to him.

Therefore it's of special advantage if he can create an inner or external place where he can foster and nurture his special need for slowing-down; a place which is stable and emotionally warm, which doesn't change much, gives him security and ensures that he has all the time to observe everything that happens to him from every perspective and with all possible feelings involved.

A person with Delay as the Goal and theme of his actual existence could be compared to a ruminant. He tells you the same story over and over. He needs—just like a valuable cow—the possibility of regurgitating that which has just been swallowed, of tasting it and digesting it and processing it again and again through his various (emotional) stomachs. If he isn't allowed to do this or doesn't take the time for it himself, he can't produce his own »sweet milk«, namely good feelings or fine ideas. If, however, he considers his needs as a stigma, a fault or burden for others instead of understanding them as a beautiful necessity, in other words, if he is ashamed of his own nature, the milk of his being will not be of great sweetness and nourishing content and he'll be unable to nurture himself and others with it.

The archaic quality of this »ruminating« process could be an opportunity for him to create himself conditions in which he can assimilate his emotional experiences without being bothered. If a valuable milk cow grazing on a flowery meadow is constantly being herded around the field with a whip, the farmer shouldn't be surprised if its milk dries up. A person with a Goal of Delay should therefore not allow his fellow men to be such farmers, and should even take care that his »inner farmer« (or his super-ego) is not cruel or careless.

It's important for all who have chosen this Goal to peacefully settle down in some cosy corner of life. They achieve this when they clearly reject the norms of a society which are oriented on haste and acceleration, on progress and material growth, because that will give them permanent guilt feelings and would seem to imply that slowness means unworthiness and fast advancement will always win out.

Energy 2

Rejection

– Prejudiced   Discerning +

The word and indeed the whole concept of »acceptance« is pleasing to you. It evokes a longing in the psyche and conveys the impression of warmth, love and security, of broad-mindedness and tolerance. You all seek to be accepted and you also realize the value that lies in accepting.

But woe be it when you hear the word »rejection«! Then something tightens inside you, immediately you become anxious and feel threatened. The idea that rejection can be something positive is foreign to you.

Embodied souls are subject to the law of duality. They also experience—consciously or unconsciously—that everything they encounter in life is polarized. If you want to learn what Acceptance is, you first have to understand how important the experience of Rejection is for the Goal of Acceptance; you must learn how crucial it is to know what rejecting and being rejected feels like.

The Development Goal of Rejection with all its difficult and unpleasant aspects is exactly the precondition for being able to understand what Acceptance can be. Therefore, setting a Goal of Rejection is the necessary preliminary stage for the Goal of Acceptance. All of you who have chosen the Goal of Acceptance have dealt with Rejection in all its facets in previous lives. This sequence—first exploring Rejection and then Acceptance or vice-versa—repeats itself several times in the course of your entire incarnation cycle. The same thing applies to the sequences of Delay and Acceleration, or of Dominance and Submission.

In this sense, what does Rejection mean? First it's important that you rid yourself of its threatening aspects. Don't be afraid. Try to understand the act of Rejection as an expression of inner strength. Explore the significance of the process that makes Rejection necessary in order to filter out truth. Then, if you hear the word »rejection«, you'll react in the same way as when you hear the word »acceptance«—fearless and relaxed.

But you always want to be accepted and you fear being rejected. You take being accepted as a sign of love and being rejected as a sign of dislike. That is a grave mistake. Also, you have a tendency to understand Rejection in a passive way; but it's just as important to reject actively, to say no to a person, a situation, an order.

Herein lies a much deeper wisdom, and this requires a great deal of courage. To say no, openly and honestly, to someone or something which doesn't suit you or contradicts your principles demands courage, but it also gives you strength and creates clarity around you.

Circumspection and discernment are linked to Rejection. They are the techniques that help you understand that Rejection as a positive, creative energy requires careful examination and patient sifting of people, professions, decisions, thoughts, philosophies, circumstances, reactions, actions and so on. It is a process where you build up or take down all the choices which make you happy or depress you, which do you good or harm you, which help you advance or hinder you. This examining and sifting belongs to the process of Rejection in the sense of a helpful Development Goal for your soul. And there's a good reason for this. For if you all too quickly depend on what others offer you, if you don't know how to say a loving, honest no, you'll walk with crutches although you don't need them, and you get weaker and weaker. If you reject the crutches, you'll be free to go where you want and at your very own individual speed.

Of course, humans who devote a lifetime to the art of rejecting sometimes make mistakes and often seem quite hard and rough in their need to say no anyway. Often they prefer to deny and reject just anything in the first place, they carry an aura of inapproachability, before they soften and are also able to say yes for their own good. The reason is that they need distance in order to see clearly.

We've said that Rejection requires a great amount of courage, for you can imagine that every necessary act of Rejection, even after loving and judicious sifting, be it ever so wise and discerning, carries with it the risk that other persons will feel hurt and offended. It's not always easy to accept and endure their reaction. But your discernment between that which is good for you and what others suggest or want to force on you in order to protect themselves or their own interests, helps you to crystalize your own essential nature, that which you are, and the goal of your own path. And you ought to understand that anyone who wants you to say or do things that you truly don't think are good for you is not really your friend.

We'd like you to place more weight on the healing qualities of honest Rejection, of being able to sometimes say no even to someone you love. Saying yes has a value only if a person can also say no, otherwise it leads quickly to falseness, subservience and obsequiousness. Being able to say no and yes are aspects of inner freedom. Whoever can't say yes is a prisoner. A person who can't say no is a prisoner, too.

If you understand Rejection as something you can learn to express without necessarily hurting or without being automatically rejected yourself, or, if Rejection happens anyway, being able to deal with it, then you'll be able to grow into an attitude which allows others to also reject your ways or proposals from time to time even if this rejection hurts or angers you.

Your great general fear of being rejected results most of all from the fact that you've coupled the idea of Rejection so closely to feelings of unlovingness. Try to separate Rejection from the concepts of coldness, cruelty and dismissal. Rejection and dismissal are two different aspects of one thing. And, of course, the Goal of Rejection has a minus pole, namely prejudice. A prejudiced person is against everything, from the start and without discernment.

We understand Rejection as a clear, loving and empathic refusal of something which isn't good for you or for others. This is of fundamental significance for growth and soul development. We define prejudice, cold dismissal or repulsion as an expression of unlovingness which results from the inability to endure closeness.

Because most humans understand Rejection and repulsion as synonymous, they react to every Rejection as if it were a painful, destructive dismissal. And you don't separate that part or detail which has been rejected by another person but tend to feel that your whole being has been put into question. Only if you yourself practice Rejection as something which can be useful and profitable in the name of love will you be able to let others also reject you from time to time without suffering.

Whoever chooses the Development Goal of learning to reject in the name of love will be confronted their whole life with the encompassing theme of Rejection, no matter if it concerns its passive or active aspects. He'll often appear to be an outsider in society. It will be hard for him to fit in. He'll feel a sense of rebellion in himself that will rub others the wrong way and which will go against their grain. He'll meet with prejudice in others and often is full of prejudice himself against his own fellow beings. But this kind of prejudice is a particular kind of fear.

People who don't go along with everything, people who assisted by their Goal of Rejection cry out instead of complying silently, in other words those who practice civil courage and are in the best sense particular about their interests and their needs, will often be viewed as trouble-makers, as exaggerated individualists or as folks who can't submit, who are either dropouts or eternal rebels who never want to get involved in anything generally accepted or »normal« and who are never satisfied with what is. But this is the fearful point of view of those who aren't in contact with their own power of Rejection. Nothing is stronger than the refusal which is expressed against black sheep. Therefore we don't mean to say that Rejection is an easy Goal. But it is certainly worthwhile, and a necessary experience for every soul.

Whoever chooses the Goal of Rejection, chooses a life of challenges that are especially encountered in the area of social clashes. Rejection also plays a great role in the private lives of such persons. They fear all the time being rejected because of their own strong need to reject. They will often take a long time before they'll allow others to become close to them and their trust is not easy to win. They are suspicious. However, if after much thought and examination they develop trust, they will remain steadfast with it.

They don't accept everything from their family or partners and therefore any person with the Goal of Rejection will be a demanding but valuable teacher for people close to him. His love is shown in the fact that he isn't satisfied with superficialities. It is deepest whenever he can display enough trust to reject his partner in something which appears at the moment to be wrong. He is, therefore, in a position to test the love of his companion in a depth that others would seldom dare do. This testing aspect is part of the Artist energy, Rejection being the Goal of energy 2.

A person with this goal will change his profession or activity, because it may no longer be good for him, more often than someone with the Goal of Acceptance. But understand how both are connected. Such a person accepts his dislikes and his criticism, his inner truths significantly more often than one who laboriously deals with the Goal of Acceptance, trying hard to comply even to adverse circumstances. Only when his fear is too great will he also reject himself or be wrongly suspicious of others. And when he's dissatisfied with himself, rejects himself, condemns himself, hates himself, flagellates himself, when he has lost his self-love, then the child, man or woman with the Goal of Rejection is dependent to a great degree on another human being who recognizes their momentary state of fear and takes them to their heart and shows them that they are not being rejected in their self-rejection.

To pursue the Goal of Rejection in a way that some balance is achieved between a healthy no and the unwanted provocation of enmity which, after all, prevents a judicious inspection of the facts, is an act of self-love which arises from a creative effort. Rejection is the archetypical Goal of the Artist. It's therefore an art to find the right form of Rejection. The art consists of rejecting without destroying, rejecting without harming oneself and pushing people so far away that contact is broken.

Judicious, discerning, nonprejudiced, loving Rejection will, therefore, always take into account that others also have fears. To combine Rejection with love and sagacity demands the art of self-criticism, the judicious examination of one's own motives and the sincere observance of proportions which result in the insight that the Goal of Rejection—namely the growth of one's soul—can only being achieved if Rejection stems not from hate or enmity but from love and self-respect.

Energy 3

Submission

– Subjugated   Devoted +

It's of special significance for a developing soul planning an incarnation to learn how it can create the kind of harmony it was used to on the astral plane even in a human body, although from the moment of incarnation it has to submit itself to the will of new authorities, beyond its own impulses, the necessities of its soul family and the intentions of the All-One.

On the one hand, it's necessary to understand that every soul—no matter if it's incarnated in a human body or not—is subordinate to a trusted energy form—for example, its soul family. The soul is used to submitting itself to the interests of its soul siblings without giving up its own incarnation goals in so doing. It's accustomed to adapting to the loving manifestation of the will of the entire development process. It knows how good it is to devote oneself to the course of events, the almost automatic unfolding, or to what on your planet is called fate but which we, from our perspective, describe as the fulfillment of a greater plan in which the soul itself plays a decisive role. Submission, therefore, is familiar to each one of you from your existence in the disembodied Astral World. However, this must also be learned in the body. That's what this Goal of Submission serves to do.

Most humans who've chosen Submission as a goal for their whole life long for a feeling of devotion yet, at the same time, fear it. However, rebellion which fights against all forms of subjugation, is inseparable from the Goal of Submission. Often, devotion will happen by itself after a fiery act of rebellion. Rebellion, in this sense, means freedom.

At first most people view Submission as unpleasant. It seems to be something like a yoke or slavery. This is because most of you now live in a time and under historical conditions where such states are viewed as torture. Indeed, no stifling sense of being subjugated plagues your daily existence, although you all bring with you experiences from a great number of earlier existences which took place under various forms of slavery or social hardship in which there was no possibility of choice or freedom of decision. The historically »normal« structures of society, whether they were a caste or rank or place, didn't question whether a person wanted to obey their laws or not. That's why many people even now fear the Goal of Submission. It sounds threatening to them, as if it were a permanent subjugation. Subjugation, the helpless, unwilling, unloving impulse to obey the circumstances, is, of couse, just the negative pole of this Development Goal.

An incarnation in a female body has additional difficulty in understanding Submission as something which doesn't contradict a desire for personal freedom or emancipation from traditional role models. However, it's necessary to understand the particular beauty and worth of such a goal, especially in its plus pole, devotion. In this area there are also unpleasant mental overlaps of the ideas of submission and subservience with some of the Chief Characteristics of Fear. Whoever experiences the fear of Self-Deprecation or Martyrdom, for example, will lay the blame for the voluntary subjugation of his own personality on someone else and will accuse him or her of practicing a system of wilful suppression.

But Submission is an act of freedom and a need of the soul, whereas subjugation, as the minus pole of this Goal, means that a person—for fear of punishment, because of helplessness, hate and fury, but also from his own weakness, is forced into resignation. Instead of practising open rebellion, such a person submits against his or her will to the will of others or to adverse circumstances, whatever they might be. Nothing satisfying can ensue from such a negative subordination, but it certainly can from the plus pole which we call »devotion«.

Devotion means the temporary dissolution of an ego-aspect, namely a fearful desire to establish one's own will, in order to protect oneself, or to defend oneself against the flow of life and the interests of one's fellow-men. When these needs of the false personality slowly lessen, when the walls that separate you from the whole disappear and the desire for openness becomes ever stronger, devotion happens by itself. It will start to be the principal energy of a person with the Goal of Submission. It will surround him like a radiance and show him more and more often how devotion can fill him or her with love, softness and openness. Devotion will give much more positive feeling than his old fear that someone more powerful could decide his fate, or make him a grudging servant.

The difficulty for a person with the Goal of Submission lies in the fact that he always fears appearing too soft, too weak or too open, for he's afraid of falling under the tyranny of another and not being able to defend himself anymore. But his own strength—which he'll experience ever more often in the course of his life—lies just in being open. It lies in the loving devotion to what has been chosen by him as a matter of personal concern and interest. Often, a more general concern can only be achieved when two or more people submit to joint leadership. This is the archetypical Development Goal of the Warrior, and the Warrior likes comradeship and acting in unison. To pursue a goal together with others fills him with a special quality of devotion.

A cart, which is drawn by six horses and led by a cart driver, can't be brought safely to its destination when all horses aren't harnessed, or subordinated to the will of the driver and therefore move in unison. So is a person unable to reach a certain place in his soul's development if he doesn't learn to submit himself and to affirm this submission by total devotion to a higher intention. But, as we said, the freedom of rebellion also belongs to this process. Whoever wants to grow into the Goal of Submission must also practice refusal and rebellion, not only in thought or idea, but in doing. For this goal carries the active energy of the Warrior.

Since Submission is the archetypical Goal of the Warrior soul role, we will use allegories from battle strategies in order to make this clearer. As long as a soldier isn't preprared to carry out orders from a higher authority or emanating from the deeper insight of his general, and, in so doing, to forego his personal expressions of will, an army won't be able to win a battle, no strategic movement will be possible. If everything gets confused and each person does exactly what he wants to or personally considers necessary, it's impossible to maintain combat strength or to achieve success and victory.

The same thing applies to people who subordinate themselves to an ideal, who join a large organization, who entrust themselves to the goal set by an authority above them since they know that they wouldn't be in a position to accomplish and achieve these higher matters alone.

Many experience their capability of devotion more in the context of a general idea or non-human authority rather than in Submission to the needs of society or the wishes of a partner. Whoever entrusts their personal will to that which he calls the »Godly« will practices true devotion. Whoever entrusts oneself to life with all its highs and lows without wanting to influence it with his ego and the powers of his false personality, whoever opens himself to the directions that come from the wisdom of his intuition, his inner self or his soul-family, practices devotion and dedication. Thus he is learning to endure a temporary transcendence of the ego, never an easy task for humans, without the fear of subjugating himself to a human power which he can't control and can't reject.

But there is also natural Submission in the personal area for every person within a family or especially in a marriage or partnership. Many resolve them without any difficulties, because they submit out of love. But for some others subordination presents problems because fear rises in them that they must submit themselves to the will of the partner or parental figure without any possibility of free choice.

If, however, they've chosen the Goal of Submission for their life-time it's of great importance to even let devotion into areas of supposedly fearful or resigned subjugation. A person with Submission as a life theme must create life conditions which offer him the possibility of submission and devotion. He must have the possibility of experiencing both subjugation and devotion als the minus and plus poles.

But Submission, being an active Warrior energy, is not entirely a passive experience. A person with this Goal will also demand—and this is to his advantage and to the advancement of his soul—that others be prepared to submit to him. For just as with all other goals, the whole breadth of experience with all its aspects must be lived.

Therefore Submission is not basically a passive goal as many fear. On the contrary, it belongs to the energy level of »action« and must, therefore, actively manifest itself. A psychologically mature person with the Goal of Submission has the special talent of motivating others to being devoted—to a cause, to a person, to an idea. But if his fear level is too high, there's also the danger that he might force others to submit to him and his will and obey him blindly. In most cases, people with the Goal of Submission have a powerful ability to carry through and have well-defined intentions. It's precisely because of this ability and talent that it is a special challenge for these people to practice loving devotion and to do so without forcing their fellow-men, subordinates or colleagues under the yoke of total obeyance.

Many people with the Goal of Submission prefer not to be too active and thereby try to avoid, from unjustified guilt-feelings, the temptation of wanting to subjugate others to themselves. They lead a life without many contacts in order not to fall too far into their negative pole. Since they themselves harbour great fears of being made submissive to the demands of society or the pressures of people, things or situations, they try to avoid this danger by withdrawing from social life, family or friends. In so doing at the same time they avoid the experience of prevailing over others and deny that experience to their fellow men. This is a way of denying one's own strong will-power and a detour on the path to the Goal's lighthouse. We do not blame anybody for it. However, this isn't necessarily the best solution. People with the Goal of Submission need the experience of socializing and being in company. They need the possibility of testing their Warrior-like powers in friendship, at work and in a partnership and of being able to freely choose between a devotion to a human collective with its higher tasks and an involuntary subjugation out of helplessness and rage.

Devotion, like no other goal, breaks down barriers and fills the heart with a radiant softness. The ability to love, which to a particular degree reveals itself through the ability to show devotion, only develops from the voluntary decision to direct one's will so that it can be realized in its most positive form.

Energy 4

Standstill

– Immobilized   Pausing +

To most of you it is a paradox that Standstill could be a Goal of Development. And it looks like a contradiction that there is growth value in standing still. You, who belong to a culture of haste and movement, have only a negative perception of standing still.

In your eyes there is nothing going on or happening in a Standstill. It seems paralyzing, unpleasant and frightening. Each of you wants to move forward and almost all are of the opinion that moving forward has nothing in common with standing still.

Therefore we would like to point out to you right at the beginning of our explanations that standing still and soul growth don't contradict each other. Standing still once every few life times provides for much more growth for the soul than perpetual accelerated movement.

Those of you who have practiced quiet forms of meditation in the right manner know the special quality of an hour in which nothing seems to happen but during which so much does indeed happen—stillness, quietness, nothingness. The exquisiteness of the golden emptiness, the liberation from any demands and challenges, the lack of any desires are so beneficial and so helpful for the development of inner powers, that a standstill with the help of meditative techniques is of immense benefit for any person who longs for and enjoys this special experience.

If we apply the quality of this brief hour of meditation in the course of a busy day to a model of your many successive incarnations, a natural wish will crystalize in your soul to include lives devoted to standing still in the cycle of ceaseless, active development. You'll be able to measure how important and valuable such a period of relative peace, a time of stillness and of ostensible inactivity can be if you've just finished an incarnation which advanced your soul development in great strides but which also caused a feeling of soul exhaustion and growth-weariness.

When you have worked hard for many hours, you need a few hours of sound sleep. During a long journey it's beneficial to spend days and sometimes even weeks at one place and to devote time not only to rest, but also to reviewing what has happened and to prepare for what lies ahead as well as cementing impressions and gathering new strength. In just such a way it's necessary to include a »life of rest« in the cycle of successive incarnations which is intended to allow a human being to regenerate after too much excitement and soul fatigue.

A life with the Goal of Standstill will proceed neither very dramatically nor tragically in the external area. Drama and tragedy are sufficiently well known from previous lives. The person is now ready to integrate all the soul has previously experienced. During a life of rest, he'll devote himself to the peaceful, quiet exploration of his own self and his possibilities.

Whoever has chosen the Goal of Standstill will, because of the reasons we've already mentioned, need much time, much stillness—both inner and outer—in order to devote himself to his development goal. Often he'll prefer not to enter a marriage or partnership, which, because of its constant natural dynamic, presents too much agitation and too many challenges for him or her. One rather tries to establish a quiet relationship with a person who doesn't even live in the same place, but which allows one to nurture some inner peace and to experience a love which doesn't depend on wild dramas and clashes to remain lively.

A person with the Goal of Standstill is well advised to create conditions of life which allow a pause. And by Standstill we mean first of all being able to sit still without being pressured or crowded, in order to allow a silent flow of emotions and insights, to take time to observe all things, both phenomena and events. Standstill means allowing one's body a great deal of rest without giving up activity altogether, developing happiness in peaceful activities, turning to music, nature, art. It is the contemplative way of life which allows introspection, flow and other aspects of life which bring peace instead of hustle and bustle.

The person with the Goal of Standstill needs a lot of time to ponder, to feel and to linger. He needs a peaceful house or apartment in which things are not constantly being changed. He also yearns for a place to himself where he can spend a lot of time just doing nothing in order to feel healthy and well and, if it's possible, his own room to withdraw to.

A person with the Goal of Standstill likes to be alone and quiet but only temporarily, not all the time. For you must understand that a person can stand still only when he's previously been in motion. And the flow will be the more effective and pleasant the stronger the previous activity has been. Therefore, it would be mistaken to assume that standing still is the only possibility and ability of a person who has chosen this development goal. On the contrary, inner and outer movement are a prerogative of the desire to pause, in former lives but also in the present one. But whereas humans with other development goals have a rhythm of much activity and little rest, a person with the Goal of Standstill needs the opposite: much rest and little activity, although in a regular rhythm.

Standing still can be defined as a cessation of active movement. This applies for all lives in the body, but also within a particular embodiment so that a meaningful, beneficial alternation should be strived for between physical or mental movement as well as sexual activity and the following phases of absolute peace and quiet. People with this goal like to work hard for a week or a month and then take a rest of several weeks. In this way, they can be very creative and efficient. But working in your time seldom allow this particular form of employment.

Activities and pauses can alternate daily in a pleasant rhythm or in greater gaps. Whoever has chosen the Goal of Standstill often feels uneasy that nothing, or not much, is happening in his life, compared to the exciting ways of other people. He doesn't even understand how it happens that everyone else is constantly on the move or in a state of change and renewal but that within himself nothing decisive seems to be happening.

The misunderstanding lies in the belief that nothing happens during a standstill. But that is exactly what happens—nothingness! This finally allows something new, for the less the external life moves and changes, the more changes take place in the inner world of the person.

If, because of external pressure, he feels called on to accelerate his life in an unpleasant manner, to arrange his work or his free time in a hurried way that seems required by his family, friends or society, which are themselves in the process of rapid movement, the person with the Goal of Standstill will unconsciously decide to become ill in order to legitimize his need for a pause.

These »rescuing« illnesses often affect parts of the body involved in movement—the bones or muscles, and in most cases they happen quite suddenly. They lead to a temporary paralysis, back problems, lumbago, a fall in which the leg or foot is broken; but sometimes even multiple sclerosis and other chronic illnesses are chosen by the soul as the only solution to prevent a person with this particular Goal from having to keep moving in a manner that is inadequate to his soul's needs. Even paraplegia caused by an accident can, under certain circumstances, be an expression of the soul's need to remain still. If a person recognizes the development Goal of Standstill within himself, he will be in less danger of creating these abrupt pauses, the stiffness or paralysis in a pathological manner.

The explanation of the causal connection between a certain ailment and the Goal of Standstill helps many to soon forgo their illness; it shows them how to integrate more moments of peace into their daily routine, to allow pauses which are demanded by their psyche. Then they can experience the necessary pausing and flow of emotions and thoughts in new ways so that lumbago, sciatica, migraine, an accident or a temporary paralysis are no longer needed.

The positive pole of the Goal of Standstill is pausing for reflection. Pausing means being still for a while—for minutes, hours, days or weeks in order to observe everything slowly and precisely; pausing in order to be able to make new plans, to gain an overview over what has been experienced, created, achieved; it means pausing to reflect and draw conclusions and to be prepared for the possibility of taking on, with a clear spirit and rested body, new duties which can't be carried out in superficial haste but only through longer-term, dedicated planning and implementation. Pausing allows assimilation and integration, the characteristic of energy 4. It creates understanding, insight and meaning. Standstill is the archetypical goal of the Scholar. The minus pole is a particular kind of immobilization or petrification. The person who is completely overworked or overwhelmed by too much hustle and bustle, too many duties and pressure, will fall into a kind of stupor where he hardly functions at all or like a robot does what he has to do without feeling or consciousness. There are cases where persons with this goal escape for a while into something almost similar to a waking coma until they have rested their completely overwrought nervous system enough to awaken again to slow but normal activity. This is an emergency measure; the important thing is to understand that someone with a Goal of Standstill reaches a personal point of exhaustion much earlier than any other people. And he keeps comparing himself to seemingly stronger, healthier, more efficient or resistant people and feels bad because he does not see why he can't be like them. But once he understands and accepts himself as having a different Development Goal, things change, he feels relieved and can relax into what is so special about him—a particular quality of stillness and introspection.

If a soul sees, under normal circumstances, no other possibility of resting and pausing and thereby achieving its Goal of Standstill, then it will decide to choose a body which, from birth onwards, is so handicapped that haste, rapid movement and external pressures to achieve something in the world of business are simply not possible. Such a handicap is often less sad and upsetting for the affected person than for the observer or family member who views the situation from his own needs for movement and thus thoughtlessly applies them to the handicapped child as if every human being in each life needed the same conditions and orientations.

Whoever observes their children and discovers one who first romps about for an hour or two and then sits motionlessly for a long time in a corner, staring into some mysterious distance without appearing to be unhappy, should consider the possibility that he's chosen the Development Goal of Standstill.

This goal isn't directly connected to mental slowness or an intellectual handicap. Quite the contrary: the mental faculties of a person with the Goal of Standstill are usually extremely active. But he's mainly concerned with himself and his inner perceptions and with the careful registration of all which he experiences. He who pauses is, as a rule, highly sensitive. He observes and registers more than he could ever tell. He registers more from the outer world than most others but needs leisure and peace in order to understand, assimilate and integrate everything in the deepest and most complete way.

And there often linger memories, awful and disturbing, from past existences which must be overcome and digested half-consciously through great efforts and sometimes severe pain, especially during the first ten years of life. Such a child, therefore, shouldn't constantly be disturbed or distracted, motivated or activated. He'll develop better and more consistently if he's simply left in peace. Otherwise he will feel like someone who is brutally awakened from an important, significant dream.

Most parents want lively, active and charming children but constantly punish them when they're too loud and active. A quiet, dreamy child is practical but it worries the parents since it doesn't fit the norm. A child with the Goal of Standstill will become overly nervous if he's roused too often from his immobilizing day dreams and his need for retreat and flow. If this happens too emphatically, as a last retreat he'll escape into autism, which will guarantee his standstill and inner peace. However, if one respects his desire for seclusion and pausing from the beginning, he won't see the necessity of fleeing into this kind of psychosis. If the soul of someone with this disposition becomes fearful of not achieving his Development Goal because he won't be allowed to enjoy as much peace and pausing as he needs, he can, in adulthood, even fall into a mental state of major depression and apathy which indeed no longer allows any movement and which is extremely tormenting for himself and all involved.

For a person with this goal, depression means a symbolic expression of refusal of any contact. This can be temporary, until the fear has passed, or it can last months or years. A doctor or family member who understands that a desire for a pause which isn't being fulfilled lies behind this disturbance, will be able to help and free this person from their frozen, petrified, immobilized state. They will—slowly—be able to breathe life into him again and to communicate to him that in the future he can make a sub-stantial pause anytime he wants to follow his personal needs and his soul's goal.

Standing still is creative. Standstill creates an inner world of indescrib-able richness, of brilliant color, of happy well being which, however, seldom or never reaches the outer world since it doesn't sense any great need for com-munication.

Whoever has someone with an obvious Goal of Standstill near him and wants to lovingly deal with him, should first of all respect the »unex-plainable« desire for a pause instead of condemning it as a nuisance. He must accept the »strange« need for silence and inner withdrawal of the partner, child, colleague, friend or family member and then choose particu-lar forms of communication which should not be violent, loud, hectic or forceful. Then he can be confident of the love and gratitude of his fellow-man and be happy that he's helping his loved one in his development and inner growth.

Growth and inner progress occur through pausing at the right moment. The paradox of this situation is only superficial. In a deeper sense each of you knows that pausing is healing for body and soul and that the fear, through such a silent standstill, of sinking in a marsh and not being able to move out again, is completely unfounded.

Love and self-respect should ensure that motion and standstill, striving and pausing, supplement each other in a perfect rhythm. Both professional and private lives ought to contribute in a meaningful way to achieving this goal if they are experienced in a contemplative, introspective and meditative manner.

Energy 5

Acceptance

– Ingratiating   Kindhearted +

Many of you confuse acceptance with resignation. This mistake goes so far that most of you are almost incapable of making a distinction between both behaviors. What you think of as acceptance is often secret, painful resignation. But what we mean by Acceptance is an important Development Goal and something entirely different.

Accepting means saying yes from a warm, full heart. Saying yes has no meaning if it lacks joyfulness. Acceptance means getting involved. From this true admittance of everything that is into one's heart, arises kindheartedness, a form of unconditional love.

It would be superfluous to put the word »unconditional« in front of the word »love« if all of you had not been trained from earliest childhood to experience love mostly as conditional love. You all seem to believe that mother love is basically an unconditional love. But throughout most of your life you have experienced love that set conditions rather than to have really been unconditionally accepted. So you had to go to the potty when mother wanted you to and you were rewarded if you were successful, but not if you weren't. You had to laugh in order to make mother happy. Then you were loved. You had to behave well and look sweet so that your mother could be proud of you. Then you were loved. You all know this and still consider that kind of love unconditional since you rarely if ever experienced something different. You learned very early to accept with a certain resignation the demands and conditions attached to love. Therefore, it isn't easy for you to understand what Acceptance can really be, how much happiness and ecstasy there can be in an unconditional yes to all that is. And we accept that as a fact. But surely you can learn. Usually you associate Acceptance with unpleasant and negative situations or reactions and people that »must« be accepted, if ever so grudgingly. It's difficult for you to imagine that acceptance can just as well be associated with something beautiful and pleasant. Acceptance and grudge don't go together. We say: Everything that is, is good. Everything that is—be it good or bad, beautiful or sad—can be accepted joyfully.

Acceptance is a Goal which at its best doesn't judge or differentiate and sets no conditions. Let's give you an example. You may have heard someone say: Live in the here and now! An excellent proposal, but if it's a demand from someone, it will carry the force of pressure and set a condition. Then you are not really o.k. if you don't. But imagine how wonderful it can be to really say yes to what is this very moment and not desire anything that is not. Then you'll understand that the idea which lies behind this call is truly excellent.

Since people with a Goal of Acceptance learn very early how to please their parents and how to ingratiate themselves to those around them, it's difficult for them to be free from a fear-driven false politeness and exaggerated kindness and to distinguish it from the concept of love as they want to practise it. We notice again and again that with a Goal of Acceptance you're convinced that saying yes is the only way to survive. Acceptance then becomes a distorted act of love, something you do for someone else to please him or avoid criticism and conflict. You do or say something kind and helpful, though often against your inclination and your intention, against your deeper insight and especially your energy. This isn't love in the sense of true kindheartedness, though, because it rings untrue.

Love as an expression of true goodness simply acts and responds without even asking: »Do I want to or not? Has he or she deserved it or not?—

I just do it because I do it. I love because I love. I act because I act. I say no, because I say no. I say yes, because I say yes, because in this instant of here and now it suits me.«

This attitude of authenticity would do a lot of you good, independent of your own Development Goal. It would make it so much easier for you to deal with life and its definite adversities if you weren't cut off so often from love because of false kindness and obsequious behaviour. You don't need to feign goodness, you are good because you exist! And authenticity is goodness.

We are not speaking against duty or true selflessness. But if you do something for another person, whether it be in a spiritual or a physical sense, check to see if you're really happy doing it. Then you'll be in the pole of unconditional love and kindheartedness. But if what you do is done reluctantly, if you have to overcome some major resistance, if you just hope to win the love of the other person, his esteem or admiration, then you're in the area of obsequiousness and false politeness. The act as such may be helpful, but it lacks the energy of love, is secretly impregnated with the energy of fear and therefore will have a much different effect in the long run.

Now we want to draw your attention to one more thing: Whoever chooses the Development Goal of Acceptance for his life and pursues it, won't be able to avoid false kindness. Trying to avoid it is useless. It is one legitimate way of trying out the minus pole of this Development Goal. Accepting people will necessarily be sometimes ingratiating. They are experts in well meant insincerity. They often have a chronic smile on their face. But they can't only stay in the positive side of their goal, the kindheartedness. Why is that so? If you, with your Goal of Acceptance, tried to be always good, that would be a clear indication of non-acceptance of yourself in your natural rhythms. Rather chose to observe yourself and become more sincere with your own emotions.

You would not be understanding and kindhearted against your inner truth if you tried to condemn yourself for not being more often or constantly in the area of sheer goodness. Souls with this Delevlopment Goal are naturally among the kindest peeple on earth; their growth potential lies hidden in their ability to say no when no is true.

Acceptance doesn't mean »swallowing everything« or »saying yes to just everything«. Supposed goodness, obsequious friendliness tries to shortcut the resistance necessary for others, doesn't dare to refuse, prevents positive friction, is filled with feelings of guilt, is a little cowardly and mortally afraid of every boundary and limitation, every »no« of someone else.

Whoever has chosen the Development Goal of Acceptance will have to spend his whole life trying to realize where his own weaknesses begin and where he weakens others by accepting everything from them. When strength is manifested in a loving steadfastness that sees the true well-being of others and also the needs of one's own self, Acceptance begins. Kindheartedness without effort starts to flower. But when you speak of boundless goodness you often mean, without consciously realizing it, a behavior that sets no boundaries or a person who can be described as very easily exploited. And boundless goodness is almost naturally equated with naivety or stupidity.

Whoever makes a great effort to be falsely polite and ever friendly because of a lack of self-acceptance of his own shadow side, often proudly says about himself: »I'm too good for this world.« He says it half out of fear and half out of self-satisfaction. Being too good for this world appears to be a very special human quality. In truth it is nothing but fear and weakness. They are the ones who are exaggeratedly generous, who give everything away and remain with nothing left. They are the overly-willing persons possessing no apparent will of their own other than the desire to constantly be at the service of someone else. They don't want to put in question their own self-image, they prefer to give in to everything and everyone and don't respect their own dignity.

Those around them, however, often view such a surplus of goodliness with pity, irritation and even with a certain revulsion.

We remind you again that the plus pole of »kindheartedness« is not unconditional in the usual sense. Quite the contrary, all those with the Goal of Acceptance are called on to differentiate clearly between accepting everything and swallowing everything. Unconditionality means in this context: »I'm prepared to love unconditionally and in so doing to respect the conditions set by my fellow-man as well as my own conditions.«

The need to accept requires courage, not resignation. It must not only apply to unpleasant situations which you or others face. The Growth Goal of Acceptance often applies first of all to yourself. Accept yourself, therefore, when you feel you can't accept yourself. Accept the fact that you can't always be good. Accept the fact that you can't always be loving. Then your heart will be lighter. You will feel wiser, for Acceptance is the archetypical Goal of the Sage.

You'll come a little closer to your goal of growth if you consciously allow yourself to be unloving at times. Or observe yourself how out of a deep fear of being rejected, of not being accepted, you are flattering another person and accept yourself while you are doing it.

The person with the Development Goal of Acceptance is called on above all to accept his fear of saying no. It won't help him if he tries to laughingly pass over this reluctance and to navigate from the positive pole of his Goal, the kindheartedness only. Whoever isn't prepared to acknowledge his own minus pole of being obsequious and overfriendly, to recognize it and to observe it as a sign of his fear to say no, will have difficulties with his goal. Whoever is ready, however, to make the observation of that fear of not being accepted the servant of his inner growth and development will make great progress on his journey.

Energy 6

Acceleration

– Confused   Comprehending +

The Development Goal of Acceleration will be chosen if a soul senses the courage and strength within itself to realize and experience more demanding situations than in previous lives. It is a particularly strenuous and demanding goal. It will bring acceleration and turbulence into the development of the soul and the incarnate personality. It includes certain constellations of the soul collective—(e.g. the Soul Family)—which, independently from the intimate needs of the individual soul, will make possible a considerably rapid growth for more than one member of that collective.

This constellation will come into being if a greater number of members of one's own Soul Family make themselves available for mutual growth through friction. It happens whenever many of the soul siblings are also incarnated at the same time and place so that contacts—both pleasant and less pleasant—can take place more often and more naturally. The Goal of Acceleration will also often be chosen if historic or political conditions present a special occasion for the soul to deal with themes which, under different circumstances, wouldn't be available to the same extent.

For example, this could concern epochs of great military conquests or times of accelerated material, economic or scientific progress, or phases of decline, as for instance the fall of the Third Reich, periods of mass migrations or massive cultural change like the invasion of a tribal society by a more developed and highly organized civilization. You can imagine how difficult it is for a human being whose entire biological program is directed toward security, anchoring and a homeland, stability and loyality, to suddenly find himself in a situation in which he's forced to repeatedly give up his settled form of existence and move on. He may no longer be able to put down roots, he will lose family members or get into dangerous situations which never would have occurred if he'd been able to stay with his people in one place.

This situation manifested itself to a great degree throughout Europe after the Second World War and also, in many parts of your earth, during the huge refugee movements in more recent times. The Goal of Acceleration often requires an extremely strenuous situation that a soul chooses beforehand in order to grow. But the growth lies not in adapting and coping somehow. It is the emotional, inner process that changes from utter confusion to new insight, clarity and comprehension and a reassessment of one's own self under confusing circumstances that makes the soul's growth accelerate.

Also unexpected, sometimes terminal, illness or being out of work for a long period puts the theme of Acceleration at the center of attention. The person with this Development Goal will have to accept and deal with every challenge with which he is confronted to further his inner growth.

Acceleration, therefore, always seeks difficult situations which demand a certain measure of courage and endurance in order that they might be overcome. But of course such growth doesn't have to take place only in difficult situations. Quite the contrary. The Mature or Old Soul who seeks accelerated development must learn not to stand still if nothing much is happening externally. People with a Goal of Acceleration will seek inner challenges if life is quiet, if things are going well for him, when everything is fine and there are no longer any external challenges which must be met. Therefore, to the surprise of friends and family, he often feels it necessary to create problems where there are none, or to make big problems out of little ones, simply because he needs a problem for his development. He sees everywhere challenges and difficulties where others see none. If these difficulties are no longer evident in the external world, he'll look for and find them within himself. Since he likes to turn to his own self, his own depths, his psyche and subconscious, he'll be someone who prefers growth in psycho-therapeutic situations and knows no peace until the reasons for his desire to advance are plumbed to the depths and he has the feeling of really making progress.

Whereas Rejection and Acceptance are outward-going, communicative Goals, being located on the Level of Expression, Acceleration (like Delay) is a Goal located on the Level of Inspiration. When life is raging all around him, the person with the Goal of Acceleration needs to become quiet and retreat in order to digest what is happening. If he goes on rotating and stays active for too long, his confusion will become overwhelming and his nerves will snap. So after each major challenge a period of quiet and integration is needed to maintain inner stability. Only this rhythmic measure leads to the beautiful, almost meditative clarity and overall comprehension of life souls with this Development Goal are seeking. This Goal belongs to the energy of the Priest.

Growth usually takes place in a stop-and-go manner. It is never linear, but takes place in phases. Acceleration as a method to grow spiritually in the largest sense uses everything at hand in order to acquire more awareness. It's of special importance for a person with Acceleration as his Goal to identify the phases of great inner growth after some major challenge and not to be dissatisfied if the psyche and also the soul need to pause for awhile before they prepare for the next great leap. It is an aspect of the Accelerator's fear to look frantically for the next challenge so he can stay confused instead of allowing clarity. Clarity is a great teacher and a challenge as such.

You know that a child who's been bedridden for a longish period discovers with amazement that he's grown several centimeters with a speed which wouldn't have been possible in a healthy state. Therefore, a person with the Goal of Acceleration often needs phases of peace, of withdrawal, almost regression, in order to prepare for a new time of accelerated development. Without a phase of integration he would constantly be confused. He would neither achieve insight nor understanding. The state of lack of understanding would remain and accumulate. No human, no animal, no fruit can constantly and continuously grow. The times of preparation are also an important element of growth. But they're not so apparent. Whoever doesn't rest falls into deep confusion and no longer accelerates.

But these periods of rest are different from those a person with a goal of standstill or delay would need. They are much shorter. Often half an hour of doing nothing or a day off will be sufficient. Acceleration is the the archetypical goal of the Priest. It is therefore essentially a quiet, inner process that has a quality of meditation and contemplation. It is obvious, though, that doing nothing, just lying or sitting with their eyes closed, is so difficult for many persons with the Goal of Acceleration that it resembles a kind of subtle torture. But it is necessary to digest all the feelings and impressions an attitude of constant challenge implies. If this is not done, a very nervous, tense and confused state of mind will be the result, and often some illness with a high fever or a few weeks in hospital are needed to ensure the necessary days of rest for psyche and soul. A holiday here and there, a week on the lakeside in a log cabin, a fortnight in the mountains, just walking and sleeping and looking into the blue skies will do miracles.

A person with Acceleration as a Goal will often despairingly ask where else he could find occasion for more growth. If several days pass without any problem or difficulty, he will be unsatisfied, but he'll also complain when exactly that difficult situation he has been yearning for finally arises. He yearns for intensitiy and for utter peacefulness at the same time. He senses within himself, and from without, a constant demand for growth that often makes him very tired and nervous. Then he would like to fight against any new demand or challenge. His standard phrase is: »I can't take any more, I am utterly exhausted.« But the next day already he is off in search of something new and exciting.

We spoke earlier about the automatic functioning of a Development Goal and said it resembles a lighthouse flashing constantly and showing the way. As with all Goals, this also applies to the Goal of Acceleration—a certain automatism is integrated into the advancement. A person with this Goal has no need to seek extra challenges; life is there all the time to present the next one to him.

Just as you can install an automatic gear in your car and then no longer have to worry about shifting gears, so there is also an automatic shift in the life of one who, in his special way, is involved in accelerated growth, a kind of Acceleration which allows him temporarily to think about something completely different than advancement and progress. And that does him good.

Meditation and moments of peace are of very special importance for people with the Goal of Acceleration, even if they present themselves in the guise of absentmindedness or laziness. If they don't allow themselves this peace of mind it will be more difficult for them to deal with the dissatisfaction that plagues them because they aren't advancing to the degree that their standard and discriminating inner norms demand.

Accelerators are often insomniacs. The pauses necessary for psychic digestion they usually deny themselves during the day are not entirely substituted by night sleep or afternoon naps. It would be best if they could lie down without sleeping for half an hour every day. Then they would need less sleepless digestion time during the night, and the plus pole of comprehension would be facilitated.

Resting and pausing and day-dreaming will often erroneously be viewed as the opposite pole of growth by Acceleration. But this isn't so, and especially not for people with a Goal of accelerated soul growth. Actively doing nothing (not sleeping) is of excellent significance for inner growth, for it is from this particular state that the deepest insight emerges. It's a special challenge to truly learn to endure the temporary powerlessness and helplessness which every soul who has chosen the Goal of Acceleration faces when he is inactive and devoid of problems.

People with this Goal often set themselves lofty, often overly-lofty demands. They long for every challenge since they think it is their decisive life's purpose to overcoming enormous difficulties, the greater the better. But they hate the confusion which proves to be the complement to any clarity and insight which they want to gain. They fight against it because they can't categorize the temporary state of unclarity and are plagued by the fear that this could be a permanent condition.

However, for a person with the Goal of Acceleration, confusion is like the fuel which starts the motor. No deep insight is possible without previous confusion. Only when one first allows the fearful feelings of having no ground beneath one's feet, and not knowing where one's going and which path one should choose, can one expect that sudden insights will appear like a comet in the night sky.

Whoever has chosen Acceleration as his life theme sometimes sees great worth in making his life as difficult as possible. However, this is a misunderstanding of the Goal. We would like to remind you that no Development Goal fundamentally has the function of burdening a life, or of making it unbearable. Therefore, we advise all those souls who feel the need of making as many quick and great strides forward within an individual incarnation to trust the dynamic within themselves and to rely on the fact that their soul, as if by itself, will seek the suitable challenges. Your earthly life already presents enough problems so that further difficulties and challenges posed by the psyche and the mind are unnecessary.

The Goal of Acceleration can be compared to the swift flight of a bird, higher and higher into the sky and nearer to heaven. A lead weight hinders that flight. Lightness, grace and the necessary confidence in the weight-bearing capacity of the elements and trust in the laws of existence are the qualities that every person with the Goal of Acceleration also possesses, like a bird, and he can become aware of it. They will manifest themselves when, in his consciousness, he allows room for the realization of his soul's disposition.

Energy 7

Dominance

– Dictatorial   Leading +

Lack of leadership creates chaos. It's clear to everyone that society couldn't successfully conquer the challenges of the age if there weren't people prepared to lead them and take responsibility. Those souls who have chosen Dominance as their Development Goal are prepared to do this by their very nature, their aptitudes and powers. They develop leadership qualities and are willing to take all the risks involved: dictatorship and loneliness, mistakes on a grand scale and the temptations of power.

In this same society in which leadership is in so dire need, every presumption of dictatorial dominance will be viewed critically and even with disapproval, suspicion and as morally reprehensible since most of those who can't affirm the Goal of Dominance for themselves personally fear the negative effects of this goal. The minus pole is »dictatorship« and dictatorship is truly a reason to distrust power.

Everyone whose soul chooses the Goal of Dominance and affirms it in bodily life must practice self-dominance to a special degree and guard against the effects his fears have on this Goal. For the temptation to view leadership as a license, as permission to force others to cede to his will and to do things which would harm them or which they loathe is especially great for someone who pursues this Goal. The plus pole, which is manifested in a responsible, venturesome leadership, will always have positive effects if the person with the Goal of Dominance has learned to master or dominate himself and to use his capacity for love to achieve his Goal. This means that everyone who makes Dominance the center of his efforts first must learn to bring his own power under control. The first step consists of recognizing how a natural desire to dominate or a tendency towards imperious behavior in childhood, youth and early adult age affect their immediate surroundings.

The person with this Goal is, as a rule, not aware of the fact that he presents a threat to others. He has the tendency to get his own way and to disregard the more weakly articulated needs of others; and if he can't do this by means of open discussion, he'll resort to manipulative measures in order to achieve what he views as his birthright. Generally his friends and family consider him or her as domineering.

These manipulations could consist of defiance or flattery, charm or refusal. The person with the Goal of Dominance will, nevertheless, seldom have to do without carrying out his intentions or fulfilling his wishes. He usually gets what he wants. Dominance is characterized by the archetypical energy of the King. Parents, partners, friends and colleagues submit because they feel they can't be a match for the massive and self-evident pressure of their opponent and with resignation give up their position. This can easily lead them to showing insufficient resistance to a young person with the Goal of Dominance, so leaving him unclear as to the boundary between leadership and dictatorship. They let themselves be ruled by him and only indirectly display their anger. The dominating person, who doesn't appreciate his impact and acts like a giant in a land of midgets, knows only that the effects of his untamed, dictatorial needs bring him a good amount of loneliness and isolation instead of contact and popularity.

The next thing that happens is that the dominating person becomes afraid of displaying his claim to Dominance. He'll still practice Dominance; however he will develop a tense disposition to the effects of his drive. He'll be shamefully aware of his desire to dominate everything and everyone and will be embarrassed to achieve another victory even if he desperately needs this victory in order to live meaningfully. But this is a necessary experience. It is a fact that pursuing one's Goal in any sense gives meaning to a life.

The Goal of Dominance is difficult to sustain in youth and young adulthood. Only in a mature age will the dominating person be able to recognize his unconscious dictatorial side, reject dictatorship and develop an authentic leadership ability. Authority, influence and the inseparably-linked responsibility will occur ever more frequently instead of the desire to simply rule over others. The manipulative behavior lessens and is identified as an expression of the fear of not being able to carry through when »carrying through« is viewed as an essential necessity.

The mature person with the Goal of Dominance will be more peaceful and secure. He's now in a position to exercise his strength moderately, lovingly and really profitably. And his self-control is now steadfast; he no longer has to prove at every opportunity that he's greater, stronger, more intelligent, more wonderful than others. His self-evident authority will communicate more about himself to those around him than his wilder domineering actions.

He now has the ability to be a model for others. He can more often assume leadership roles out of experience. He won't have to fight emphatically for recognition of this leadership for it will be alloted to him in a natural way. Because of this, the level of his fear drops and he no longer has the need of using dictatorial methods to achieve with will-power what he couldn't achieve with love.

If such a person can find little or no possibility to try out the role of ruler, leader or dominating person because of certain reasons of social imprinting, education or neurosis, he'll let others rule him. He'll achieve his Goal of experiencing Dominance by letting himself be dominated. Then he'll develop feelings of hate and rejection which he directs at others who can better dominate and lead than himself. He'll therefore have problems with authorities, with powerful and dominating people, whether they be in school, society, politics or the home environment, where he'll make father figures or enemies of all those who live their Goal of Dominance.

The person with the Goal of Dominance tends to be jealous of all those who can better articulate their leadership abilities than himself. If he can recognize the Dominance of others without being too frightened by it, he'll make them into a model, an ideal or idol, a leading figure upon whom he can orient himself. In early adulthood, however, he'll have to put them into question in order to find his own authority and leadership ability. Otherwise, he'll always hide behind the greatness of these leading figures. He'll nurture his weaknesses instead of taking responsibility for his own strong personality.

The concealment of one's own strength and powers leads a person with the growth Goal of Dominance to an attitude which finds expression in petty or malicious forms of control and exercise of power over those he views as subordinate and weak. He should take care that he doesn't suppress his family like a house tyrant and that he also doesn't use fear, punishment, physical affliction or chronic illnesses to make everyone dance to his tune.

It's of great significance for him to develop a feeling for the correct balance. He can, unchallenged, assume a leadership role within his circle of friends and colleagues if he doesn't try to achieve his goals with too fearful a pressure on others. He should always remember that his Dominance will only be disputed, envied and torn from him, or will result in punishment if he uses dictatorial methods to carry it out. If he succeeds in creating a firm but still friendly-loving system of rule, which doesn't constrict them but promises them freedom without abdicating leadership, then he'll be an excellent father, mother, head of department, intensive care nurse, manager or politician.

The self-control of which we've spoken will have a positive effect on the Goal of Dominance. The more a person with such clearly dominating tendencies moderates them consciously, the more he can exercise his strength in a meaningful manner. And if he succeeds in reconciling self-criticism, self-knowledge and self-restraint with his growth Goal of Dominance, he'll develop into a personality who commands natural respect, who's loved and respected, who can be offered leadership for large groups of people since his fellow-men recognize and realize that they're in good hands.

In the area of personal relationships the person with a Development Goal of Dominance needs partners or friends who, on their part, have a healthy self-image and who are filled with a natural ability to carry through. If the dominating person meets too little resistance he'll either unconsciously fall back into domineering behavior and won't be able to moderate himself, or he'll punish with contempt his partner's lack of resistance to him.

In order to really love a person with a Goal of Dominance it's necessary to set limits on him and to emphatically point out to him when he practices dictatorship and thereby places others under a regime of fear. We've said that the person with the Goal of Dominance is often hardly aware of the effects of his power and that it's therefore difficult for people near him to rebel against him.

He accuses those who are less dominant or more timid, of lack of will-power or lack of self-confidence; on the other hand he fears the Dominance of others. If you rebel against him and his attacks, he'll feel you're trying to take over his leadership role. He'll feel threatened and attacked like a king who is confronted by a rebellious generals. In private relationships this can result in major fights which can only end in a peace treaty when both parties realize that they were acting out of fear and not love.

Parents can learn to set clear limits and boundaries for children who seek to rule the family without curtailing their leadership role altogether or even breaking their will; for a person with the Goal of Dominance needs from the very beginning a realm in which he can be the undisputed leader. If parents notice their child has this goal, it's good to provide him an area in which his Dominance, his will power, his leadership role, his cleverness and his abilities to carry through remain undisputed, and which can be observed with happiness.

A child with the Goal of Dominance also needs within his circle of friends the possiblity of leading and should only be criticized or punished if he unbearably constricts or pressures his comrades. Otherwise, the child will soon feel pushed aside, he'll find out that no one wants to play with him and he'll have to escape into power and greatness fantasies in order to test at least in the imagination of his mental realm the goals which he couldn't test in society. Boundaries are necessary but too strict rules harm the leadership will of the child and result in the fact that for years he'll have to deny his natural powers or he'll feel forced to find neurotic outlets for the application of his capacity to dominate.

We stress once again how necessary it is for every social structure to entrust leadership responsibilities to those who have a natural and healthy authority and who practice Dominance in responsibility and love. Therefore, those who have chosen the Goal of Dominance are especially called on to assume leadership responsiblities whether in private, social or political sectors, in trade and industry or in management. Whoever possesses these powers should nurture their abilities and practice them in self-control and responsible leadership.

The natural and visible inner strengths, which are accessible to such a person without effort, free him from the necessity of showing how good he is or of having to forcefully carry through against the will of others. The more a person with the Goal of Dominance trusts his positive influence and his powerful personality, the closer he'll approach his Goal and the more fulfillng will be his existence.

As long as inhibited expressions of his mighty Goal are his only outlet, a sense of dishonesty and difficulty, of meaninglessness and unfulfillment will be pervasive. Only the affirmation of the Goal of Dominance frees a person from the fear of not being able to show his natural leadership qualities. Then he can breathe freely and rely on the concept that his energy is needed and he is loved just the way he is. He'll experience a wave of admiration and support which confirms his leadership abilities and removes the fear that he could cause harm with his power, his wishes, his abilities and his instincts.

Modes

⑤
Power

− patronizing   + authoritative   − anxious   + prudent

Expression Level

②
Caution

⑥
Passion

− fanatic   + charismatic   − inhibited   + restrained

Inspiration Level

①
Reservation

⑦
Aggression

− belligerent   + dynamic   − fixated   + persistent

Action Level

③
Perseverance

④
Observation

− watchful   + vigilant

Assimilation Level

IV The Seven Modes

The Mode determines the best way in which an incarnate soul reaches the individual Development Goal. It also indicates the way in which a person lives his life most powerfully.

The information you've received so far about your soul pattern has already produced a coherent and meaningful picture: However, it's like a black and white photograph or a charcoal drawing. Now the Mode brings color to the picture.

The Mode is not only the most appropriate way and means by which you move toward your Goal—that's its main intention—but it's also the way and means by which you color all your experiences and intentions in a specific life. Therefore, the Mode has a great deal to do with the joy of life. It moderates the all too severe challenges which a soul often sets for itself in the special exuberance prior to a new incarnation.

The Mode can also be used as a corrective measure in the dynamics of a soul Matrix. For example, it can envelop harsh contrasts and potentially conflicting energies in a protective mist or fog. Or it can bring color and contrast to a picture whose depths of field are too flat. What would life be without these colors and contrasts!

The Modes represent a system of temperaments, a possibility, therefore, to describe and determine the tempo and mood with which you live best and shape your life best.

You've already heard that the Mode strives to concentrate on the fulfillment of your individual Development Goals. These Goals are often difficult and contradictory and, as a rule, the Mode steps in to help you, to support you in the pursuit of your Goal and to give you further impulses on how you can use your energy in the best and most meaningful way in order to reach with ease the Goal your soul has set.

We want to explain a few aspects of the Mode. For example, whoever has chosen the Mode of Reservation shouldn't think that because of this he is obliged to show restraint (the plus pole) in all life situations, or that he is condemned to be inhibited all his life (the minus pole). And whoever has chosen the mode of power doesn't have to insist on asserting his authority everywhere. They'll do that anyway most times. It's much more important to constantly remember: If I act from the plus pole of my mode without any special exertion, I support my Development Goal without having to work directly on this Goal.

Let us explain: If you have chosen Rejection as a Goal in your soul pattern you can achieve much through restrained rejection, if Reservation is your mode. It's enough to concentrate on this plus pole of restraint. That is your most efficient way of rejecting what's not good for you. But if you have united the Goal of Rejection with a Mode of Passion, then you can rely on your charisma (the plus pole) to show you the best way to reject. Because of your fiery, impressive aura, your rejection will be achieved as if by itself without any great rhetoric or actions. The Mode is an aspect of the Matrix which makes things easier and more relaxed.

And how can you tell if you're in the plus pole or minus pole of your Mode? The mode in it's positive aspect is a source of joy and well-being. Whenever you find contentment in supporting your Development Goal in your own special way, and whenever this gives you a feeling of ease and inner freedom, you're in the plus pole. And since this plus pole is always viewed as pleasant and beneficial by yourself and others around you, it's easy to activate it. It is still easier for you to do this if you remember all the difficulties which burdened you in the past because of an all-too lengthy period spent in the minus pole of your Mode.

Of course, as elsewhere in the Soul-Matrix, nobody can constantly avoid the minus pole of his Mode. However, if you become aware of its typical energy, it's easy to glide over into the zone of the plus pole, from inhibition to restraint, from fanaticism to charisma, from surveillance to clarity. In the first half of your life you'll be in the minus pole of your Mode more often than in the plus pole. The reverse will be true in the second half of your life. This is the natural fruit of self-experience. To live more and more often according to the plus pole of your Mode makes life easy.

Energy I

Reservation

– Inhibited   Restrained +

Whereas the passionate person brings his totality to all areas of his life, the person with a Mode of Reservation withdraws into himself in all areas. He doesn't allow himself to be carried away by his personal needs and feelings. He knows how beneficial it is for himself and the world around him when he restrains his power, his will, his covetousness as well as his anger, fury and desire. But when he not only restrains but hinders and inhibits them for fear of their power, he starts muting his personality and his whole his being too much. Then he can no longer emerge from his shell, or act in the freedom which lies in restraint but becomes a slave to his own inhibitions.

Restraint and inhibition are the plus and minus poles of this Mode of Reservation. They arise out of the necessity to control an already existing strong energy, especially of feelings and emotions. For restraint and inhibition would be completely superfluous if there was nothing to control.

Many people with this mode have a shy inconspicuous aura when they're governed by fear. Because of the terror of revealing themselves, they try to make themselves invisible. This results mainly from the angst of being carried away by their energy if they are in an uninhibited state.

Therefore, the inhibited person builds so many dams and puts so many locks in the strong current of his powerful energies that he assumes he has them under control. In reality, however, the dams and locks have him under control. They've become autonomous, and it's not easy for those who have been inhibited from youth on, to dismantle the many barriers in order to again make their energy flow powerfully and move freely.

The inhibited person is the river and the lock keeper at the same time. This lock keeper is an extremely shy and overcautious figure. He only acts on instructions from above. And when the higher authorities neglect supervision, he'll prefer to let the river of his energies dam up or allow the whole country (his emotional life) to suffer from drought and become infertile before he'll take a decision which carries the danger of him being punished for acting on his own authority.

So someone with a fearfully restrained Mode of Reservation prefers to wall himself in within his inhibitions and to take into account in so doing that his inner landscape will become desolate. He only feels secure within his self-built prison walls and, if need be, speculates about the idea: »What would life be like if I didn't have any inhibitions?« But he shies away from actually testing the possibilities. On the other hand, however, his psyche senses how wonderful it would be not to have any inhibitions and to be able to flow freely.

Many people with the Mode of Reservation suffer badly because of their inhibitions. They are convinced that they'd be better off if they didn't have any inhibitions at all. In so doing they imagine a misleading ideal. Being passionate or very outgoing isn't a choice for people who've decided for a life-time on the Mode of Reservation.

Now there are many ways and means of dismantling inhibitions, and one of these is alcohol. Often people with the Mode of Reservation who want in some way to free themselves temporarily from their inhibitions reach for the bottle. For a good quantity of alcohol in a short time frees the inhibited person, at least temporarily, from his prison. His tongue loosens, his limbs become more nimble, he does things he otherwise wouldn't dare do. He begins to boast and show off, and overestimates his powers to the same degree as he underestimates them in a normal state. For it's very difficult for him to just restrain himself, stop drinking after a glass or two. The relaxation and excitement which suddenly flow through him with the strong stream of energy are so enticing that he doesn't even think of rationally restraining his impetus. The same effect can be observed with sleeping pills and illegal drugs, for the inhibited person is often extremely tense because of the efforts to keep his dams constantly intact and chemical means relax him; with their help, the tension automatically dispels.

The shyness of the inhibited person is different from that of the arrogant person. Inhibited people, as a rule, don't realize their true strength. But they certainly have the possibility of transforming it into a healthy reservation. While the arrogant person is highly aware of his potential, raises himself above others and builds a wall of fear which is intended to separate himself from them, the inhibited person often truly isn't in a position to reveal himself since he can't give up his natural Reservation.

The reserved person prefers to mute all areas of his life. Even when he's relaxed, he's never exuberant; he remains quiet, he takes his time, he seldom immediately reacts to anything. The less he lets himself be ruled by fear, the more pleasant his reserved manner appears. It isn't hostile, it isn't cold, it is simply calm and collected, and very sensitive at the same time. This is the Mode belonging to Energy 1, it is archetypical Mode of the Helper/Healer.

It sometimes resembles the behavior of the Mode of Caution, but is more emotional than intellectual, and even more reserved. It isn't intended to weigh the pro and contra of a situation but more to test one's own feelings at a given occasion. It is less about objectivity and an adequate judgement; it's more a matter of the self-restrained person bringing into harmony his own needs, moods, feelings and sensibilities in a certain situation. And since this demands a behavior which doesn't immediately react or undertake something, the reserved person is someone who first withdraws into himself in order to feel things over before he makes a decision.

We remind you that this Mode belongs to the polarity of inspiration. This means that the restrained, reserved person is in contact in both the plus and minus poles of this Mode with his inner voice and also with higher inspiration. And, as you know, listening to voices which can't be heard by the body's ears, needs an inner stillness. One mustn't lose oneself in too many distracting activities.

Therefore, the less the reserved person is governed by fear, the more he will long for peace and quiet. He needs time to feel. In order to near the loving plus pole, he needs to be able to seek advice within himself, to test and sound out his vibrations, his emotional response to occurences. And the more frequently he allows himself to reach a decision only once he's certain and clear of what best meets his desire, the easier it will be for him to emerge from his extreme inhibition and to direct his energy outwards, be it ever so reserved.

Since the Mode of Reservation is associated to the archetypical Soul Role of the Helper/Healer, the reserved person is waiting for a directive from his inner voice, in his higher self or from God, from everything which could inspire him. And only when he receives this inaudible, invisible directive, is he prepared to act. This doesn't mean that this mode is mainly passive. Reservation just takes time to test emotionally which actions and decisions are appropriate. The cautious person, in contrast, thinks much before he acts.

Reservation, therefore, is a highly-positive and important component in the Matrix if it is expressed in a relaxed and peaceful restraint. It will be adverse to a person with this Mode if it's expressed mostly in inhibitions, which prevent the natural flow of energy to such an extent that fear is the motivation for all decisions.

However, just as dams and locks no longer needed can be torn down, so can harmful inhibition be broken down. It's not only the reserved person himself who can examine and observe under which conditions his fear diminishes, or what conditions he needs at his workplace or in private life in order to avoid sinking further into fear and instead allowing relaxation to take place. Friends, family members and therapists can contribute significantly to reduce inhibition and transform it into positive self-restraint. They must first realize, however, that a person with this Mode will never be completely free of inhibitions, will never want to be the center of attention and will always avoid making decisions without first consulting his feelings. He simply is not passionate or temperamental.

If a therapist doesn't expect that a naturally reserved man or woman become a playboy or femme fatale or that he would display passionate behavior, he can achieve much to help the inhibited person loosen up. But if someone, even a parent, forces a too inhibited or even a moderately-reserved person into a situation where he's obliged to give up all restraint and to act temperamental against his will, a deep lasting hurt will result; this only drives him back into his painful inhibitions rather than free him.

But respect for this person's inborn Mode will win lasting affection. It's especially difficult for people who are strongly governed by the Modes of Power, Passion and Aggression to deal patiently with the Mode of Reservation, for restraint is often foreign to their nature. They believe that even a mild form of restraint is due to an unhealthy shyness or unresolved problems. The real problem here is that strongly action-oriented Modes have little experience and little understanding for the more passive, quiet Modes.

But usually a Mode such as Caution, Reservation or Perseverance will be chosen by the soul if, in previous lives, experiences have been made with more externally-oriented modes. Only after someone really has aquired the powers which need to be restrained, can he truly dedicate himself to this process. A soul at first chooses, once or many times, extrovert modes like Power, Passion or Aggression, and only when it has exhausted the possibilites of these action-oriented states of being will it withdraw and, from a newly-won distance, try to mute and contain these powers of expression, inspiration, or action with their dual counterparts without losing them entirely. Another option would be to choose the assimilating, neutral Mode of Observation as an interim solution.

It's of great importance that a reserved person learn to live with his Mode and to assess it positively. His fears and inhibitions sometimes suggest to him that he could achieve his ideal personality if only if he could learn to conduct himself in a passionate, aggressive or powerful manner. But he's yearning for Modes which, for good reason, aren't accessible to him. We say for good reason, and remind you once again of the very conscious desire of the soul to choose this Mode of Reservation in order to experience something new.

The reserved person will best be able to free himself from his inhibitions if he recognizes the worth of his basic Mode of behavior and doesn't force himself to sway from this position. For him Reservation and Restraint are an anchor and a source of wisdom. The frantic covering up and ignoring of his natural and meaningful limits will lead him back into areas which he explored long ago and which now, in his present incarnation, would sooner lead him away from his Development Goal rather than to it.

For we constantly remind you that acting and being acording to one's own Mode describes the very best way in which a person reaches his development goal. The reserved person can and must therefore allow himself a relaxed, peaceful and quiet form of restraint. He'll make himself happy by coming closer to himself through the constant observation of his true feelings and the contemplative listening to the voice of his intuition.

Energy 2

Caution

– Anxious   Prudent +

Caution is a mode which prevents an incarnate soul from thoughtlessness, from too much spontaneous reaction, from too wildly a pursuit of his goals without taking into consideration that he is now again a human being who must live with the finiteness of all things.

Earthly finiteness means that you have to take into account many factors which limit you, which won't obey you, which you cannot master. Included among these are your own fellow men. And the second thing which you must take into account is your own modality of being, your biology, your moods, your impressions, the limits of your personality, that which is possible at this moment and impossible in the next, that which you've planned and that which you believe life owes to you.

There are also all the limits which your society has set—laws, morals, social rules, your individual upbringing, your society's attitude to education; your gender role is equally decisive. And finally, you must take into consideration the limits which are imposed on your own species' biology, your body chemistry, your physical ties to the earth and the cosmos.

If you don't consider these factors in a way your intelligence asks for, you'll constantly experience that the goals you wanted to achieve won't be met simply because you have not acted cautiously before reaching them. Or if you achieved these goals for a short period, in retrospect you'll not be happy with the result because you tackled something too demanding, you over-taxed yourself, or thoughtlessly disregarded the other needs. Then they'll strike back, they'll put limits on you they'll make sure you are put in your place, and you will be frustrated, angered, dissapointed in whatever you had planned to do.

But if you let the Mode of Caution prevail, if your soul has chosen it for a life-time, you'll always be more prudent, you'll take into calculation whatever might stand in your way. You will broaden your view so that you won't go through life wearing blinkers or only seeing what is directly before you. Thus cautiously you can bring many things at once into careful consideration, next to you, behind you, over you and under you, in order to value without overrating them.

Being cautious means being realistic in a creative way. Being cautious means being far-sighted. Many can only achieve their Development Goal if they allow themselves to take into thorough calculation at times what lies to the right or left of their path, not ignoring the facts of life but considering them realistically. Caution tells you: »Now you're going too far!« Or: »Now you've done more harm than good!« Prudence exhorts you: »Wait awhile. Go slower. Test the ground and floor on which you walk, for it could be that you're treading on a marshland and must take care that you don't sink. Once you're stuck in a marsh, it's harder to extricate yourself and again move toward your goal than if you take a few careful steps now in order to find firm ground on which to stand.«

Prudence tells you: »Not everyone can walk on water. Most, if not all, drown. Caution advises you to take a boat or to choose a larger ship, perhaps even a oceanliner, if you want to sail the seas for a great voyage. The further your Goal is from you and the more difficult it is to achieve, the better you must prepare, the more careful and prudent you must be if you want to reach it.«

For example, if a person with the Goal of Dominance has chosen a Mode of Caution to experience it, it is especially useful to use it while controlling his desires to act like a tyrant. If he's chosen another of the active Goals, for instance the Goal of Acceleration, it's often necessary to cautionsly apply brakes or to reduce the tempo so that excessive growth doesn't lead to a relapse or setback.

The Mode of Caution has, of course, two sides. It possesses two poles like all other modes and all other Matrix elements. We've already spoken about the positive pole of prudence as such, which always emanates from love. Prudence is deliberateness, intelligent cautioning and loving consideration. Deliberateness allows the weighing of possibilities, prudence gathers strength before the great leap. Deliberateness doesn't aim at curtailing the powers and prematurely breaking off before the essential Goal has been achieved.

But whoever lets himself be guided by fear, easily falls into overanxiousness and will approach everything and everyone anxiously with much too great a caution. He will excessively fight against any form of overtaxing and will therefore seldom or never find out where his limits are and how he can overcome them. A very fearful person with the Mode of Caution always finds good reasons to withdraw from the challenges of life, to turn away from them, to isolate himself and to tell himself from morning till evening: »That's too much for me. I can't do that. I'm not up to that. I better let that be. It's too dangerous. It might be a mistake.« For his fear leads him to transform healthy caution into unhealthy anxiousness.

An overanxious person in the negative pole of this Mode will all too often decide not to attempt anything at all. He'll prefer to live on a pilot light, he'll prefer to be inactive, lethargic and timid and to always seek good reasons not to act which arise from his fear. A gray aura of shrunkenness is created around the overanxious person, who retreats like a shy animal from all difficulties, challenges, perceives dangers everywhere and would prefer most of all to simply hide away in the labyrinth of his mind. In contrast, the aura of a cautious person who nurtures his positive pole of prudence is peaceful and often also has a rosy glow if he recognizes the excellent effects of his prudence on himself and others.

An anxious, overcautious person will tend to see threatening risks lurking all around him. It is a fact, however, that life does consist of unpredictabilities, and if he wants to live life positively, he must at least take a part of these menacing possibilities into account. But he sees hazards and perils lurking in every action and movement. He tries to keep distant from dirt, from aggression, from violent discussions. He doesn't go out on the street because he could fall. He never eats what might possibly not agree with him. He avoids fresh air because he could catch cold. He doesn't go to the doctor because he could catch some virus there. Or he goes there often to get tested for some yet unknown complaint. His whole life consists of considering what adversities could happen to him, what could threaten him - and what, in our view, could make him alive. But he shrouds life in the idea that something intense or risky could make him sick, menace or kill him.

As a parent or teacher an over-cautious, over-anxious person is a great obstacle to the independence of a child. The favorite expression of a person with the Mode of Caution who nurtures his fear is: »Take care wherever you go! Take care that nothing happens to you! Take care that you aren't knocked down. Take care that you don't fall and hurt yourself. Take care that no one angers you. Take care that you don't catch a cold.« In reality this mostly means: »Please, for God's sake, take care that you don't hurt or aggravate me!«

But if a person with the Mode of Caution turns his thoughts in the direction of love, if he can chase the ghosts from his fantasies, if he again finds access to his liveliness, he can be a very good, very deliberate, prudent and sensitive father or an appropriately protective mother, who doesn't keep the child separated from life but teaches him how to approach life in a protective, sensible and positively cautious way.

A person with the Mode of Caution should be aware—and for this he needs time to deliberate for a few minutes or hours—that prudence always helps him come nearer to his Development Goal, be it Acceptance or Delay, Acceleration or Submission, Standstill, Dominance or Rejection, and that he will always feel well if he handles his impulses deliberately, reacts prudently, takes time to check everything, doesn't say yes or no immediately but approaches his next step cautiously. This is a very mental Mode because it mainly employs the thinking apparatus; it is the archetypical energy 2 of the Artist.

He should consider that positive Caution can certainly protect him from many real dangers and rough spots; anxiousness, however, cuts him off from life's threads. Deliberateness or prudence are always present if a person with the Mode of Caution can breathe freely and peacefully. Overanxiousness, in contrast, can be immediately recognized if the breath is shallow, forced, if the voice becomes small or strangled and the view becomes narrower. Since the person with the Mode of Caution tends to withdraw from the hubbub of the world in order to think and evaluate, it will be easy for him to observe his breathing and the movement of his eyes.

And if he's in a relaxed state or, through calm breathing, has been brought from a state of overanxiousness back to his quality of prudence, he should get used to asking himself: »Is this danger truly real? Am I really threatened? Must I react as fearfully as my fear suggests? Do I have to avoid life in order to protect myself until I no longer feel any joy? Must I really be so cautious that I become gray, inconspicuous or invisible? Haven't I discovered that I am most open to attack, fall on my face the quickest, stumble or hurt myself when I'm in this overanxious state?«

The prudent person should not give up his Caution, for that's not being asked. But he can transform anxiousness into self-love and love for others. Imagine, for example, a doctor or therapist who doesn't practice caution or prudence and gives too much medication at one time. Or an incautious healer who so challenges the defense mechanisms of his patient that no healing can take place. You'll realize that this can't be good and that it would be better to proceed prudently, in tentative steps, in order to avoid provoking too strong a resistance. Imagine parents, who demand significantly more from their small child (with a Mode of Caution) than he's capable of and who overtax him. In the worst case, the child will flee into paranoia, which can be viewed as the most radical expression of overanxiousness.

Caution, the Mode with the ordinal number 2, is a highly significant and eminently important element of life. Caution protects you from harmful risks, from thoughtlessness, foolhardiness, from threats to your life, from carelessness and unlovingness. Caution is an expression of love if it's deliberately expressed. Be cautious with yourself and others without being anxious. Then you'll be able to use and apply this Mode from its most beautiful side. A person with the Mode of Caution will be able to integrate himself very well into a community, he'll spread a pleasant aura if he isn't fearful like a mouse and protects himself and holds himself back from everything and everyone. In your time when everything is approached quickly and often exaggeratedly, deliberaton, prudence and caution are qualities very much in demand.

»Wait a moment, please, let's not decide too quickly!« is the motto of the prudent person. »Let's think this over for a moment!«

Energy 3

Perseverance

– Fixated   Persistent +

We'll explain to you later on that the Mode of Aggression (energy 7) is borne by a very powerful kingly energy. The Mode of Perseverance with the Warrior-like energy 3 is located on the same level of powerful vitality. It belongs, as does Aggression, to the polarity of action. It differs from Aggression, however, in that it doesn't manifest itself in a shoving, jerking or explosive way, but, on the contrary, is capable of a particularly even distribution of strong energy over a long period of time—over days, weeks, months and years. Humans with this Mode are constant in all things—love, work, mood.

Whoever chooses this Mode tends to strive for his Development Goal with unshakeable persistence, no matter what this goal might be. We're speaking here not only about general soul development, which for its fulfilment needs a whole life-time, but also about plans for everyday life: constance in projects which concern one's profession and family, all a person undertakes in order to achieve a certain result for the next week or the next year, and which demand a patient, waiting behavior that doesn't at the same time diminish an alert attentiveness. Seldom can a person with this Mode of Perseverance be accused of inconstancy. On the contrary, he is sometimes inclined to chide himself for not showing enough persistence. One can observe, however, that a person with this mode has trouble letting go of something. Lack of perseverance is not the problem. For if the plus pole is well understood by the term »persistence«, the minus pole of »fixation« tends to let everything remain as it was, not to change anything, not to allow anything new to take place and, above all, to prevent any change which comes from without and also changes which occur over the years through the natural development and change in one's own personality. In this the minus pole resembles the obstinate behaviour of the Chief Characteristic of Stubbornness, but its energy is less stiff. It is much more vital and tough, as Perseverance is the archetypical Mode of the Warrior.

A person who lives his Mode of Perseverance from the negative, fear-possessed pole, has great difficulty accepting change, for once he has undertaken something and prepared himself for it—whether it be a job or a marriage, an apartment or a friendship—he insists that this arrangement no longer be disturbed, that it maintains its definitive form and doesn't make him fearful through unpredictable events, through changes that he must become accustomed to or through flexibility to which he feels forced to adapt. A person with this Mode counts on the constance of things and situations. He would like them to promise inalterability. For he can only live that particular fixation of his Mode which is motivated by his fear if the object doesn't move so he doesn't have to move either. This fear of change has something rigid, lifeless and unalterable about it and therefore we describe the negative pole by the term »fixation«. It describes the rebellious, almost aggressive resistance that this pole contains when confronted with the fear of change.

How meaningful and helpful Perseverance can be in its positive pole, in it's unerring persistance! These are people prepared to concentrate for months and years on a project and to persistently continue no matter if, during the course of their days, they sense a desire to do something else, get bored or if they don't experience daily happiness in carrying out their project. They are responsible and committed. They stick to their project and carry it through to completion.

We'll give you a few examples in order to show you how decisive positive Perseverance is for the functioning of your society and also for certain cultural achievements. The compilation of an extensive dictionary, for example, demands not only exact planning but, above all, a patient persistence until the vocabulary which the lexicon must contain is completely assembled from A to Z. Only a person with the Mode of Perseverance would ever think of working twenty or more years on such a project. The painting of the Sistine Chapel demanded a comparable planning and an endless perseverance not only in the maintainance of consistent artistic accomplishment but also the physical readiness to work for years continuously at the same object. Sportsmen who train their bodies for years and decades in order to achieve a certain prize, or great musicians, must also have the Mode of Perseverance, since no one else would neglect family, friends and pleasure and devote his life to hard physical training or many daily hours of practising. Ambition alone can never provide enough energy over a long period of time for a project in order to achieve lasting success. Perseverance in its positive pole is also exhibited by politicians who, from morning till evening, tirelessly do their work on many various places on earth, who race from air terminals to meetings to working dinners without displaying significant symptoms of fatigue and without breaking down within a few months as someone without this special Mode would do.

Perseverance in the sense of a steady persistence and a completely even flow of energy makes possible such a stressful, demanding way of life. This even form of energy consumption and energy creation is connected to the Mode of Perseverance. It can't be explained alone by a thirst for glory, ambition or a striving for power. The Warrior Mode ist helpful here.

But this Mode should also be mentioned where people devote themselves to projects which other's would shy away from. Whoever patiently cares for his sick spouse for many years without losing his ability to love or falling into a routine or cold fulfillment of duties, is just as persistent as is a person who decides despite an unfavorable domestic situation, to continue his education, to finish his studies, and to begin a research profession at a university, a project which takes more than thirty years to plan and carry out in order to be successful.

A collector, who in his youth begins to put together a collection and spends his life persistently gathering all objects which could help complete it, no matter what they might cost or where they may be found, will also, as a rule, have the Mode of Perseverance. He displays persistence because it makes him happy to add a new piece to his collection. If this happiness isn't present, if the accumulation of new additions to his collection only serves to pacify his compulsive fixation, then this is an example of the negative pole of this mode, the unalterability of an occupation begun decades before. For then such a person can't stop thinking that his collection must be completed for he otherwise would find neither peace nor sleep and above all isn't flexible enough to imagine that there are other activities, perhaps of higher value, than the collecting and cataloguing of objects.

The sentence «That's the way it is« can convey two attitudes. The happy, loving positive energy helps a person adapt in a lasting manner to a given situation and face it without resignation, without developing resistance and without making himself a slave. In contrast, when the sentence »That's the way it is« is filled with disgust and a person views the inalterability as a burden or torture but holds on to it as a justification of his lethargy instead of suspecting that he's in a fearful state, he is in the negative pole of his Mode. If he's acting close to the minus pole for longer periods, he makes himself to a large degree insensitive. Then the circumstances and whatever he at one time began determine his life instead of giving him freedom and joy. He is no longer master of the situation. Whoever can't let go when the time has come, no matter what he's holding on to, harms himself and displays false perseverance. Whoever doesn't let go, even though holding on forces him into fear and unlovingness, pays homage to fixation. He clings to his principles and cuts off his vitality, which is naturally subject to change. Perseverance must act and keep moving. Perseverance wants to achieve something lasting. It dispenses its actions in an even, patient and economical manner. If a fixated person prevents his activity or those of others, one can assume that he's reacting from the fear-possessed pole. He's given up his freedom to change. But Perseverance is only meaningful when changes, which mark life and existence, can be included in meaningful permanence.

If a person with the Mode of Perseverance wants to avoid being governed by his fear, and seeks more and more the positive aspects of perseverance, it will be helpful for him to observe how often he says the following things: »That just can't be changed. I have to accept this. I'm under a thousand practical restraints. I feel like I'm acting under orders« and so on. But once it's clear to him how he himself makes the situation unalterable and unchangeable by fixating it he will see that there are other possibilities of being perservering which don't deny his vitality.

Perseverance is the Mode of the Warrior energy with the ordinal number 3. This means that a certain amount of fighting spirit is included in the Mode of Perseverance. To perseveringly devote oneself to something and to enduringly fight for something are important elements of this Mode. If the courage to do battle wanes and things appears hopeless to most people, the person with this Mode becomes active. And if once in a while he, too, loses courage he can remember that change is a basic component of all life in the microcosmos and macrocosmos and that neither he nor the situation in which he finds himself are excluded from this cosmic law.

If he convinces himself that there's no possibility, either small or great, of changing a situation, his fear of being incapable of action will grow. If, however, just as a hypothesis, he takes into consideration that what seems unalterable (poverty, illness, depression) could be influenced at least in a small way and that its structure changes constantly anyway (even if he who insists on unalterability, doesn't want to see this or realize it), then he can emerge from the fearful paralysis which was caused by his fixation. He can steer his Mode of Perserverance again to the flexible area, which will help him loosen up, will free him and let him breathe a sigh of relief and make him capable of action again.

The smallest change helps bring new courage and new strength and, above all, fresh vital energy into his life, into his body. A person with the Mode of Perseverance who spends too much time near his minus pole tends to petrification of character and also to the formation of stones in his kidneys, bladder or gall. Constant movement dissolves petrification and, therefore, a person with this mode should take care that both his mind and his body be in regular movement, for there's more in constant, persevering exercise than the acceleration of his circulatory system and the elimination of poisons. Persistent, constant movement of the limbs also keeps the mind and the Mode in motion.

If he changes his stride, a change in his viewpoint can't fail to appear. Therefore, peaceful sports activities are also appropriate for those with this Mode who have rheumatism, arthritis and other paralyzing illnesses. They can distance themselves from their fear of inalterable painful stiffness if they remain in slow and constant movement.

The most magnificent blossoms evolve from this Mode if a person tenaciously observes himself and turns regularly to his inner-most being. He develops from this regular, constant self-observation a persevering growth plan for his life, for his personality, for his intuition. His inner voice will show him the way even if his path doesn't yet have a definite goal and appears bumpy and thorny. Only through striving persistently for a long-term change—whether this be through a form of psychotherapy or a form of meditation, or a determined will to direct one's own power toward a long-lasting change of insight or character-perseverant people achieved more than those with other Modes. Here Perseverance is a guarantee for the happy completion of a growth project. For a person with this Mode in a Mature Soul Age, there's no more beautiful occupation for his Perseverance than to devote himself to introspection and his soul growth without being inconstant or changing his methods all too often.

When the soul has chosen the Mode of Perseverance it has at the same time expressed the desire to devote itself persistently to its own development. Only when someone doesn't give up easily, will he enduringly enjoy the fruits of his actions and thoughts during the same life-time.

Energy 4

Observation

– Watchful   Vigilant +

You can easily recognize people with the Mode of Observation by their lively facial expressions and especially by their eyes, which can barely focus for a second on an object or a face without immediately moving on. It's not easy for them to concentrate on one individual thing, since this Mode requires that they pay attention to many things at once, simultaneously be concerned about everything surrounding them and tirelessly direct their energies at the multitude of objects of their interest.

Whoever has chosen this Mode often appears a little unsettled. His channels of perception are wide open. His mind is like a video camera in a supermarket, it registers everything without drawing conclusions or getting involved. It's difficult for an Observer to deal with all the innumerable impressions which flow through him incessantly and to digest them without being burdened. Therefore, the Mode of Observation is coupled with a tendency toward digestive problems and insomnia. The Observer needs a great deal of time to process what his senses have communicated to him. Not only his eyes, but also all other senses provide him with information. This is overwhelming if he doesn't like to take time to integrate it. He thinks something might escape his attention. His sensory archives are bursting with information and all too often need to be checked and reorganized. If there's no other way, he'll spend half the night reviewing the day's events, the joys, pains and excitations in his mind, and to check them again until he has catalogued them. Only then can he find peace, only then can he let himself rest, only then can the night descend before his inner eyes.

The Mode of Observation allows a person whose soul has chosen it to see everything, to sense all details of smell and taste and touch and all emotions without having to immediately react to them. His chakras are wide open, but he remains neutral. Now the main issue is how he later on processes the fruits of his observation: whether he fearfully stockpiles them to protect himself from imaginary harm (this we call being watchful) or evaluates them calmly, letting them flow through him and passing them on as events which lead to insight and clarity (then he's vigilant).

As long as a person constantly examines his external and internal world with the eye of fear, he'll remain imprisoned in the restlessness which results from this. His tendency to constantly watch and survey everything that happens or that could happen to him, his habit of continuously being on the watch for possible dangers, potential attacks, or threatening injuries, turns him into a chronically distrusting personality, even though he likes to view himself as trusting. He believes there is really one thing only he can trust: the constant surveillance of his life situation and his surroundings so that he can easily and adroitly avoid any attacks, problems and difficulties. Indeed, this Mode provides a certain protection. Very seldom something happens which the observer hasn't noticed announcing itself somehow. The worst he unconsciously fears, namely that he could be attacked from behind without having been alerted, will destroy his self-confidence completely.

The greater his fear, the more diligently he trains himself to keep an eye on all potential adversaries, on enemies he suspects in every person and in every situation. He employs all his senses, all his bodily energy centers like a radar to spot possible dangers in order to eliminate them often weeks and months before they could actually happen. One can see from this that it isn't easy for a person with this Mode to relax. In his negative pole, he's either busy processing impressions from the past and catalogueing them as harmless or threatening, or he's projecting possible threats into the future, preparing himself for them, observing minutely every symptom that could indicate the emergence of a serious situation. Often he comes to hasty conclusions. »Watchfulness«, therefore, is the key word for the minus pole, the fear of the Observer. The person with this Mode will keep everything observingly under his control. He doesn't want to rule, he doesn't want to exercise power, as his energy is the neutral 4 of the Scholar. He simply wants to know where he must be prepared should the worst happen.

Even though there are fundamental differences between the minus pole of this Mode and the basic fear of joyfulness (the Chief Characteristic of

Self-Sabotage with its self-destructive quality), there are also certain parallels, especially the habit of drawing false conclusions from observations and pursuing preventive actions against disappointments. The dire suspicion that something could go wrong if one doesn't control it will often be falsely confirmed by the tense surveillance, which has an eye on everything. Constant observation and fearful watchfulness are truly strenuous. You can imagine that a person, whose interior resembles a nuclear plant control room with thousands of monitors all in operation, can't easily let go. He fears turning his attention elsewhere or falling asleep and thereby facing the danger of making a crude, fatal mistake by overlooking something important because he no longer commands a view of everything. And what he fears is comparable to a personal nuclear disaster. Therefore, he views his watchfulness as highly appropriate. This being the Mode of the Scholar, the idea behind it is: I must know it all.

It's of decisive importance for a person with this Mode to make perfectly clear to himself that his fears of being unexpectedly hurt or wronged are paranoid. His world in no way consists only of enemies whom he must constantly survey day and night.

But if his fear decreases, a person with the Mode of Observation can moderate his habit of surveying everything and transform it into an extremely precise, enduring gift for observation and introspection. If he doesn't observe out of fear but rather out of love and relaxation, many correlations, many insights will be revealed to him which would easily be overlooked by others. Since he has the ability to relate many things to each other, to both observe and analyze them at the same time without getting emotionally involved, he can draw unexpected syntheses and develop surprising knowledge.

A person with this Mode also tends to practice self-observation and if he uses this ability positively and lovingly, he can attain great and lasting success in achieving clarity and insight into his inner motivations, methods of suppression, resistances and psychological fallacies seldom accessible to people with other Modes. Observation as a Mode has an ability which is very suitable for a scientist or researcher. It doesn't matter what the subject of the research is. It's decisive that it suits excellently an activity in which experiments are carried out, first evaluated and only afterwards interpreted. The strenghth of this mode lies in its capacity for neutrality.

Although the Observer can be very lively and is enthusiastic about each of his discoveries, he often appears as if he can't focus on one thing for very long. His particular gift, however, is his ability to focus on many different things at once. In truth he has a lot of patience. He oftens sits peacefully, is quiet and appears to be far away or day-dreaming. But his perceptive abilities are running at high speed. His capacity for Observation is seldom exhausted. He sees and senses everything at the same time, tries to categorize it and appears in so doing to be sometimes distracted. He's accustomed, however, to use his vigilance or watchfulness to the point of overstimulation and to think nothing of doing so. That makes him feel nervous and over-wrought.

The Observer often submits to his temptation to constantly formulate his observations and to inform others about them. He is indeed curious since he wants to see and understand everything and gain certainty and clarity. If he observes something he doesn't understand, he likes to ask questions. »What are you doing there, what are you thinking, what are you feeling?« he'll ask. He does this because he realizes that he can't automatically interpret everything correctly—not because he doesn't have any idea of what he has observed, but because he wants to mollify his fear of not having seen enough, all the many uncategorized individual facts.

It's better for a person with this Mode to question and make sure rather than to draw wrong conclusions. However, when others feel they are constantly being observed and interpreted, they become nervous or aggressive. Their own fears will be awakened by the impression that the partner, friend or colleague doesn't miss a thing, that he watches, surveys and observes every-thing, that he has his vigilant feelers turned in all directions and intrudes deeply into them and their private sphere. They might think that their inner intimacy is being destroyed by the constant questioning and drilling or even mute control.

This Mode of Observation with the neutral energy 4 of the Scholar has a peculiar trait. For although the Observer sees and senses and therefore »knows« everything, he finds it difficult to quit his neutrality and draw active consequences from what he's observed. He remains passive, sometimes almost paralysed when it comes to change something. It is sometimes appropriate to shake him out of his lethargic neutrality and push him into doing something. Friends and family can do that, but often life presents the necessary challenge. For although the Mode of Observation is necessary and helpful as a quiet, static behaviour, so is the resulting activity necessary.

The Observer finds it difficult to turn off his mind. His senses are always wide awake. But that's exactly what would gradually release him and his fear. If he succeeded in pulling in his feelers, of shutting himself off, and spending an hour or a couple of days in meditative pursuits, he would begin to feel less threatened. He could more easily rest and sleep. Both watchful-ness and vigilance can cause insomia, of the restless or more quiet type. There's so much to review during the silent hours of the night! Often this does not even take the shape of coherent thoughts.

Observation is the most common of all Modes. The general distrust which results from the statistical frequency of this Mode permeates all spheres and branches of your society. You can judge alone from the fact that many people can't bear to sit with their back to the door in a restaurant or waiting room, how much tension arises when people are forced to assume such a unprotected position where they can't keep things under visual con-trol. And it is amusing that people with this Mode dislike intensely to be observed by others. This Mode can often be traced back to unpleasant sudden experiences in a past life which a person wants to avoid at all costs in his new incarnation.

A surveillance which results from pure fear doesn't bring the result that lies in the great positive potential of the Mode of Observation. This Mode will legitimate its essential purpose only if it is lovingly applied to the discovery of one's own self. It is helpful only if it maintains its function in the neutral observation of others, an observation that should help them know themselves better, more clearly perceive reality and win insight that appeared inaccessible before. In the positive pole, vigilance equals the loving, non-judgemental self-observation of an experienced, highly conscious meditator.

The ability to observe can do much good in all areas of life. Whoever takes the time and has the necessary patience to direct his sensitive, perceptive channels to the positive recognition of connections with the astral and causal worlds of consciousness, and thereby achieve clarity, and who also especially tries to remain in the moment and to perceive what is happening now and only now, will be able to make the best of this Mode and use it for the well-being of himself and his fellow-men.

Energy 5

Power

– Patronizing   Authoritative +

If we use the expression »power« to describe a Mode, we don't mean in the first place a temperament, an influence, a way of acting, but rather a state of being. Being powerful is basically different from exercising power.

You automatically assume that whoever has power, also abuses it, and you understand power mainly as political power, or as a form of suppression, enslavement and hegemony. To be powerfully vibrant, however, is different from exercising power over others. Therefore, we ask you not to fear the Mode of Power as a state of being and not to reject it as something that a person basically has no choice but to abuse and employ to the detriment or damage of his fellow men.

Power is a necessary factor in a system in which human togetherness, society and association form a basis for mutual growth. A person whose soul has chosen the Mode of Power in order to strive toward his particular Development Goal is a person who must find his natural, inner authority.

Power as a Mode with the energy 5 is the archetypical energy of the Sage. And as you can imagine, the Sage is a soul role which possesses a considerable amount of authority, influence and power of example as long as he shapes his life close to his essence. The Mode of Power means to have an ability to exercise power wisely. Power—wisely practiced and exercised—leads without effort to a healthy and much needed authority.

You all know examples of people who are especially honored, respected and loved because their authority emanates and radiates from within. They don't have to place people around them under a yoke or force them to do something contrary to their wish and desire. The peaceful, relaxed positive authority of a person with the Mode of Power is convincing to everyone and truly pleasant, so that they don't have to protest against it. They don't have to subjugate themselves to the Mode of Power but can simply recognize the behavior of a personality who, in a responsible manner, takes over responsible leadership and carries it out in such a way that everyone develops confidence in being able to make his contribution in an intelligent, encompassing, goal-oriented context.

The powerful person has the duty of transforming his Power into an authority of this kind. In order to do this, he must learn to resist the temptation of making decisions for others and suppressing them in fearful attempts to exercise power at all costs in a patronizing way even if fear results from the rejection of his actions or manner of speaking.

Instead of acting wisely, a person who hasn't found access to his natural authority will all too easily succumb to expressing his need for power by knowing everything better, spoon-feeding others, holding them on leashes and making them dependent on himself instead of granting them freedom. At the same time he'll despise them for the fact that they made themselves subservient and allowed him to dictate to them. On the other hand, his fear of not exercising power and influence doesn't make it easy for him to give up making decisions for others.

A person with the Mode of Power is patronizing in a rather rigid and sometimes stern manner as long as he lets himself be ruled by his basic fear or in combination with a Goal of Dominance. He has to live his desire for power, but doesn't trust himself to bear the consequences. He doesn't believe he can truly be an authority for others and therefore strives all too emphatically for respect and recognition by restricting them and wanting to integrate them into his sphere of influence. Of course, they feel controlled instead of trusted.

The ideal image of a powerful person is one whom others trust in love, admiration and dedication because they sense that under his patronage they'll be able to find their potential, their self-confidence, their own leadership abilities without getting entangled in a fearful derailment. The powerful Sage has no joy in abusing his Mode of Power. But he enjoys the happiness which arises within himself and others if his Power results in great aims being striven for and arrived at together. Power in this positive sense gives security.

A person with the Mode of Power who is tormented by too great a fear will, in contrast, do everything to take away the freedom of others, to silence them, to enslave them psychologically or physically, to take away or withhold their decision-making ability, to constantly give them the feeling that only he can determine their well-being and that no one but him realizes what is good, helpful, or necessary. He can, however, also live the minus pole passively, as is possible with all matrix elements, and let others have too much power over himself and to make decisions for him. Then he allows them to patronize him.

The powerful person who acts out of fear will be able to create rules and laws which disempower if he's in a key position in political, religious or economic sectors. The greater the fear, the greater is the rigidity of a powerful person. He expresses this by regulating all and everything, creating unnecessary rules, contracts and laws so that an individual who feels subordinated to him has little possibility of making his own decisions and following personal impulses. In private or family areas, the powerful person who lets himself be ruled by fear, is a family member, friend or partner who compulsively assures that no one has any freedom of thought or action, that everything has a certain order preestablished by himself, that no one except himself takes certain far-reaching decisions.

But if someone else threatens to dispute his Power, he feels excessively forced into a position of helplessness, and tends to subversively recover his Power by creating a situation in which he again is the only person who knows what to do and who can take decisions that others must acknowledge. This can go so far that a person exercises his Mode of Power in the role of a sick family member by setting completely rigid rules; it's he who decides on his diet, his times of rest, the administration of medicine, the room where he stays and many others things. In so doing he assures that those around him can only go on tiptoe and are suspended in perpetual fear of doing something wrong. He will not even acknowlege that the doctor might know better. The sick person's control is exercised by confining the living space of his healthy family. The person in fearful, patronizing control is certain that he could never achieve greater authority than by exercising power over his nearest and dearest.

This negative exercise of the Power Mode is sometimes confused with tyranny or dominance (belonging to the kingly energy 7). However, the motivation is different. Power as a Mode lacks the majestic self-will. The fear of not being able to realize himself as an authority and not being able to live his inner wisdom, forces the powerful person to create a system of internal and external regulations and control systems with which he not only takes away the decision-making power from himself and others, but, above all, prevents himself from assuming sincere authority and exercising it in an authoritative, but in no way authoritarian way

A fearful, powerful person is sometimes satisfied if people around him, in professional or private life, are ill so that he can disempower them by stipulating everything he believes right for them in order to relieve the overpowering burden of his inner regulations. And if the rules he's set for the recovery of the sick persons—without consulting them—aren't observed or are even openly ignored, he'll feel all the more offended in his authority. He's certain that he knows better than any doctor or the patient himself.

Since the Mode of Power belongs to the level of expression, one can't dispense with actually exercising this power. The powerful person will have to communicate and display it either positively or negatively. If he tries to suppress his need for powerful authority and influence, or for patronizing, controlling and knowing better, things will go wrong. For him this is a completely natural and legitimate need, and if he tries to not admit it, to conceal it, he'll be forced to express his Mode in an unpleasant, harmful manner.

Many who've chosen this Mode will feel relieved if they allow themselves to really live their authoritative impulse happily and joyfully. If you recall that you chose this mode in order to better arrive at your Development Goal and, above all, to make a meaningful, necessary and much desired contribution to the human and soul community, it won't be so difficult for you to acknowledge your Mode. You'll be happy in exercising authority, and to let others happily experience a person who makes a powerful impression, has powerful vibrations, and an unforgettable personality, without appearing unloving, without taking away the air and freedom of others.

Whoever has the Mode of Power as a motor for their Development Goal will have to get accustomed to being an example for others in the course of his life. Initially, he'll have to deal with his shyness and inhibitions. But he'll only be able to reach his purpose if he shows himself and casts others under his wonderful spell, transmits his powers to others and lets them take part in his life's work.

A person with the Mode of Power doesn't do himself any good by isolating himself. For Power can only be displayed in an interchange with others. Otherwise the powerful person will become helpless and passive and fantasize about »What would happen, if I only could tell them what is right?« He will raise or humiliate himself, allowing others to live for him that authority which he doesn't dare live himself. He'll then react bitterly and angrily at all those who confront him with their own authority. He'll come into conflict with his elders or betters, with civil servants and shop-keepers, with the management of his firm or the nurses in his care unit. He'll feel ruled by any powers over whom he has no influence. Therefore we urge anyone who has chosen this Mode to come to terms with its possibilities and consequences and to create a small or larger forum in which they can practice their powerful personality and authority. Thus they can function as an example for the community.

Energy 6

Passion

− Fanatic   Charismatic +

Passion as a Mode is an expression of totality. It means great readiness for spirited action, enormous temperament and energetic richness. A person with the Mode of Passion is to a high degree imbued by his duties and pleasures and enthusiastic about his aims, his plans and his interests. The ordinal number 6, which is assigned to this Mode, is a part of inspired, priestly energy. The inspiration which characterizes the passionate person gives him a kind of strength that surprises himself. It emanates from this priestly position among the seven Modes.

You've all heard that passion tends to create suffering. The passionate person can suffer from the profusion of his enthusiasm and his totality, for it stirs him on, doesn't take into consideration his constitution, and sometimes leads the person to go far beyond his physical capacity. A passionate person often ignores his individual limits through sheer rapture.

Passion principally fills the spirit and affects the person ecstatically so that from time to time he loses the ground beneath his feet, the connection to real possibilities and to a pragmatic accomplishment of something, setting dream goals that are difficult or impossible to reach.

In any case, the passionate person has the tendency, when he's motivated by fear more than love, of dominating his environment and moulding it by trying to harness it for his own purposes, his radical desires, his highflying ideals, without asking if others really want to share them. Therefore, the passionate person appears fanatic in his fear that his fellow-men might not share his electrifying opinions and goals and enthusiasms since, filled with priestly energy, he believes in the higher inspiration of his ideas and can't recognize that what he considers right only applies to himself and not to those whom he wants to change, convert, enlighten or cure.

The passionate person is a stressful companion when his fear causes him to force someone to share the ideas who isn't at all captivated by them. Since he's almost prepared to die for his ideas and ideals, he demands the same willingness from others to make sacrifices. If it comes to this, however, he'll prefer to let others die and to save himself since he's more than one-hundred-percent convinced of his mission, no matter what it might be. He could be wanting to convince you of a new kind of health matress, a special vacuum cleaner, an ecological or political movement, some unheard-of insight in astrology, a radical philosophy, a revolutionary kind of diet.

As long as those around him have the possibility of defending themselves against the fanaticism of this frantic missionary or reformer, he can't do a great deal of damage. He'll be dismissed as a cranky, odd, all-too unconventional person. Woe be it, however, if the fanatic assumes a position which gives him a great deal of power—whether it be in the political or religious sector—for then it can happen that he will literally walk over bodies in order to railroad through the ideals and goals which he personally considers the only true ones without giving a thought to the physical or mental sacrifices others must make in order to support his personal truth.

The passionate person often is a great orator. He possesses a fantastic persuasive power. He can be a demagogue when he dares to propagate his plans to a larger public. If a person with the Mode of Passion acts from love, his powers will move in a direction that will be able to change just as much in a positive way as it could create damage in a negative way were he motivated by fear. In his charismatic positive pole he will be a great preacher—about anything from health topics to gardening, from military strategies to moral values. He can also be an excellent salesman.

The overwhelming aura of a passionate person has an enthusiastic and motivating effect on his fellow-men. The more a person with this Mode develops a peaceful and warm personality, the greater is his charismatic effect. But he himself has a certain difficulty with this since the strong effects of his personality confuse him at first and frighten him because he fears he could misuse his charisma and unintentionally use it for bad purposes. Therefore, it's important for him to know that his charisma can't cause any damage as long as he lets his totality flow in happiness and freedom. His passionate ways will pose a danger to himself and others only if he senses that strain, tension and all-too-much willpower is tied to the accomplishment of his intention.

Humans seem to link the word »passion« first of all to sexuality. Until now we've intentionally ignored this in order to show you that physical-sexual or erotic passion is only one of many possibilities of living this Mode in a positive or negative form. Often a person with the Mode of Passion tends to restrict his temperament to a certain area, in order to control it, since he's afraid it could overwhelm him, explode and be as eruptive as a volcano whose fiery lava buries and destroys everyone, including himself. Therefore, you'll notice that a passionate stamp collector is seldom a passionate lover at the same time, that a passionate cook or gardener concentrates his energy on his hobby. Passion as a Mode is directed not only at other people. It's more often concentrated on an abstract idea or an object which appears harmless.

To desire a person passionately is much more dangerous, because refusal can hurt.

The less a person with the Mode of passion trusts himself, the more shamefully he'll deal with his charismatic potential, the more restrained and hidden will be his Passion. It could hardly be detected except for a glittering in his eyes when he mentions his hobby or secret longing. His fanaticism or charisma is like a glimmer in the ashes, able to set a house or city on fire at any time.

The passionate person has to work less than others to achieve his aims and realize his plans. The clearer it becomes to him that his energy flows the best, is most powerful and clearly directed when he's relaxed and doesn't do much to convert and impress his fellow-men or convince them of the power of his ideas, the more they'll be impressed by him, the more they'll be captivated by his charisma, and the more he'll be given respect, support, admiration and attention. Only when the passionate person believes that he won't be able to achieve what he needs in a loving way, will he fanatically assure in a harmful way that he'll get attention and admiration.

Passion as a priestly Mode carries with it the danger of missionary enthusiasm and arrogance. We've already said that the passionate person is a representative of totality. He's often blind to the needs and affairs of his companions since he's so completely filled with his own convictions that he can't take into consideration differing opinions or rejects them as insignificant and annoying. The passionate person happily enjoys these illusions. He likes to imagine that everything in the world dances to his tune and develops according to his plans. Therefore, there's a barrier between himself and the people he's trying to recruit for his purpose. When he's too breathtaking, they fend off his fanaticism by seemingly agreeing with his plans and thereby mollifing him like an insane person in order to create some free space in which they can breathe again.

People with the Mode of Passion are passionate about everything.

And sometimes they suffer from their own temperament. Nothing leaves them cold. Their mood is never even. In rapid succession, they are rapturous, almost manic, and then quite suddenly disgusted and utterly sad. They rise to heaven every day and fall from the clouds just as often. They are thrilling, spirit-stirring and inspiring personalities but at the same time can be tiresome and exhausting for those who dont't share their sudden mood changes.

Whoever has chosen this Mode will reach his Development Goal best if he knows how to guard against fanaticism. Passion doesn't easily give up. It possesses a high ability of concentration. The Development Goal remains the focus of efforts for one's whole life. The totality of the Mode of Passion assures incessantly that energy is focused on personal growth and that all other interests are subordinate to the Development Goal.

If the passionate person wants to avoid having his Mode guided by fear, he should keenly react to the attempts of others to repel his fanaticism. He can realize that he's in danger of overwhelming his spouse, child, friend or business partner with intensity if this person indicates to him that it's all too much, that he's tired, he needs peace and distance, or if he silently withdraws with a yawn. Then the passionate person will know that he tried to force someone to do or think something without taking into consideration the other person's mood, needs and ability to take things in. If, in contrast, he notices that his partner or audience have glowing cheeks and shining eyes while listening to him, are positively stimulated, ask more and more questions, or have an alert, curious expression, then he'll know that he has captured his audience with his charisma. It's good for him to seek his reflection in others. This mode needs the outlet of expressed enthusiasm. Keeping silent and subduing one's fiery temperament wouldn't be helpful.

Certainly there are also quiet, secret or inconspicuously lived Passion Modes. But they are usually the result of certain inhibitions, due for example to the fears of Self-Deprecation, Self-Sabotage or Martyrdom. They don't dare show themselves, to communicate or to let others take part in the Passion Mode. They don't trust their own charisma. Only when this Mode is carried by a positive, candid ardour can the passionate person be completely satisfied with himself alone. He then finds fulfillment in the inspiration which his own being provides. But in most cases, the passionate person wants to share his enthusiasm with someone else, even through an indirect form of communication, whether it's a book that he writes, a musical score he composes or an idea he introduces into the world via the internet.

We want to point out to you once more that the passionate person is, by nature, someone who doesn't have to worry about making an impression on others. The effect is constantly there without him having to do anything about it. »Being« is the key to his charisma, »doing«, in contrast, leads him to fanatical measures.

Independent of where the passionate person directs his ardour—a stamp collection, political or religious reform, a scientific research project, the order and cleanliness of his apartment, a love affair, his job, his children, eating, art, travel, gardening and many other things—, he'll always be carried away about everything. He gathers strength from the objects of his interests and gives other people strength through the inspiration of his experiences, his knowledge and his charisma.

Energy 7

Aggression

— Belligerent   Dynamic +

Of all the Modes, Aggression has the most energy. And this is also the difficulty of this Mode: bringing so much impetuosity under meaningful control. The eruptions which are naturally connected to this mode must be channeled and led in a direction that isn't destructive. The Mode of Aggression is even more outwards directed than is Passion. Seldom, and only when a personality is psychologically disturbed, is this Mode used against oneself and one's body.

This Mode has an extremely creative dynamic if it's used properly. Aggressive energy produces a basic behavior which shoves and pushes, it wants to achieve something, it doesn't let go and takes what it wants.

Aggression has a dynamic impetus that forces one to act. It can only be kept passive with effort, and feels in an inadmissable way restricted if it's forced to keep still. It wants to be expressed and, being an eruptive, dynamic energy, it's productive in the broadest sense. Symbolically it represents the sperm and not the egg. And just as sperm is a basic phenomenon of life, so is Aggression an inalienable element of vitality. A person who can't come out of his shell, a person who doesn't want to achieve anything anymore, who no longer feels any impulse to identify himself with this masculine principle is as good as dead. Liveliness and aggressivity are closely united and from this there results another necessary linkage of Aggression and health. For the immune system is closely connected to the ability of the body-cells to fight off negative influence in the most aggressive manner.

Dynamism as the plus pole of the Mode means that something is in motion, and if it's not in motion, it will be put in motion. To be healthy also means being in motion. If energy flows properly, if the juices are flowing, if a person feels a natural impulse to move, if he wants to act and is capable of action, if he's open toward his fellow-men and the constant change of the world around him, then he's healthy.

But the ability to defend oneself on all levels also belongs to the phenomenon of a healthy dynamic and lively Aggression. Here it's less a matter of a passive form of delimitation or refusal. It's a positive aggressivity, a dynamic of preparedness to emerge from a defensive posture and to actively set your own borders, to defend them by attacking the opponent, forcing him back or effectively holding him at a distance.

The dynamically aggressive person is in the best way capable of staking out his territory and successfully warding off any attack without weakening himself. What distinguishes him from the cautious person, the restrained person, the passionate person or the powerful person is the dignity and natural strength which he applies and the preparedness to show his Aggression Mode, to expose himself to counter-attack without losing face. He shows a great deal of courage.

Someone who lives his dynamic plus pole without the constant fear of being condemned as harmful and violent, creates respect. He'll be admired for his readiness for action and his civil courage and will rarely encounter the rejection he fears in weak moments. But we have to admit that it isn't easy to live the Mode of Aggression in a purely dynamic energy-rich way, for the energy contained in this mode is unpredictable, explosive, often overwhelming and hard to tame. Therefore, a person who has chosen this Mode must experiment a great deal with various attempts at channeling this eruptive energy.

He'll often experience that he overshoots his goal and attacks his perceived opponent to defend his borders rather then actively setting limits without offending his fellow-men so deeply that no further negotiations are possible.

Therefore, it's of special importance that a person with this Mode learns to deal lovingly with his aggressive emotions. This positive approach will be viewed in two different ways in your society. The many inhibited and fearful people among you would prefer to turn off any aggressivity since they're not in touch with their own desire to attack, their fury and hatred and are reluctant to come into contact with it in themselves or in others.

But when we speak of Aggression as a Mode we don't mean aggressive actions which are expressed in acts of violence. We mean neither physical, verbal nor psychological violence, but only the ability of a person to employ his aggressive dynamic-creative energies in the best possible way to change and influence the world so that everybody can profit from them.

Some people want to ban all aggressivity from their lives because they fear Aggression in the form of injury and violence, which they basically reject on philosophical grounds. Experience shows that this doesn't work. Others, often well-meaning therapists want to release a person's aggressions and do it in such a way that they provoke its expression. They misunderstand the fact that aggressivity is basically a form of energy and that this energy ought to be released without destroying a person or a thing. Because of this error, they foster mainly the minus pole of the mode, belligerence. They believe they can free the natural Aggression Mode of a person from its chains by challenging him to unrestrainedly seek clashes and fight to one's heart's content. In so doing, usually the heart's content is left on the track and nothing remains but reluctance and frustration, because the Mode of Aggression wants to construct, not to destroy.

We in no way want to say here that a good fight in the sense of a fruitful clash doesn't lead to the release of energy. Quite the contrary: a person with the Mode of Aggressivity is always belligerent, when he's afraid or tense.

He needs a verbal storm and the banging of doors more often than others. It is impossible for him to avoid touching his minus pole every now and then. He therefore needs an opponent, a colleague or a partner who doesn't take this purging ritual all too seriously and who happily welcomes the positive fresh energy which results from it. It is good to acknowledge that the lava is fertile after the volcano has erupted. However, if a person with this Mode is constantly seized by fear of becoming a victim of the reactive violence of his fellow-men and projects his own misdirected energy on his surroundings, he'll seek fights whenever he can. He'll pick a quarrel because of the high-handed idea that every clash is justified, providing he can free himself in the fight from the inner pressure which threatens to suffocate his life-energy. Thus the smallest event is often enough to cause a fear-possessed person's aggressive energy to overflow, to lead to an explosion which frightens every-one, including himself, and leads to actions which are no longer easy to con-trol. The fight which the belligerent person seeks degenerates into angry words or violence, into bodily injury and even into a desire to kill and some-times the satisfaction of this desire. This all serves only to release the enor-mous energetic powers that are blocked if they can't find a positive, and regular, outlet.

Ideally parents should be advised to challenge the natural aggressive im-pulses of a child who obviously has this Mode and to allow it. But in most cases this isn't possible. Aggressivity is labelled as undesireable, scares many and will therefore be made taboo very early on so that a child is seldom enough in a position to test his powers. His basic energy—whether creative or destructive—can hardly be observed and finally brought under a healthy control.

The Mode of Aggression has the ordinal number 7 and therefore belongs to the essential Soul Role of a King. As a Mode it occurs relatively seldom, and therefore we stress once more that this Mode shouldn't be confused with the natural aggression every person—no matter which Mode he's chosen—possesses as a basic expression of his vitality, his self-defense, his fury, his hatred. The Mode with the ordinal number 7, how-ever, implies that there must be a certain dominance and claim to power contained therein. At the same time it's also an energy that can affect and achieve much, especially in areas of life and society which demand powerful expressions of thought and will, dynamic ideas, the ability to carry through and a courageous pressing ahead in unknown areas.

The person with such a Mode is the born pioneer. He'll venture forward where others fear to tread. He'll avert dangers by ignoring them. He can be an example and a model of courage for others. He represents the type of kingly commander who puts himself at the head of his army and risks his precious life to lead his army to victory—even against a superior enemy.

If a person applies his inborn dynamic in an advantageous and loving manner, he'll achieve more than he could ever imagine. He'll never belong to those who lurk in the background. Such a person is no grey eminence but glows in the gleam of his own light as long as he succeeds in bringing under control his belligerence and does not suspect enmity and opposition in all areas of life.

For this is what often torments a person with this Mode: he suspects others of aggressions and aggressive intentions if he doesn't trust himself to let his energy flow freely, when he puts too many inhibitions on his own creative desire to attack, when he can't free his energies from the thought that they could overpower him, become independent and lead to destructive actions.

The creativity and destructiveness which are contained in this Mode shouldn't be separated from each other. However, a person can very well differentiate between that which is creative in the sense of bulding a better world and that which destroys the vitality and joy of himself and others. Both sides belong to his potential. This is a kingly Mode and must be employed with great responsibility.

Often influential political or economic leaders have this Mode; trade unionists or great inventors, founders of industries and sports champions profit from it. If you want success in a competitive world, this Mode is useful.

If someone with the Mode of Aggression wants to come into better contact with the positive pole, dynamism, he should become accustomed to observe when he projects his own Aggression on others. The more he finds that the world aggressively opposes him, cuts off his rights, injures him and infringes on his territory, the clearer it will be to him that he isn't realizing his own energy positively. The more often a person becomes the victim of violent acts or bodily injuries, the more obvious it becomes that he is inhibiting his own aggression, has falsely channeled it into some apeasement policy or peace ideology and, therefore, must delegate it to other people and also to institutions. Whenever these elements appear conspicuous, if, for example, a woman is repeatedly beaten or raped, or a man several times is the victim of robberies or gets involved in car accidents again and again, or if his colleagues mob him without reason, it would be worth investigating whether these apparent victims have been too careful in never being aggressive, in acting subserviently or remaining quiet instead of admitting the kingly energy within themselves and showing others their teeth. A person with the Mode of Aggression will easily become a victim if he doesn't allow himself to live his Aggression creatively. He risks his health and liveliness if he lets others live this blocked, suppressed energy. He sometimes becomes a victim because he's too noble to attack or defend himself. He pays homage to a false, ego-possessed ideal of gentleness or superiority. He's afraid the world will fall apart if he raises his voice or beats his fist on the table. Whoever has all-too-many apparently justified reasons for never showing aggression, and more than that, whoever thinks he doesn't have any aggressive feelings at all, should fundamentally consider the hypothesis that his natural Mode of Aggression is buried.

Many of the souls who in former lives were overly-inhibited in expressing sound aggressivity choose this Mode now in order to view the theme of
power, influence and violence from a side that doesn't necessarily lead to
destruction, for they had experiences in previous lives in which aggressive
actions leading to death and destruction played a central role. Often a soul
is prepared to change its attitude and to gather new experiences with the
positive energies ofthe Mode of Aggression.

For when one wants to give up an old habit of turning every provocation into physical violence, if one wants to transcend this impulse, it's seldom
adviseable to eradicate it completely. It's much more instructive to view it
in a different way, to judge it in a new manner, to consider possibilities of
reacting differently and, with the basic components of human vitality, to
experience aggressive powers positively.

Whoever does this has the chance of achieving great influence and
aiming for powerful effects. This fact alone should make it worthwhile to
remove the grey cloak of false gentleness and to risk becoming visible in all
of one's attractive dynamism. The inhibitions which one removes are in most
cases a hidden armor intended to bind the fear-possessed liveliness which
appears all too dangerous. If people with the Mode of Aggression control
their belligerence and instead give expression to their dynamic force out of
love, they become figures of immense vitality, of overflowing creativity and
enormous influence on this world.

Mentalities

⑤ Idealism　　　　　　　② Skepticism

− vague　　+ visionary　　− distrusting　　+ investigative

Expression Level

⑥ Spiritualism　　　　　① Stoicism

− gullible　　+ verifying　　− resigned　　+ tranquil

Inspiration Level

⑦ Realism　　　　　　③ Cynicism

− guessing　　+ perceptive　　− humiliating　　+ critical

Action Level

④ Pragmatism

− rigid　　+ practical

Assimilation Level

V The Seven Mentalities

Mentality, as part of the Matrix or soul pattern, describes the attitude of a person toward his individual reality and to the world as he understands it. Mentality is mental structure. This concerns ideas, patterns of thought, interests and judgements which he develops and employs in order to understand his existence.

No man living is capable of looking at the world from all seven mental perspectives at once. This is the reason why the soul chooses one of the Mentalities as a focus to understand the world, truth and reality deeper. In another life the perspective can be changed so that in the end the mosaic of perception is complete.

The Mentality of a person shapes his world outlook and the understanding that he can gain from his life. Since this concerns more or less closed systems with which everyone tries to describe life in general and their own life in particular with a certain claim to sole rights, the inborn mentality serves to set up a mental scaffolding of securities within which one moves without being forced to change one's basic attitudes and views all too often. For such a change would cause a great deal of insecurity.

Therefore, the Mentality belongs to the soul pattern chosen before incarnation, and you'll notice that although an individual can change the weight and severity of his mental convictions, he can't change his basic outlook on life itself.

It's obvious that even small children in a group all have very different possibilities of mentally processing the little incidents of their daily lives. One wants everything to be different and better than it is, another accepts with great equanimity whatever happens, a third will be naive and trustful, yet another will check to see whether his perception is justified and if he can believe that which is being offered him. This basic behavior is not the result of moulding or education but an expression of the soul's desire to classify the mental attitudes within the whole, abilities which are only given to humans capable of an inner distance to what they experience.

Each of the seven Mentalities provides a system of doctrines or beliefs. Through this system reality as a whole is not only described and understood, but also shapes on its part the individual reality in a way that a person feels certain that: »This is the way it is, no other way. The interplay between me and life, between me and the world, between me and the universe functions this way, and no other way.«

The difference between the Mentalities with their partly conciliatory, partly radically delimiting convictions, shapes relationships, for it's not easy for extremely differing Mentalities, e. g. a Skeptic and an Idealist, to find a joint basis on which they can understand each other. People who share a similar or the same mental structure understand each other better than those who have differing or conflicting mentalities. Since the mentalities come into being from birth, these differences also lead to tension and friction between parents and children, betweens siblings, school comrades and friends.

On the other hand, relationships based on an affinity of mentalities, like pragmatism and realislim, or idealism and spiritualism, create a natural network of ties which allows the striking up of contacts far beyond the usual. It lets people communicate with each other regardless of national borders, races and languages. Since the Soul Mentality of a person is not only expressed in thoughts but also in specific brain waves, it's easy for people who share the same mentality to enjoy a sense of harmony, solidarity and loyalty.

We would like to develop a symbolic picture to help explain such an

occurence to you. To each mentality can be assigned a specific geometric figure, for example, a triangle, a square, a cylinder, a ball, a circle, a pyramid, and
so on. If two or more people of the same Mentality are together there's a
thought pattern among them which corresponds to this basic form: several
triangles, or a number of squares.

People sense that when they say: »I get along well with this person. I can
follow him. We understand each other easily. We have the same wave length.«
This effortless understanding is based on the automatic creation of identical thought patterns which lead to a feeling of congruity. It is no coinci-
dence that the Mentalities are named after philosphical schools of thought
where those who shared a particular outlook on life could meet and talk and
feel mentally at home.

But it's not always speaking that leads to this congruity. Verbal communciation is only one of many methods to create this mental harmony.
People with conflicting Mentalites often talk past one another. Each person
tries to make himself understood and senses clearly that the person opposite
him has a blank look or gets irritated as he doesn't have the possibility to
produce immediate understanding.

Mentality is a mental factor and has nothing to do with nationality,
education or upbringing, intelligence or schooling. People with the same
Mentality feel drawn to each other no matter where they come from, and
often are surprised that they like and understand each other although their
background and education are so different.

Energy I

Stoicism

– Resigned   Tranquil +

Can you imagine an Idealist who could do without wanting to improve something? He is never quite content with what is, whereas a Stoic is convinced that, basically, everything is fine the way it is. And even if he has fear or pain, he doesn't try to change it immediately. And if it's not fine the way it is, it simply is the way it is. For the Stoic, there's no doubt about that.

A person with a stoic Mentality takes life the way it presents itself to him. He behaves passively toward the world, truth and reality as he experiences them. He sees his salvation in this attitude, he regards it as the best possible posture. The acceptance of what is allows him to understand the world as correct and well-ordered, as an expression of a higher or godly will and an inspired wholeness. To reject this or to deny this makes no sense to him and can't make him happy. He looks for a meaning and a higher order in all life's vicissitudes and tries to remain tranquil.

Of course, if a person with the basic attitude of Stoicism, a Mentality with the energy I belonging to the archetype of the Helper/Healer, and therefore to the energy level of inspiration, perceives his life as a long series of unpleasant, painful events which frighten his body and mind, he'll very easily fall prey to a resigned form of stoic passivity. Then he'll try to make himself insensitive to fear and pain, to avert his anguish through taking on the behavior of a victim thus expressing in a bitter way his inability and refusal to change what has happened to him.

A fearful Stoic, therefore, believes that fate determines his life, that he has no part in shaping his life, that he must only in some way try to come to terms with events and survive as best he can. He withdraws from society, becomes ever more passive, falls into a stifling resignation in order not to have to deal too much with his problems. He doesn't even wail, as if he feared to bring the wrath of the gods upon himself through loud lamenting.

Resignation leads very easily to a low-frequency energy which makes him physically ill. Such an attitude of accepting everything without taking a stand, leads to life not being lived, only endured. The resigned Stoic believes that this angle he chooses for his view of existence best protects him from even worse torments by arbitrary powers whom he is neither capable of recognizing nor assessing. The resigned person with this stoic Mentality therefore finds life a drudgery, a vale of tears, wretched, a perpetual punishment which he can only escape from through passive resistance.

But people who have chosen a stoic Mentality in a particular life have the possibility at any time of accepting their difficulties with tranquility. A positive imperturbability creates great inner strength. A Stoic not governed by fear is neither at odds with whatever happens to him, nor does he harbor expectations of great changes which he could create. And if he succeeds in developing such tranquility, he'll acquire the rare ability to live in the moment and to realize that all events, all feelings, all reactions possess exactly the same validity and worth.

This form of tranquility, of composure, which has little or nothing to do with resignation, makes one happy in its own way. It's an expression of a special form of curiosity and is fulfilled in the observance of each facet of daily life as a manifestation of the entirety, the AllOne. A Stoic can be tranquil no matter if he's sick or healthy, poor or rich, sad or happy. He remains in the middle, undisturbed. He isn't exuberant, he isn't exasperated. He's simply interested in finding out how his being reacts to the most differing conditions and life experiences. He doesn't want to interfere in the course of the world or in his own affairs. For if he does, how can he find out about the significance of it all?

The passivity of the tranquil person possesses an immense calmness, a peace, which doesn't exclude a significant effect. This effect should be differentiated from active influence. The Stoic distinguishes himself by the fact that he doesn't see any sense—neither direct nor higher—in influencing events actively. He realizes the positive potential of the essential, of just being. He views active change as an impermissible manipulation of the manifest greater will. And if he consciously rejects influencing things, he'll remain tranquil. If, however, he feels only helplessness and powerlessness in view of what he perceives as the ruling whole, his passivity will turn into a limpness, lethargy or resignation. Of course a person with a stoic Mentality knows both conditions, both perceptions. He will experience tranquility and resignation. But most of all he sees himself confronted with the fearful reactions of his fellow-men, who fail to understand his basic attitude, whether it be tranquil or resigned. At times he'll be either admired or pitied, but mostly he meets misunderstanding since people in his environment have a doctrine that activity is better than passivity in any case. But the Stoic experiences a gain in not fighting his fear or covering it up through activity or through actions—an attitude which demands respect even though only few will share it.

We can say that there are many more resigned rather than tranquil Stoics. However, it often happens that a person with this Mentality frees himself in an advanced age from his many years of resignation and develops a tranquil, composed attitude. Youth and composure don't go well together. A necessary preconditon for becoming tranquil is the overcoming of many challenges and difficulties. Only one who faces life and his fate courageously can find out how he'll react when storms are raging.

A Stoic will often assess that he's confronted more than most others with painful experiences in his life. But only then can he discover his ability of choosing between tranquility and resignation. And we'd like to point out here that a tranquil attitude as an expression of self-love in no way goes without tears or laughter. Only the resigned person, despite his pain, sheds no more tears and, therefore, is also no longer capable of laughing merrily. He isn't in a positive sense indifferent to everything to the same extent, but he's insensitive to everything that happens.

The stoic Mentality with the ordinal number I, belonging to the archetype of the Helper/Healer, is linked to the Principle of Support. Therefore, it's understandable that the Stoic can't and doesn't want to manipulate the events of life. He wants to support what is happening with some greater, mysterious purpose. He feels in service of existence, like a person who must be obedient to life itself, or God, in freedom or compulsion, in any case obedient to directives which are felt as coming from above. The Stoic who is filled with fear will interpret these directives as a fateful blow and moral punishment. The person who loves himself and life will view the same events as a bond in a loving relationship between servant and master. He doesn't have to decide everything himself, he can and should ask for directives or inspiration. And if he finds his master not only in people but also in the loving, godly whole, he can be carried on the waves of his existence like a ship whose passengers trust their captain. As soon as they sail onto unknown waters, they can calmly view all events without losing trust that they will reach safe harbor at the appropriate time.

Just as the Spiritualist, the Stoic is convinced of an order that encompasses him, and trust in this higher order is his life's elixir. The Spiritualist fears exploring and testing his belief. He trusts blindly. But the Stoic allows life to put him to the test. The tranquility, which is the core of his Mentality, makes him a useful tool of creation. On the whole, the Stoic does without a personal will directed against the course of his life. He neither fights nor rebels. He likes to swim with the current. He accepts whatever should happen to him and, in so doing, finds himself—as long as love prevails over fear—in harmony with his own being and the whole of creation. If someone asks him: »How can you remain so tranquil with all these problems you have?« he just smiles. That is his secret.

Energy 2

Skepticism

– Distrusting   Investigative +

The Skeptic seeks truth like everyone else but he's not sure what form this truth takes. Where can it be found, what does it mean and does it really exist at all? He makes doubt his tool of finding truth. Often, however, the method of doubt also releases him from his need of being able to know exactly. Doubt is healthy, but distrust (the minus pole) is generated by fear. The more a Skeptic distrusts, the more he feels lost. He questions everything, even his doubts, and therefore no longer possesses any orientation. He loses the trust in his own perceptions that every person needs in order to be peaceful. And although a person who doubts and distrusts is someone who can never be accused of harboring illusions, he, nevertheless, misses a firm term of reference and trusts neither himself, nor others, neither fate nor the existence of a greater order.

The Sceptic doesn't really want to rely on anything, but sometimes he also is incapable of relying on anything. Then he feels abandoned by God and the world. However, he often forgets that it's only the fear of having to rely on something for good which makes him so uncertain and lonely. He is a seeker of truth. But sometimes he doubts he can find truth because he doubts that it exists. He is a seeker of certainties and security, and sometimes, through his Skepticism, through his constant questioning he penetrates into areas which allow him to see truth in a depth and sharpness of focus which is usually hidden from others.

And if we speak of truth, we mean the individual truth of one's self as well as general aspects of truth to which he devotes his attention. There is also the suspicion that some higher, universal truth might exist which the sceptic postulates but certainly doesn't want to submit to without questioning it. He's a doubter, but doubt can be a helpful medicine or a harmful drug. The Skeptic doubts either because of inner freedom and self-love or because of fear, and accordingly his questions are shaped either by an investigating mind or a destructive mistrust.

If a sceptic asks »What is love?«, he can do this in two different ways. He can observe himself and his fellow-men and explore their motivations, their actions, their expressions, can question them out of the desire to determine the essence of love. He can ask about everything he perceives: »Is that truly done or said out of love or is there a layer of fear behind the apparent expression of affection and understanding?« But if he doesn't have any trust in love, he'll from the outset put into question that it even exists. He won't trust his own feelings, he'll look distrustfully at every impression, suspect falsity behind every attestation of love. He'll feel safer if he assumes that no one can love at all (or him) since he can't find any true love in himself and he'll refuse to dispute this. He doubts that his perception could be wrong, since he's certain that others are only suffering from illusions.

Doubt is mental, it is a form of thought. No animal can doubt. We welcome the possibility of doubt and view it as one of the most important aspects of human expression, for doubt leads to self-recognition as long as it isn't used as an instrument of self-destruction. Doubt creates a distance of a human mind to himself and to his world. This distance, in its mature expression, allows growth.

The Mentality of Skepticism makes an extremely valuable contribution to humanity with its habit of questioning, investigating, uncovering illusions, of forsaking gullibility even if this makes other Mentalities uncertain. It is valuable even when the Skeptic poses penetrating, often bothersome questions which serve to shake the hopes of the Idealist, the beliefs of the Spiritualist, the certainties of the Realist. The Idealist is dissatisfied if he determines that his ideals seem too difficult to fulfill for the time being,, however he doesn't doubt that they are attainable in the end. A Skeptic, however, on the basis of his Mentality will investigate: »What validity does this ideal have? Is it possible to achieve it at all? Is it necessary? What purpose does it serve? What damage can it do? How can it be disproved? Who can destroy it? Why does a person need ideals? Wouldn't it be better to forgo them in the first place?«

And he overlooks in all his Skepticism that doubt also represents an ideal attitude for himself. He uses it to penetrate the deepest layers of truth, and his Skepticism can only fulfill its function if it presupposes that there exists something which is worth such penetrating questioning.

The Skeptic can be a deeply committed religious person even though he would doubt this if asked about his convictions. He finds the godly through searching for it within himself and outside himself. He discovers it by removing the layers which faith, traditions and the desires of mankind have covered over it. Through his incessant searching questions he creates a highly individualized impression of what truth means to him, and since he has worked this out for himself, no one will be able to disuade him of his results unless he himself discovers new doubts and uncovers new layers.

The Skeptic longs to look at the innermost core of all being. All of his doubts, questions, his investigations and his distrust are shaped by this longing. His worst fear is having to realize with horror that all his searching and longing were futile.

The Skeptic with the ordinal number 2 represents the archetypical energy of the Artist. Since an Artist is concerned with expression of form, it's clear that scepticism strives for the purest form. Just as a sculptor who patiently and arduously chips away the non-essential from a block of raw stone, has an idea of what he wants to create and isn't satisfied until that idea has found concrete material expression, so the sceptic patiently and often until exhaustion works on the unformed block of his ideas until he's seen the core which is no longer prey to doubt.

His ability to doubt is both friend and enemy. Since the Skeptic's power of self-reflection is strong, he is called upon his own capacity to investigate the vibrations of fear and love which lead him to constructive or destructive doubt and question his own motivations. If fear has driven a person to the point of doubting whether there is love and truth in the world, it would be good if he didn't stand still there but allowed himself to doubt the results of his investigations, or he'll become embittered. For it's possible that all his fears will magically be transformed into inner certainty. It's possible that he may realize at last this doubtful view of existence as one of his fallacies, and he'll find himself asking with constructive doubt: »Why shouldn't I, too, have access to love and be loved and acknowledge the truth of the godly?«

Energy 3

Cynicism

– Humiliating   Critical +

Many of you view the Mentality of the Realist as the ultimate. Much as you highly value a realistic attitude, you have a low opinion of the attitude of the Cynic. You fear it, you condemn it and, because of an incomplete understanding, regard it as a destructive, almost pathological attitude.

Our view differs from yours. Therefore, it is necessary that we ask you to accept for once that a cynical Mentality is just as important, just as valuable as are all other mentalities which create the energy aspects of the soul pattern. It's the Cynic's aim to bring truth and reality into harmony with knowledge. He doesn't doubt like the Skeptic, he doesn't believe like the Spiritualist. His mental approach to grasp what needs to be understood, is provocative ignorance: »I don't know.« He wants to reach an absolute knowledge through applying the method of not knowing.

Therefore, he's very critical of all forms of hope, belief and speculation. He can hardly understand how a person could believe something that he isn't absolutely certain of. And in order to be freed from this tension, he prefers not to know, to react critically to any given thing. As long as he does this from an authentic, cognitive impetus and remains loving and open, he has the effect of a rebellious moralist who succeeds in rousing his fellow-men, makes them think and confronts them with their basic questions and illusions.

If, however, a Cynic falls prey to his fear of finally finding confirmation of his existential lack of knowledge, he loses the ground beneath his feet, denies the ultimate existence of that which he used to value, and the ability to know in general. He also reviles or humiliates those who believe they know. Thus a demanding Cynic becomes a petty fault-finder and critic. Because of his own fear of uncertainty he'll find fault with everything and everyone, including himself. He'll be dissatisfied, ill-humored and destructive, he won't accept anything that could convince him that there is anything worth loving, worth knowing, worth living for except his certainty that everything is superfluous, futile, unimportant. This attitude appears to him to be his salvation from doom, and he fights for his survival by pushing everyone away from him who imagine that they know what could help him in his despair.

Just as the Realist, the Cynic is convinced that he represents the only true, the only real world outlook and that all others are only suffering from naive or malicious illusions. As long as he's in the minus pole of his fear he sees in his fellow-men enemies who want to lure him onto the slick ice of certainty in order to let him slip even more roughly. Then he'll take revenge by humiliating them.

Most of you know cynics from their manifestations of the minus pole. You suffer from their humiliating remarks, from their denuding looks into your holiest convictions. You're scared to listen to their derisive remarks, their sardonic laughter at your most intimate views. That a loving Cynic could exist seems like a paradox to you. But it's also completely possible for people with this Mentality to show love through their fundamental philosophy by directing their readiness and ability to be critical onto areas of existence which are unclear, false and harmful in order to purify them.

A Cynic assumes in the positive sense that he doesn't know anything until he's been completely convinced that what he sees or what is presented to him really is the way it appears. And by nature he's not easily convinced. This makes him a person with valuable steadfastness. Anyone who wants to convince him is constantly required to develop clarity on his part, a firm point of view, to offer conclusive proof in order to develop the steadfastness of his viewpoint which wouldn't appear necessary to him in other circumstances since no one except a Cynic would react to them with so much criticism and resistance.

The Cynic, being a Warrior Mentality, is more active than the Skeptic. Where the Skeptic expresses doubts or keeps them to himself, the Cynic attacks, he penetrates and pokes and unmasks. He doesn't rest until he gets an answer that will mute his criticism and satisfy a mind so thirsty for knowledge. Otherwise he will mock, sneer, disdain and jeer. While the Skeptic asks doubting, probing, but mosty careful questions, the Cynic doesn't restrict himself to questions. His method consists of direct provocation and denial. He thereby leads his opponent to produce evidence. And its very important to him to separate true being from surface appearance. In his own unusual way, the Cynic, therefore, is even more serious and honest than representatives of other Mentalities, since for him the true being of a person is neither apparent nor simply structured. It consists of many aspects and shimmering facets. A Cynic seeks the truth behind the truth.

A cynical seeker of truth with his basic critical position is the only one who considers it possible and natural that truth and reality may, from different viewpoints, possess different indisputable qualities and that there might be more than one truth. As long as he succeeds in living with the uncertainty of not knowing and it gives him pleasure not to commit himself, he won't be overcome by negativity. However, as soon as he hates himself and the world for the fact that there's no certainty, that truth doesn't even exist just because he can't find it, he'll turn into a desperate, hardened, sharp-tongued person who massacres and debases everything that pleases and moves others.

A Cynic who's filled with self-hatred can hardly bear that his fellow-man is satisfied or happy. He'll try through a direct, fundamental denial of this state, completely without argument, to expose this subjective happiness as a lie, for the fearful cynic happily applies the technique of exposure. And since he in no way wants to suffer from illusions which could cover up or falsify the essential truth, he poses—as long as he doesn't think and act destructively—a massive challenge for all those who, as Idealists, Spiritualists and even Realists, are moving in the minus poles of their own soul matrix. He worries them since he offers them no absolute truth of his own to replace their illusions after he's destroyed them. It's a sign of his Mentality that a Cynic's motto is the principle of uncertainty and the endurance of uncertainty.

The Cynic has the ordinal number 3 on the action level and represents an aspect of the Warrior archetype. For this reason he likes to attack and often behaves in an offensive way. He wants to convince and be convinced, if necessary with force. He wants to actively deal with things. Unmasking something or someone gives him pleasure. His penetrating, his nagging, his insisting shows the combative strength of this attitude. And just as a metal saw can break through material of great hardness and resistance, so the Cynic succeeds in exposing even psychologically deeply-buried resistance or self-deception, as long as he doesn't all too threateningly or destructively clash against the fears and sensibilities of his fellow-men. But when he directs his Cynicism against himself and incessantly massacres his own inner and external values, his belligerent attitude will be so dismissive and offensive that the Cynic is left alone and will eventually fall on his own sword.

A cynical person always has a sharp knife in his hand. He can use it to cut away social tumors, he can apply surgery in order to heal, as well as strike with it in order to kill. He cuts away everything that could make sick or grow rampant and which doesn't belong to the essence of a person or a social group. He's a great mental surgeon and therefore makes his contribution to the healing of mankind. But since people fear him and his knife, they'll only trust him if he makes his incisions with a calm, loving hand and if he's prepared to bandage the wounds which he for good reason opened. Then he'll be sought out by all who want to free themselves from the superfluous and harmful, who want to discover the truth about themselves and to penetrate their undisguised authenticity.

Energy 4

Pragmatism

– Rigid   Practical+

The Pragmatist occupies energy position 4 in the soul Matrix and is connected to the neutral position of the Scholar. As such, the Pragmatist views
with a certain distance and equanimity the differing Mentalities of other
people, and not only these but all phenomena of life, especially the belief
systems with which the ways of the world, truth and reality are understood
in the most variable ways. He observes all this and then asks: »What's the
purpose of it? What good is it? What can I do with it? How can I apply it?
What effect does it have and what will it change? Is it practical? Does it
work?« For a Pragmatist puts the effect and use of an attitude or an act in
the foreground. An idea which can't be applied and has no concrete consequences or visible results isn't of any worth to him.

The Mentality of a Pragmatist, therefore, is neither based on belief, hope,
knowledge nor doubt. He concentrates on application. He prefers to to comprehend truth and reality from the many varied possibilities of application
and to use those that truly seem capable of making his existence understandable and his daily life easier. He seeks a practical solution to the problem which
every human fundamentally has, namely the dilemma between the practical
demands of his physical manifestation and his many great ideas, expectations
and memories that are linked to being human.

The Pragmatist is ready to apply on himself what had been explored or
handed down by those before him. He tries out, observes and takes notes
like a scientist performing experiments on himself. But he'll also be interested in including concrete results of others in his investigations. As far as he's

able to determine that an Idealist, Spiritualist, Cynic or Stoic is getting on well with his world view, he'll become curious and want to investigate, to systematize, evaluate and to put their experience into a transferable, applicable form. If a Pragmatist determines, however, that any method—whether it's intended to increase consciousness or to lose weight—isn't successful or too complicated to be useful, he categorically rejects it and neither recommends it to himself nor others.

The Pragmatist falls into ecstasy if he realizes that something works! Then he senses that the world has been made richer, has received a gift of enduring worth that is not just theoretically interesting but has been practically tested and thereby anchored in reality as an empirically-proven truth.

As function-oriented as the Pragmatist can be, he's also tempted to reduce everything to practicality if he's fearful and loses his curious outlook. He then limits his former global approach to what is possible in the immediate here and now. The narrowness of his horizon becomes apparent in the fact that he can no longer neutrally observe and examine if what he tries out may have a positive effect on others, even if he personally isn't successful. This turns him into a morose, reserved person who is impervious to anything new. He's rigidly encapsulated in the idea that experiments are senseless since the world will never change, that it's not necessary to try out something new because the tried and tested of the past is still somehow practicable and must suffice. Then the Pragmatist becomes stiff and rigid, he is no longer flexible or curious. The old and tested can be a habit to be kept even if it no longer has any positive effects, sends no fresh impulses, no longer causes feelings of happiness or satisfaction. It remains there just because it's always been there.

The pigheadedness with which a pragmatist holds on to traditions or habits if he has an all-too-great a fear of change can be seen, for example, in an irksome practice of meditation. Every day at the same time, at the same place, year-in and year-out, with no visible results. He may also hold on to ways of nutrition, work places, relationships, ways of dressing and fashions, all of which were valid and helpful long ago and functionally adequate at that time but which have long since lost their function and have become a superfluous ballast.

This can also apply to well-worn reactions and automatically-produced emotional attitudes which at one time were reliable but which no longer suit the reality and inner truth of the personality or occasion. So the Pragmatist moves between the poles of his happiness in practical experimentation, on the one hand, which is directed at the testing of something new, and, on the other hand, a fearful rigid attitude which rejects whatever is new, hangs on to the already-tested in order not to give uncertainty and change too much room.

The Pragmatist loves his habits but he also shows love for himself when he can replace old habits with new ones. However, if habits rule him without him noticing it, he has to a large extent forgotten his self-love. Therefore, it's good for him to be prepared to voluntarily change his habits: for instance through travelling or moving or changing his work place. In order not to be paralyzed in ritualized ways of action, it would be good for the Pragmatist not to continue his beloved uninterrupted, usual life-style for ever.

As long as he insists rigidly on finding the same conditions at his place of vacation as he does at home, or if he notices that massive difficulties are caused for him at his work place by a change of colleagues, the installation of a new machine or a structural change, he can realize that his rigidity is cutting him off from life with its constant pulsations.

A person with a pragmatic Mentality makes, just as much as all other Mentalities, an excellent contribution to the functioning of the whole. For if the Realist, Cynic, Skeptic or Stoic constantly tend to test reality and truth according to their content, the pragmatist has the task of making their theories concrete, to generalize them, to filter out the essence of the various theories and test their applicability.

The Pragmatist wants to take the essential, which he distils in order to free it from the validity of the moment, and to give it a timelessness which keeps its basic value. Because of this, he likes to explore methods and achievements of the historic past to free them from the mist of oblivion and make it apparent that they haven't lost their validity. A Pragmatist, therefore, often is also an historian. He loves the ancient, the tried and tested, but has to take care that he doesn't become its prisoner.

The Mentality of the Pragmatist corresponds to that of the Scholar archtetype. The Scholar is a careful observer. He remains neutral and, therefore, doesn't like to get involved in the mental clashes that occur among the other Mentalities. He understands and accepts them all. He's only interested which validity the various basic ideas of reality contain. To him the truth is what a person can apply. What really helps is real. The pragmatic person is a secretary and historian of the most varied, differing elements of knowledge. Without his commitment, his honest, impartial service, much would remain theory, utopia or wishful thinking. He is the instrument through which all that is imagined is transformed into deed, action and effect.

Energy 5

Idealism

– Vague   Visionary +

For the Idealist everything that is, is imperfect. He complies with it but isn't satisfied even if he accepts it for the time being. An Idealist experiences his satisfaction and fulfillment in rising above the present state of things, in the idea that it has by no means reached its perfection and is therefore capable and worthy of improvement.

The Idealist looks ahead and above. He has a vague or a clear vision of what's achievable, desireable and beneficial. This applies to himself and also to his fellow-men. And it applies to the material world as well as to the immaterial world.

All Mentalities try to discern truth and reality, describe it, integrate and form it. The Idealist doesn't see truth where he is, but always where he isn't. Truth, absolute and eternal, exists for him like a luminous writ high up in the sky. His endeavors consist of learning to read it and to apply the teaching that is contained therein. He has no doubt at all that truth, clarity, justice and love exist. He only deplores that no one seems to live by it. He himself sometimes is estranged from these values, which he feels determine all existence, and at times he is cut off from them. However, they are not foreign to him. But his ideals are always far, far away—in the past or in the future. Often he lacks grounding, his mind is only rarely in the present moment. The fact that in his eyes nothing, including himself, is all right as it is can sometimes create a fundamentally malcontent character. On the other hand, the Idealist is full of hope that things might change for the better, although not always does he have definite proposals to make. His ideas for the future remain vague, his ideas about the past are vague, because he insists on a vague romantic view of olden times and is not interested in historic studies which might reveal how it really was. His view of the present is equally vague because his eyes are not focused on it. Nevertheless, whenever the Idealist puts his feet on the ground and in this positive energetic state develops his visions of a better world, like an astonomer gazing into the universe, he is profoundly in touch with the yet unawakened potential of mankind. He is the one who dreams those dreams which one day may become true.

The greater the distance between his momentary reality and his ideals, the more difficult it will be for the Idealist to be satisfied with himself and what is. The Idealist is an eternal seeker. It's his secret, though, that he doesn't really want to find. For to find it would quell his longing and seeking. But the Idealist doesn't want to live without this longing. Whenever some of his ideals become reality, he immediately creates new ones and places them far away so that he can constantly strive toward them. His path is truly his goal.

The Idealist is unhappy, therefore, in two diffferent situations. He is sad when there's nothing left he can aim his ideals toward since he finds himself temporarily in a state which meets all his dreams. This is completely unreal to him, and suddenly his basic emotion of nostalgia is superfluous. And he's also unsatisfied if he's distanced himself too far from his own ideals so that his feeling of personal worthiness suffers and he falls prey to his own contempt.

A person with the mentality of an Idealist is often caught between the desire or compulsion to fulfill all his ethical standards and the realization that he isn't capable of doing this and that there's also hardly anyone around him who can meet the norms he sets. Then he experiences bitterness, sadness and disappointment. He can punish himself severely for all the transgressions of his idyllic ideas. And therefore he often appears not very fond of himself, he keeps finding fault, and only finds himself again if he discovers a new approach to his own ethical or practical norms. He senses a new little happiness if he can confirm himself or be confirmed by others that in the end he isn't as far away from the heavenly goal of perfection as he had feared.

Since an Idealist isn't happy being »here«, he seeks to be »there«. Out of pure fear of not meeting his own ideals, he tries stubbornly to suit them at least externally. He wants everything to be better, greater, truer, more perfect or more beautiful, including himself. Then he appears to be ungrounded and vague like a person who has many balloons in his hand and lets himself be lifted in the air by them. He no longer has any contact to the basis of his reality. He appears nebulous surrounded by the pink clouds of his hopes; he doesn't want to admit that there is a distance to the real world now. The Idealist is often an illusionist. He suffers from illusions about the position he finds himself in compared to his heavenly ideal.

However, if an Idealist is honest with himself, if he identifies his ideals as visions and doesn't condemn himself when he doesn't achieve them, if he doesn't condemn his fellow-men when they don't meet his personal norms of perfection, then he's surrounded by a sweet luminous glow, the glow of oneness.

He merges with existence, he dissolves the barriers of his individuality to the whole without losing his identity. Being one with himself doesn't mean that he no longer seeks and strives. That he will never give up. It means rather that he realizes which station he's at on the long journey between his fear and his love.

The Idealist looks into the distance and he always looks upwards. His eyes often have a starry gaze. Therefore, he also realizes more clearly than others what is possible. He experiences better than other Mentalities the whole great potential of mankind and the world. If there were no Idealists who intuitively comprehended that potential and believed there was access to it, this heavenly door would remain closed. The Idealist, therefore, knows the place, points out the way and opens the door with the key of his hopes and dreams.

The ordinal number 5 shows that the Mentality of the Idealist represents a variety of the archetypical Sage energy. The Sage knows that for mankind there is something more, something greater, wider, better and higher than the reality of the moment, and that it's possible and desireable to find access to this distant sphere. However—although his ideal in its transfigured form is constantly before him—the Sage is therefore wise because he lovingly admits that he himself is only a spectator, an observer, a person in his total imperfect humanity.

Therefore, the wise Idealist loves his weaknesses. If he can love his own fallibility and his shortcomings, it's easy for him to also accept his fellowmen the way they are, without, of course, wanting to keep them that way. He shows them what they can eventually achieve and accompanies them gently along the path to the light. He takes them by the hand, not by setting an unapproachable, severe example and letting others think that he's already fulfilled the norms and conceptions, but by waving to them from where he's standing and encouraging his brothers and sisters to stroll together with him on the path of perfection.

Energy 6

Spiritualism

– Gullible   Verifying +

Idealism desires and dreams. Skepticism doubts and asks. Cynicism denies
and probes. The Spiritualist just believes. He believes that all men are good.
He believes that the divine spirit is to be felt everywhere. He believes firmly
in truth. He believes it's contained in every manifestation of existence and
that it's his task and that of all mankind to uncover it. He senses the holiness
in all earthly manifestations and longs to get in touch with the forces of the
invisible reality around him. Spiritualists are the esoterics of all times and cultures. The Spiritualist believes he possesses intuitive insight into eternal truth.
But often he doesn't know the truth although he is convinced of its presence
in everything. If a person has chosen the Mentality of a Spiritualist in order
to observe the reality of the world, he subscribes to a basic spiritual position
in life. This means he hopes to come into direct contact with the dimensions
of the godly spirit.

Spiritualism also means feeling constantly inspired by the spirit of
creation. The Spiritualist feels one with it. He finds no fundamental separation between that which inspires him and that which he is. He views himself
as a small wheel in the living mechanism of the universal clockwork. He feels
touched and guided. He believes he is never alone. The godly, the spiritual
principle, the universal will are trusted ideas for him and nothing makes him
more insecure than realizing that another person can consciously dispense
with these universal integrations, that someone would want to deny that he
exists within a spiritual context, which he, the Spiritualist, feels is irrefutable
and proven.

And this is what the Spiritualist fears most: having to discover one day that, despite all his trust and inspired sensations, he is alone in the world. That he might realize his separation from the whole and that the whole in the end doesn't watch over him like a mother or father, but refuses to protect him from all the perils of life. And since he's secretly tormented by this fear, but can't admit any doubt in his basic belief since this would go against his Mentality, he sometimes decides to become a devotee. He devotes himself to the teaching of an enlightened master who sees the truth, he devotes himself to his own supreme convictions, to any idea that appears comforting to him, he surrenders himself without skepticism, without the slightest doubt. He simply decides to be a believer. For only when he rules out any uncertainty can he prevent his fear of an unpleasant awakening.

We view the Spiritualist as a person who, out of pure fear of verifying the truth, finds salvation in a belief system that promises to provide security from his own doubts. Therefore, he often believes in authorities, dogmas, systems. In no way is he only concerned with spiritual dimensions. He tends to believe everything that is presented convincingly to him. A Spiritualist will, without realizing it, fall prey to every declaration of truth and security, no matter if it concerns love in a partnership, financial arrangements, a happy future, prophecies, offers from insurance agencies, gestures of friendship or the diagnosis of a doctor. He needs to trust.

The Spiritualist, therefore, can be gullible and naive. He delights in magical thinking. He believes his trusting nature will protect him from disappointment. He'd rather accept being taken in by something or be deluded by someone rather than giving up his credulity or putting into question his personal security system. For this reason he depends to an extreme extent on convincing declarations. He needs reassurance. He wants to believe, after all, even when evidence speaks against it. He longs for promises that are never broken, neither by God or the saints nor by his guru, for assurances by his own parents, his spouse, his insurance agent. Whoever is prepared to convince him of something will find in him a submissive supporter, a person who places great expectations and hopes in him and constantly signals in many ways and means: »Please don't disappoint me so that I can continue to believe and trust in you!«

But since sometimes, despite all his efforts, he finds out that the vows of people aren't dependable, he focuses his religious hopes on his God. This happens from a need for a creed on a spiritual authority whom he views as more dependable since it's high above mankind. He believes in the loving qualities of life or in the personal protection by his favoured saint, or in a talisman, not because he has true trust but because he simply can't bear the thought, the idea, the feeling of not being able to rely on anything.

Now you can imagine that we, on our part, in no way deny the existence of a loving, protective authority who guides and protects human beings. We couldn't ever do this since we've been convinced of its existence. The Spiritualist doesn't suffer because he doubts that there is such an authority, but because of his absolute wish to believe it. He suffers because he prefers to be devout, to remain naive and gullible, instead of asking for proof. And he's afraid of the answer. The Spiritualist shies away from the risk of falling into emptiness. He avoids finding out if this protection, this leadership, this overwhelming love really exists. Therefore, he must believe blindly. He confuses trust with some kind of blindness.

However, this is true only in times when his fear wins out over his ability to trust. If a person with a spiritual Mentality feels well, if he's secure in his loving plus pole, he feels completely competent of undertaking certain risks in order to find out if the bridge between him and the all-loving spirit will also support him. His boat, which truly takes him on the shore of inspired safety, is the wish and the will to test, to verify, to experience in the place of blind belief.

His questions aren't identical to the doubts of the Skeptic. The Spiritualist doesn't ask: »Can I really trust you? Perhaps I shouldn't trust you.

Who knows if you're worthy of my trust? Who knows, maybe you're only deluding me? Perhaps it's not good to trust you at all.« The Spiritualist must employ a different testing method. He will feel better if he can test that along his path there really is a bridge crossing the abyss of delusions, if it's safe or crumbling. He has to verify his beliefs and dogmas about the world and the various aspects of reality despite all his fear of never reaching the other shore or of finding out that no one is waiting for him there.

The Spiritualist should gradually take leave of his naive devotion and find out whether that which he believes is really there for him. If he believes his spouse loves him or his boss appreciates him, why not put it to the test? His growth lies within this. And if he gives priority to neutralizing his fear of truth through devoutness, and in such a way creates his own reality, he'll have to ask questions in order to receive valid answers. Such an insecurity, such a risk is very painful for him since he always places immense value in his unquestioned devotion and firm belief which raises him above his unbelieving comrades. As long as he's a devotee and doesn't pose any questions, he thinks he can stand alone on a rock in a raging surf.

And like a ship-wrecked person, who's just been rescued, doesn't think immediately of asking the name or nationality of the ship that rescues him, so is the Spiritualist content when he realizes that there's something better than his isolation on the arrogant rock of devoutness.

The Spiritualist who wants to set out on the path of loving verification leaves the rock of his naive devotion and opens himself to new, trusting questions. These questions don't doubt the possibility of help from the spiritual forces but ask: »Am I prepared for once to really be guided? Will I really accept the help of the spirit world or of my soul family in which I believe so firmly instead of holding it in reserve for the day, which I hope never comes, namely the day I do need help? Do I have the courage to find out if it will then be granted to me?« For only then can he have the spiritual experiences which are so important for him.

The Mentality of the Spiritualist is part of the archetypical energy of the Priest. It has the ordinal number 6. And if you connect this Mentality to the Priest's soul role, you'll realize why the Spiritualist has such great fear of one day realizing that his belief system has disappointed him, that he is an insignificant speck of dust after all and nobody out there cares for him. For at every moment the soul role of the Priest lives under the impression of godly guidance, inspiration, of unity with higher realms, the beyond, the existence of an all-encompassing truth. And if a Priest begins to question what he so blindly places his trust in, he feels so confronted with his own distrust—another word for naive devoutness, but it sounds more offensive—that he starts doubting his own essential calling. He could just as well give up. The attitude of a loving Spiritualist, however, is akin to the soul role of the Priest in its positive pole, when blind devotion to the godly or higher authorities becomes quiet and trusting experience of its reality, open to verification. Trust and examination don't exclude each other. Trust is a gift of love, credulity is an expression of fear. Blind faith destroys trust.

Truth exists, although it is manyfold. It's accessible to humans and doesn't shy away from questions. All Matrix-elements with the ordinal number 6 characterize people who fear destroying the aura of the holy with their probing and seemingly irreverent questions. They think they'll lack respect if they examine their beliefs. But truth will appear clearer and more beautiful once it's freed from the veils of fear and from the cloudiness of gullibility. The Spiritualist will experience moments of rapture and quiet beatitude if he risks being really trustful, if he tests the promises of the world and dispenses with the false security of his naive desire to believe.

Energie 7

Realism

— Guessing   Perceptive +

Just as all other soul Mentalities a Realist is concerned with truth and reality. He easily perceives truth and reality and the ways of the world. For him,
reality is obviously where he is at the moment. It isn't in the distance,
neither above nor beneath him, neither within nor outside himself. He
experiences himself in a complete integration with the real.

Therefore, he's convinced that there's only one dimension of reality, and
that is the one he, as a Realist, can perceive. The people surrounding him
also view him as a Realist, because they realize that he rarely suffers from
illusions, that he constantly examines the reality of events, of his own experiences, wishes and plans. He asks: Are they realistic? Are they in touch with
the facts? Are they in accordance with the possibilities of the moment?

The Realist perceives, where others wish, doubt, hope, believe or
endure. He perceives and achieves in his perception a depth, width and clarity that can be extremely helpful in dealing with many phenomena of life. But
there's one thing a Realist doesn't perceive: the limits of his own ability to see
things clearly.

This leads to someone who quite seriously denies other Mentalities their
potential for perception. He views them as dreamers who, although they
possess endearing qualities, unfortunately aren't in contact with reality. He
doesn't realize that there are in fact realities other than the ones he views as
real, realities that call for different points of view than the one he can offer.
And another thing also often escapes him. It's difficult for the Realist to
perceive the exact moment when his quality of perception loses its clarity

and purity and is reduced to guessing. Therefore, it often happens that he realizes something which is accurate and correct but expands it into a decorative wreath of conjectures and speculations which no longer corresponds to reality. And when his fear is strong, he even becomes suspicious. He then thinks that he's the only one who knows the truth while all others are trying to deceive him.

The borders between perception and presumption, between clear vision and supposition, between real visibility and misrepresentation are fluid as long as they're viewed from the perspective of the Realist. Other Mentalities, however, sense immediately when the borders are crossed over and the Realist begins to imagine, guess or even to fantasize. It happens that he starts presuming and guessing once he no longer trusts his usually dependable sense of realism. He'll then ask: Am I dreaming? Or: I think I must be drunk or going mad. Then he's utterly confused.

Since a person with a realistic Mentality is so irrefutably convinced that his world view is the only true and real one, he sometimes deceives himself about the extent of his clarity of perception. Then he sees more than really exists. We don't say he sees something else—he actually sees more. This means that he sees something which is right but in his exuberance over his recognition, makes more of it than there is. Then in his confused and fearful state he begins to regard everything that he perceives as true and real, and it's difficult to again dissuade him from this since, if he's anxious and in need, he tends to despise those who don't view reality the way he does. He considers them naive or over-fearful, unrealistic and even stupid. Why should he trust these people?

A Realist, therefore, has difficulty allowing the validity of areas of perception other than his own. But his attempts to comprehend reality as such and to understand himself as a part of this more comprehensive truth or reality are definitely real and honest. And if he considers the possibility that his perception could sometimes be clouded by fear and become speculation, his vision will again become clear and he'll recognize connections, causal chains, motivations, hypocrisy, illusions and lies more quickly than other Mentalities.

The Realist has a great longing to be free of false ideas and vague conjectures. Everything which is false or sounds false bothers him and he wants to distance this from his life. If he sees clearly and his ability to perceive is motivated from love and relaxation, he provides valuable help to his fellowmen and places the greatest worth on intellectual or emotional honesty. For him, honesty means separating reality from the imagined.

Like the Skeptic, he also likes to ask: »Is this really so?« But in doing so he doesn't have a nagging doubt. He simply needs to uncover the truth, which exists as absolutely for him as for the Idealist and the Spiritualist. The Skeptic doubts at long last whether there is any truth at all, although he fears receiving a negative answer. The Realist seldom doubts, maybe too seldom. There's little place in his system for self-questioning. He tries to observe what is until he recognizes it. In so doing he doesn't seek help from without but trusts that he has all the possibilities within himself to establish direct contact with reality.

A Realist arrogantly places himself above other Mentalities since his ability of perception often isn't sufficient to evaluate the worth of ways of observance which differ significantly from his. He also suffers from the contempt of those who refuse his presumption. But if he convinces himself that variety has a place in his world view he can generously include them as aspects of his reality. But the attitudes of the Idealist, the Spiritualist or Stoic remain to him exotic additions which possess justification only as decorations for his own view. He feels a bit closer to the attitude of the Skeptic and that of the Pragmatist, but he often can't understand why the Skeptic asks all those questions when everything is already clear to him, and what the Pragmatist means if he wants to examine the feasibility of something which he himself has already recognized as realistic.

The Realist isn't concerned with making something out of reality. It suffices him to be perceptive and be happy about it. Often he has a lively fantasy which appears sometimes frightening to the Pragmatist. The Realist is also a little frightened by his fantasies since he senses that secretly he tends to regard them as real. He very quickly puts the products of his imagination within the framework of reality. He conjectures happily in the future and past and determines, as through an unnoticed short-circuit: »That's the way it is.« If a thought, an event, an action develop real aspects for himself, they are real to him and he transposes these differing ways of looking at things to his understanding of truth. Therefore, he's completely confused if he's reminded that the point of departure of his supposed unalterable realistic attitude or way of viewing things is a product of his own fantasy.

The realistic Mentality is archetypical for the energy and soul role 7, the King. A king can practice political realism or he can create a world—since he's powerful—in which his own ideas and laws prevail and thereby develop into a closed system. For a king, reality is either an absolute mirror of his perception or the result of a realistic consensus. If he observes his realm, he can recognize the truth of connections and expressions, and above all the fear of his subjects which leads them to say and do something different than they think just to please him. However, if the king himself has too many fears and worries about his prestige and authority, he won't be able to perceive the lies and flatterings and will imagine that this is the truth.

There's another way of viewing reality—the willful assumption of untrue and treacherous motivations in his fellowmen—out of pure fear of putting one's own conception of the world into question. The archetypical King tends to regard his own way of perception as absolute. He denies others' realizations or curses them as mendacious.

A person with the Mentality of a Realist who is in touch with his energetic plus pole has a broad field of action in which he can test the clarity of his perception. A self-loving Realist who's prepared to put his own clarity into question, to discuss it with other people, to wash his glasses once in a while, so to say, and again and again to look into something, will make an indispensible contribution to the well-being of the whole.

Reality, recognized in truth, is freeing, supportive and nourishing. The manipulation of reality through the denial of other points of view and down-looking on them is harmful. If the Realist does this, he is destructive.

Just as the Spiritualist, the Realist also places his hopes on concrete experience. But he's less concerned that testing reality could mortally disappoint him. What the Realist fears most of all is the unreal. He's frightened by everything that he can't grasp or understand. He dismisses it and doesn't acknowledge it. In so doing, he forgets that he often sees more than there is. But he sees it only on the level of perception or supposition, not, however, on the level of hope, doubt, belief or unquestioned acceptance.

A Realist can very well remain in contact with true reality if he's pre-pared to be slightly suspicious of his power to perceive. If he broadens his ability to see things as they are, through the integration of all those positive effects the plus poles of other Mentalities (being tranquil, investigative, crit-ical, practical, visionary or verifying) have on society, mankind and the world, life becomes easy for him. A Realist views himself as far-sighted and toler-ant. He can become that, be that and remain that if he doesn't exclude him-self from the great totality of human truths by regarding himself as the only one capable of recognizing them.

Centers

⑤
Spiritual

– telepathic   + inspired

⑥
Ecstatic

– psychic   + mystical

②
Intellectual

– hair-splitting   + thoughtful

Expression Level

①
Emotional

– sentimental   + sensitive

Inspiration Level

⑦
Moving

– hectic   + untiring

③
Sexual

– seductive   + productive

Action Level

④
Instinctive

– thoughtless   + spontaneous

Assimilation Level

VI The Seven Centers
and Patterns of Reaction

The word »center« describes the place from which a person directly reacts to his environment, to the world outside him. The seven centers connect who he is to how he is. This concerns first of all the linkage of the soul pattern (MATRIX) to the corporal reality of a person. Two levels meet here: the energetic and the physical. The centers can to a certain degree be associated to the big hormone producing glands of the body, which in the Indian tradition are called »chakras«. These places are not only energy centers but also body locations which are working in differing ways in different people. Just as a chakra is connected to a certain gland, so is the center or the place from which a person at first reacts, linked to a particular place in his body.

By the word »reaction«, we mean a direct reponse to a still unfamiliar, new, joyful or frightening situation, a response that emerges from those centers of a person which function the best and most trouble-free. This can be a location in the head, the chest or lower-body. The Reaction Pattern consists of a combination of two centers. We therefore distinguish the »centering« from the »orientation«. They present a relationship of approximately seventy to thirty percent. So different persons, for example, can react to a given situation intellectually-emotionally, or moving-emotionally, or emotionally-instinctively. The centers 5 (spiritual center) and 6 (ecstatic center) have no part in the reaction pattern of the human body. They are, however, active in situations of strong intensity, especially in deep relaxation and extreme stress.

The localization of the Reaction Pattern, as it is assembled from two chakras or energy centers, is the place where direct reactions take place and from which this reaction is given expression. This pattern, therefore, has the function of transforming events into physical feelings in order to communicate to a person a special sense of identity.

The localization of the reaction pattern in the body gives a person the impression that he is challenged in his strength and to the best of his talents if he encounters a situation which he's called on to overcome. The physical aspects of the Reaction Pattern and its localization in the body are also connected with the original survival mechanism which stems from the primeval brain. The primeval brain is connected to all endocrine glands and was originally intended to conquer in the most direct and rapid way all situations by activating the appropriate physical glands.

Now the survival of a person in the modern world is no longer so often immediately threatened as in the era of the Neanderthal. The even activation of all the seven centers lost its original function and therefore Homo sapiens became free for tasks which contribute to the forms of expression of an individual in his society. A suitable differentiation has been created which no longer is intended to assure that all chakras function equally at the same moment. Thus cultural milieus were produced, for only the different individual Reaction Patterns with their clearly separate energies allow a multitude of possibilities to arise in which such varying creative responses as artistic, philosophic or healing impulses can ensue.

We suggest the concept of »Reaction Pattern« in order to make clear we're talking about the combination of two supplementing elements: centering and orientation. You should anchor in your consciousness the important fact that your Reaction Pattern is an alliance of two localizations in your body. The immense variety of human cultural achievements is based mainly on the variability and differentiation of these patterns. If humans didn't react to one and the same situation so extremely differently, one in an emotional manner, another intellectually, moving, instinctively, sexually with their various orientations, it would be impossible to interpret that situation, and, in a cultural sense, cope with it creatively.

On the other hand, it's often difficult to really understand the Reaction Pattern of another person. You'll often reach instinctive barriers which, on the basis of your evolutionary history, convince you that only your own Reaction Pattern can guarantee survival and that all the others are less capable of holding their ground in this world.

But since each of you secretly believe this we think it's appropriate to view this fallacy with humor. It's really not necessary that each of you understand each other as well as if he were the other person; it's much more important and necessary to realize and to respect that each person is unique in his own way and, through this uniqueness, possesses a fundamental justi-fication for his existence.

The centers especially seem to invite you to succumb to various temp-tations. You might, for example, despise and devalue that which you can't do as well as another. The intellectual, therefore, tends to slightly debase the emotionally centered person. The emotional person, on the other hand, is particularly proud of his feelings and punishes intellectual, heady persons with contempt. An active, moving or sexually centered person who lives bodily life consciously and full of relish might be jealous of the intellect-ual's accomplishments, but will also give him the feeling that he moves in regions which, in an essential sense, are unreal. So when the Reaction Pattern operates out of its negative pole it creates a great deal of misunderstanding and secret boasting which we would like to see moderated and don't consider necessary although we understand it as part of of your evolutionary history.

But you've now developed in so many areas of your existence away from the original functions of your body. It seems to us that it's time to view the minus poles of your reaction pattern with some healthy self-criticism. On the other hand, it will be more understandable to you why you identify so strongly with your own Reaction Pattern and so seldom can really respect the Patterns of others. You identify, as before, strongly with your body. And whenever you fear that the survival of this body is in the slightest way threatened, all your defense mechanisms are activated.

To become conscious of the various Reaction Patterns serves self-observation and growing self-understanding even more clearly than many other elements of the Matrix. You can sort them and test them daily. As a rule, the Reaction Pattern doesn't pose a problem. You can easily accept yourself as a person who reacts emotionally, intellectually, or movingly. The Reaction Pattern, therefore, makes it possible to develop a self-love which accepts yourself in a way that the specific and individual combination of energy centers demand.

It's helpful in so doing to never reproach yourself for reacting to a certain unexpected situation in your own individual way, or to think that it would have been much better to react in a different way, like other people do. This would only hinder the spontaneous reaction and would lead you to don a mask which would distort your immediacy and make you in the end implausible for others. Accept, therefore, how your reaction pattern is localized in your body, respect this localization, foster it without believing that you must be different. The centers and the localizaton are a gift your soul has given you, where you can be sure that your matters of concern will be best and most clearly articulated.

We've explained to you that the centers create a connection between the soul energies of the Matrix and your body, which, by the nature of things, plays an especially important role during an incarnation. Centering and orientation create the Reaction Pattern. The centers 1 (heart chakra) and 4 (survival chakra) communicate to you the ties to the earth, the planets and the conditions which you've chosen for your path. They create the contact to the earth sphere and to your fellow-men. They set definitive, beneficial boundaries which, as a rule, you always have at your disposal and which make you human.

The centers 5 (third eye chakra), 6 (crown chakra) and 7 (solar plexus chakra), on the other hand, have the function of not allowing these boundaries to turn into walls over which you can't look and through which you also have no permission to pass. They guarantee, however, that you always remember your astral homeland, that you cannot convince yourself that you are just an animal, simply because you have an animal body. These spiritual, ecstatic and moving centers create, when they're activated and open, a porosity for ego-transcendence. In each of you these two centers are always prepared to be activated. They can lead an incarnated soul for a time, usually a brief time, beyond its limits of consciousness so that its relations to extraterrestrial dimensions, to the future and the past, and to the wisdom of a great number of soul siblings or old friends from former incarnations don't get lost. They can't be uninterrruptedly open, like other chakras, however, without harming the necessary connection of a person to his body, to the earth. Every single person—independent of the Reaction Pattern he's chosen for an individual incarnation—has access to both the spiritual as well as the ecstatic center. They are ready at any time to be touched and opened, but can't often be actively activated by you. You can only allow it to happen. The will be activated whenever they are needed. They'll only open under extraordinary conditions of life, in situations of extreme intensity, through tension, severe fear and boundless happiness, through pleasant or unpleasant stress as well as through unusual relaxation or deep meditation.

The minus poles of these centers, the telepathic and psychic states are not negative as such. Their »negative« quality stems from the fact that they can also be used to influence someone out of fear, they can be manipulative and cunning. But the spiritual center 5 and the ecstatic center 6 have no part in the Reaction Pattern of the Matrix.

The corresponding glands, the pituitary gland and the pineal body, don't develop in the same way in all people, and, if they're never or only seldom used in the way we've just described, they can gradually atrophy. Children usually have glands (including the thymus) which are still flexible and work willingly. But just as everything which isn't used ceases its service in the body, so can the pituitary gland and the pineal body also be estranged from their original activity. On the other hand, it's possible to activate these almost atrophied glands and their functions through increased attention, awareness, an outpouring of energy and the readiness to desire, trust and value that which they can communicate.

It's somewhat easier to integrate center 7 (the moving center), which can be a centering or orientation. The moving center 7, which in contrast to the centers 5 and 6, can be a part of a Reaction Pattern during ongoing movement like marathon running can lead to a kind of ecstasy, just as the centers 5 and 6 do, and it allows a moving-centered person to experience sudden, temporary altered states of consciousness, for instance, during a dance, a long run or sports training.

Energy I

The Emotional Center

– Sentimental   Sensitive +

All people have feelings, sensations, emotions. But only part of them are emotionally-centered or oriented. An Emotional Centering means that a person reacts to events or to other people emotionally, from the first center (the fourth chakra, the heart chakra) and, in such a way, his feelings take precedence over acting and thinking. This provides a characteristic, though individually varied, emotional response to everything he experiences. Usually the first reaction is stunned silence. This kind of emotion is not at all ebullient or impetuous.

The emotionally centered person uses his mental abilities or engages in physical movement only after his feelings have sorted out a situation. So if he's is confronted with a happy or distressing event, he at first can neither say anything nor think or move. He can only speak and sort out his thoughts after he's felt silently, and he can only move when his feelings demand expression. He often thinks his reactions come »from the belly«, but this is not so. He misunderstands the sympathy or antipathy of his unreflected emotions as being instinctive, when in reality they come from his mute heart.

Emotionally-centered people are sometimes talkative and lively when their emotions aren't highly affected and activated. On the other hand, the more the emotional center is touched, the more mutely such a person will react, and it can be that he'll appear nailed to the spot or frozen, and that his limbs can only move again when the primary reaction has occurred. If need be, spontaneous shouts or violent, instinctive gestures, may occur. Physical expressions of happiness or fear like grimaces or tears shouldn't be confused with the emotions. It's a kind of jerking or flinching gesture, like clutching one's heart, slapping one's mouth or forehead, seeking sustain on the nearest wall. These movements have a strong emotional expression and immediately become rigid again without leading any further. Passing out is another option for emotionally centered people, both male and female, when the emotions are overwhelming.

The emotionally-centered person has a rich, often secretive and more often half-conscious inner life which he protects the more deeper it touches him. Two basic types can be identified. One who directs his feelings outwards through wordless crying, laughing and showing fury. He often appears uncontrolled to people who are intellectually-centered, but in many ways he's usually more relaxed and freer than the second type, whose feelings are so intense, so overwhelming that it's difficult for him to deal with them since his emotions threaten to swallow him up or drown him. He's therefore concerned about keeping them under control in order not to be constantly ruled and threatened by them. All soul roles can be emotionally centered, a Warrior just as well as a Scholar.

Since the emotionally centered person first feels and then thinks or moves, he needs the possibility of retreat. He can and must repeatedly be alone to process the fullness of his impressions, otherwise he'll soon suffer from physical or psychological digestive complaints; a small drop will soon become too much for him and overflow his inner system. At the same time, however, he seeks out every opportunity to feel more, to sense more and to ride on the waves of his emotions.

He views the intellectually-centered person as a little cold, even if admirably responsible and controlled. He likes to ask him for advice but seldom feels deeply understood. It's difficult for him to endure and maintain emotional distance, since he identifies with his emotions to such an extent that for him being alive and having strong feelings is synonomous.

Despite this, it's an important and necessary step in the learning process of a person with an Emotional Center to not expect everything from his feelings, to not overload them with demands which they can't fulfill. Therefore, in the course of his life it's beneficial if he succeeds in achieving a small or greater distance from his emotions—especially those long past—in order not to make them his master. The more temperamental, outward-oriented emotional type is often found among the soul roles of the Artist, Sage, Warrior or King, while the quiet, withdrawn type is represented by the Priest, Scholar and especially the Helper/Healer, whose emotional center with the ordinal number 1 is archetypical.

Both types are warm-hearted and have an aura that invites others not only to come a little closer to their own emotions, but also teaches them how good it is to come into contact with spontaneous forgiveness and generous direct understanding which isn't overloaded with any discussion. For the emotionally-centered person understands how to create and maintain great closeness, even if it often causes him some fear. He's dependent on this intimacy for his well-being. He understands without needing to find a reason for this, because he feels so intensely. His comprehension, his understanding of another person is quick and direct and this ability gives him a security which is reflected back by the other person. But his rejection, his prejudice, his revulsion can be just as strong if he feels attacked, if his sensitivities are touched and his fears activated. Then he reacts and rejects just as emotionally without considering the consequences and without checking his mental reasons, and he can be a bitter enemy just as he can be a warm-hearted, forgiving friend. The emotionally-centered person can instinctively find access to his fellow-men through empathy. Irrespective of this he often lacks a sensitive understanding for one who feels completely differently from him. His very existence confuses him, his abilities aren't sufficient to put himself in another's person's place since he isn't neutral enough and has little distance. Then a silent rejection soon sets in, which, however, is felt as an emotional wound by the other person.

Basically an emotionally-centered person seeks tenderness and understanding more than pure sexuality. For him the nearness which can result from a sexual embrace is always more important than the activity itself. Each touch, each intimacy, is in the first place intended more to awaken his emotions, to let him indulge in hopes, dreams, memories and other fantasies rather than to satisfy his elementary lust. His heart's desire is to reach his partner and to be reached by him or her emotionally. »Let's never part« stands at the forefront of his desires. Only emotionally-centered or emotionally oriented people know these extreme needs for a romantic heart attachment and eternity of sentiment, for harmonious merging and unity. Therefore, their feelings are all the more easily injured once they realize that not every partner shares this particular desire. This is especially true for all those who combine an emotional centering with a sexual orientation in their Reaction Pattern.

This center in its minus pole produces very sentimental people shedding tears of joy or compassion or crocodile's tears at any moment. But among emotionally centered persons you can also find the most sensitive, high-strung, empathetic and warmhearted human beings.

Emotionally-centered people love deeply and hate deeply. They can hardly understand how others can speak light-heartedly about love and hate and it's even less comprehensible to them that there are people who are capable, through convincing arguments with themselves and others, to keep their emotions in check. However, they themselves also know enough ways and psychic techniques in order not to sense their feelings if for one reason or another it isn't opportune or appears too dangerous. They can be masters of repression.

The often chaotic ability to feel allows this type of emotional person to accept life in its whole disordered entirety. He sees and recognizes connections that lie beyond a logical system and he's open to the beauty and the fascination of the unspoiled, the immediate and the contradictory.

The heart-chakra of the emotional person is especially active both in its more open or more closed state. Often a wide, broad chest of women or a strong torso and arms of men are an expression of their desire to enclose the whole world in their hearts and to embrace the universe in its chaotic entirety.

The extremely high sensitivity of an emotionally-centered person makes him receptive as well as vulnerable. It provides him the most beneficial moments of openness if he's learned not only to trust his emotions but to admit and express them. If an emotional person fears his own feelings and doesn't dare to admit them unfiltered, he'll easily descend into sentimentality. He then falsifies the feelings and covers them up with all kinds of protective shells, which are composed of moralizing, religious and romantic set pieces that satisfy the great need of constantly riding on the waves of intense feelings. The direct identification of feeling to being alive leads him to seek excitation everywhere and to turn away from the moment—which doesn't always provide excitement—in order to indulge his longings in the past and the distant future.

Emotionally-centered people take everything to heart, both happiness and suffering, and, therefore, in later years often suffer from heart and circulatory illnesses, high blood pressure, also from lung complaints like asthma, illnesses which can be traced back to the severe mood changes and the irregular pulsations of the organs connected to emotions. The lungs are often affected since emotions and breathing have a direct connection and the quiet type breathes superficially or holds his breath in order not to be overwhelmed by feelings.

The emotional center is assigned to the thymus gland.

***

The combining of an emotional centering (1) with a sexual orientation (3) in a personal Reaction Pattern shifts the emotions to a highly inspired-creative sector which can stretch from a great love of children to the cultivation of new plants, from the composition of touching music to the rearrangement of whole landscapes. Even if the emotionally-centered person is in the first place concerned with nearness and fusion, a sexual orientation fosters the direct experience of physical, sensual feelings without over-emphasizing the romantic components, so that a significant erotic activity can lead to a grounding which an emotionally-intellectual person will lack to the degree to which he wants to free himself with his reasoning from the threat of his emotions.

An emotionally-centered (1) and, in addition, intellectually-oriented (2) person will have an easier time with his reaction pattern in bringing his feelings into congruity with verbal expression. An intellectual orientation makes the emotions appear more restrained, but, often leads to a person denying or rationalizing his emotions in order to suppress them, depending on their severity and hurtfulness. It should be said here that centering has nothing to do at all with intelligence. An emotionally-centered person, no matter if he's moving or intellectually-oriented, can have just as high an intelligence level as a primarily intellectually-centered person. But his intelligence will be expressed differently—not primarily in intellectual areas but in all areas which presuppose a sensitive and direct feeling, a kind of emotional intelligence.

The combination of an emotional centering (1) with a moving orientation (7) produces people who need to show their feelings by strong expressions—floods of tears, peals of laughter, telling gestures and impressive grimaces. They can't hide their feelings. They easily lose control when emotions become too strong, go into hysterics, have tantrums or feel like they want to die right away. They must act out. They very strongly express their emotions with violent movements, with sports, intense gestures, lively grimaces. When angry, they may go running or clean up the basement, before they're ready to speak about it. They may react by hurting themselves, breaking their bones, having car accidents, heart attacks, migraine, vomiting or taking drugs to escape confrontation. It would be better for them to argue aloud or go for a walk or scream and shout to ventilate their feelings. In the positive pole they can be very touching, because they show their feelings so directly, they are excellent actors or opera singers, great poets or novelists and temperamental but emotionally honest parents.

The emotionally centered (1) + instinctively oriented (4) person is the most direct and spontaneous of all. But it's difficult for him to distance himself from his feelings. His reactive feelings are highly impulsive and he frequently regrets the thoughtless haste of his remarks and actions. On the other hand, he also has a great instinctive knowledge of people, an emotional intuition, which is expressed elementarily. He can look into their hearts and know them. He's drawn without questioning or doubting to everything which seems positive and pleasant to him and, with just as definitive a signal, keeps away from everything which might be dangerous.

Energy 2

The Intellectual Center

– Hair-splitting   Thoughtful +

We speak of an Intellectual Centering if a person's upper body—the head, organs of speech, the brain, the eyes, ears and throat and thyroid are especially filled with energy. This centering doesn't mean that a person isn't able to feel; it only describes a shifting of accent. But one can be intellectually centered without being intelligent. This combination produces people who talk a lot but mainly superficial nonsense.

Expression and creative ability are moved to the intellectual area. They're manifested mainly in the products of thought and through the organs of speech. The Intellectual Center (2) corresponds to the neck chakra and is connected to the thyroid gland. The forehead chakra, in contrast, concerns the spiritual center (5) and the abilities of the third eye.

Intellectually-centered people like to think, to reflect, to argue and discuss. They take joy in each new idea they pick up, produce themselves or dissect. They feel exquisite pleasure if they set about to create thought structures or to tear them apart, to create connections or to analyze in a precise manner. They have an active mind. They are interested in understanding the world and in deciphering the messages of existence so that it gives them satisfaction not only to understand them but also to capture and express them in thoughts and words.

While the emotionally-centered person often has difficulties expressing himself verbally and these difficulties become greater the more he is confronted with his depth of feeling, the intellectual person finds it easy to bring forward what he has grasped and to speak about it, to communicate it and to stimulate others to think with him, to perfect his often astounding thought patterns.

Of course the intellectually-centered person wants to be admired for his mental brilliance. But there's also a type of person who keeps his thoughts to himself or who thinks too much and doesn't dare present the results of his analysis for examination.

Intellectuals in the sense of a Matrix centering have good reasons to offer for everyone and everything. They rationalize to the point of hair-splitting. Causal links from apparently definite cause and effect chains appear to calm them and they seldom notice—usually only in retrospect—that they've fooled themselves or imagined something in order to rationally conquer their fear of the illogical, the chaotic. They also sense, without really being able to grasp it, that they've argued beyond their own human reality. They constantly attempt to rationalize their own sensibilities and feelings or to neutralize them through »sensible« measures. They seek reasonable, logical arguments and explanations for all the pains of the body and the psyche. That seems to appease them but there's still a certain amount of unease, which confuses them because they sense that even with all their rationality they can't always reach the truth.

The intellectually-centered person needs time to reflect. He can spend this time alone or with others. If he withdraws to put his thoughts in order, or to read a book, he prepares himself in this tranquility to present his results and to turn them into deed. However, it's often just as satisfying for him to receive new stimulus in an exchange, dialogue, in discussions with others. This is a process which refreshens his thoughts, provides new impulses and sharpens his mind so that the enrichment which he experiences in this exchange can, in turn, be used to nourish him in the stillness of retreat and to compare or integrate his ideas with those of others.

If he doesn't find time or doesn't take time to reflect, he's often forced to shape his abilities via swiftness of thought. He has a habit of thinking with lightening speed. This seeming brilliance sometimes turns his natural thoughtfulness into a fearful intellectual bustle which is aimed at coming to a conclusion as quickly as possible in order to avoid mistakes and thereby quell his fear. His thoughtfulness, which is an expression of his highest willingness to love himself and the world, comes up short. However, many intellectually-centered people believe that their greatest strength and their brilliance lie in the speed with which they can put their thoughts in order, understand connections and make decisions. They are proud to see that others are slower thinkers.

We've already indicated that many of these intellectually centered persons—whether they're educated or not—cultivate an intense reflection. This also means that logic and reason appear to them to be the highest virtue. They become very uneasy and insecure if they run up against the limits of their logical analysis. However, the more fearful and uneasy they become, the more they persist on the all-encompassing validity of logical idea progressions and thought connections, so that they increasingly refuse to take into consideration illogical systems or, something which results from this, to allow chaotic »unreasonable« feelings to take their rightful place. They hold on tightly to the supposed rules of rationality. They raise reason to the level of divinity, consider it the measuring-stick of all things and attribute to it a healing power that other people who don't have an Intellectual Centering can only shake their heads over.

The two brain hemispheres of intellectually-centered people are not equally active; the left half works more powerfully while the right half of those who are emotionally centered works better and is better supplied with blood and energy. The intuitive, spiritual center in the middle between the eyebrows, the third eye, is accessible in the same way to both, but one uses it more to clarify his thoughts, while the other uses it more to integrate his feelings. So it's mostly the neck chakra which is at the service of the intellectually-centered person. It includes mouth, teeth, ears, even eyes. It regulates the intake and output of information, the processing of impressions and the clarification and classification of knowledge which is communicated through speech as an expression of thought.

This Intellecutual Center has the ordinal number 2 and represents a variant of the Artist archetype. As such it is highly imaginative, creative, often funny and witty with a lot of scurrilous fantasy. Such persons like to invent what has never been thought up before.

These regions are often excessively put into service and overtaxed. The greater the fear of an intellectually-centered person of not being able to understand and making himself understood, the more possiblities of physical weaknesses come most clearly to light: ear-aches or inflamed organs of speech, tenseness of the neck, eye ailments, headaches, thyroid problems, tooth-ache, changes in the brain like giddiness or tumors, even dementia as well as problems in smelling and tasting. These often result from an over-emphasis on mental energies such as rationality and the ensuing hairsplitting. Intellectually centered persons develop the idea that the strength of understanding lies in the first place, or exclusively, in brilliantly solving the problems of life and overcoming the drawbacks of being human without taking into consideration that being human means much more than being able to think and to find easy explanations for the secrets of life.

The Intellectual person secretly fears the full use of all his senses. He employs them mostly to keep his mind in order and to make sure and assure that he still has his world mentally under control. He sees to it that nothing happens that he couldn't rationally classify and control. In so doing, he cuts off the possibility of realizing the world in its fullness and entirety and forgets that perception means more than an intellectual classification and mental understanding.

If an intellectually-centered person deals with areas which aren't touched by fear but which activate his ability to love, he can fly with the wings of his spirit into the highest regions of world and self-observance. He has a philosophical access to the universe since he's a friend of knowledge and insight. He can not only explore the interplay between all manifestations but also recognizes and describes them to the extent that a human being can do so. His thoughtfulness is highly productive.

He's great in clarifying and explaining, in providing a clear, systematic analysis, and he isn't easily deceived when it comes to differentiating imagination, fantasies, ideologies or closed belief systems from a critical, tested, calming assessment of the recognizable factors. His critical ability allows him to test accepted ideas and, should the situation arise, to determine that they're overtaken, limited or marked by dogmas of faith.

The emotional person is little bothered by this. The intellectual, in contrast, is deeply troubled if he must determine through his reflection that he was deceived, but he expresses this disappointment by altering his view of what was at one time accepted as fact. He is not emotionally hurt, just intellectually shattered.

His mind is active, he is a lively and sympathetic observer. The components of his being also give him the ability to meditate because he is able to observe the movements of his thought with interest. Although it's difficult for him not to think, he often gains a distance from his thoughts and thinks about thinking as such, sometimes even recognizing its limits. And he often longs to be able to feel intensely while the emotionally-centered person would like to be freed from the storm of his feelings and envies the clarity of view of the intellectual.

A person with an intellectual centering poses many questions. He is curious, he wants to grasp and penetrate all secrets of life by thinking about them. He seeks the connections between the world and God, between mankind and the cosmos by putting them in the vessel of a philosophical system or world view, to be able to gather them and observe them. The sharpness of his view, the incorruptibility of his judgement and his desire for intellectual honesty make him a contemporary who can help his fellow-men not to fall prey to illusions which can result in sentimental emotionality, a hectic bustle or ill-considered ways of behaving.

As long as an intellectually-centered person directs his cognitive faculties, his thoughtfulness toward positive desires and wishes and gives love its legitimate place in his thoughts, he's in no danger of using his sharpened ability to think against himself and his fellow-men by trying to justify everything. If, however, he rationalizes all and everything, he's often spectacularly unhappy. Whoever is close to him can help him find his way back to clarity if he carefully points out to him that the mind isn't capable of understanding everything and cannot solve all problems.

***

In order to understand the difference between an intellectually-centered (2) and at the same time emotionally-oriented (1) person and an emotionally-centered but intellectually-oriented person, it's good to keep in mind that the parts have a ratio of seventy to thirty. Then it will be easier to realize that an intellectually-centered person with an emotional orientation at first reacts thoughtfully to everything that happens and only later observes, or even registers at all, his feelings (while for the other type of person the opposite would be true. He first reacts emotionally and only afterwards attempts to clarify and understand why he reacted the way he did; thought and analysis only come into play when the feelings have reacted). The intellectually centered person only begins to feel after his thoughts and his feverish attempt to classify and understand everything have calmed down.

The intellectual person with an emotional orientation feels most relaxed during short phases free of thought, for instance, while meditating, before falling asleep, after awakening, during physical activities or while listening to music. It's also easy for him to feel if he compares or identifies his feelings with others while reading.

An intellectual person (2) who has chosen a moving orientation (7) tends to require strong and even movements in order to direct his thoughts on the right track and to put them in order. He can best perceive, imagine, reason and draw conclusions if he walks back and forth while talking on the telephone. When he has a problem, he best takes a walk, gesticulates, travels, engages in sports activities or also does housework. Many women, for instance, reach the best results of their reflection while they dust, hoover or iron. They'll feel unsettled if they have to sit still to reflect. And the same is true for people who are driving. The moving orientation demands movement not only in a physically active sense but also in the passive sense of being moved. The most suitable thing for a person who has an intellectual-moving reaction pattern are types of sport activities that require regular movement, for instance, biking, hiking, or rowing, while dancing would be more appropriate for an emotionally-moving person.

Whoever reacts intellectually (2) with a sexual orientation (3) likes to think about creating something new, something unheard-of, to create the unimaginable. He's creatively engaged in these areas. He combines unknown or even revolutionary ideas with a great vitality in bringing them into being. Such an intellectual is often very active sexually, not because of the physical movement but because the tension before and the relaxation afterwards are especially creative phases for him. Something playful grows within him and that he must capture this in firmly defined, clear thoughts. He is also very flirtatious and sometimes prefers the suspense of a verbally intense erotic exchange to the actual sexual/genital encounter.

The intellectually centered (2) and instinctively orientated (4) type is a clever, somtimes even cunning person who has no interest in complex ways of thought or philosophies but uses his thoughts and ideas for commerce and profit. He is a good gambler or fund manager. He doesn't have to understand all the motions of the stock market, he just follows his instincts and later is verbose in explaining the unexplainable. His thoughts, senses, strivings are all successfully oriented toward material areas. He thinks about how he can achieve comfort, fame and prosperity, and since his thoughts are always instinctively concentrated on the best possible methods of achieving what he wants, he's often successful—as long as the circumstances of society don't prevent him. He survives not only better than others, but completes the most profitable business deals, no matter under what circumstances. He directly understands what the market demands and what his fellow-men need and want, and he has many clever ideas of how to meet these needs and desires.

Energy 3

The Sexual Center

– Seductive   Productive +

Although almost every body has sexual glands and almost all people are or have been sexually active, only a relatively small percentage of people are sexually centered. We tell you this right away at the beginning of our explanation in order to make clear that a sexual centering, an emphasis of the Reaction Pattern on this center, is not the same as sexual activity.

Nearly every person is, or was, fertile but only a few people are aware of the kind of strength that lies in the fertility of a Sexual Centering. This is a strength which makes one capable of action and dynamisms, a strength which is creative on a very elementary level, a strength that can unceasingly bring forth new things (comparable to eggs and sperm), if that center is consciously activated and used. However, like all other centers, this one, as a rule, is not perceived consciously when it's open, but will only be used unconsciously. Frequently it will be viewed, especially by females, as a threat, a limitation or an embarrassment which should be hidden rather than expressed. Sometimes people are ashamed of their sexual power instead of applying the potency which is bundled there as an elementary expression of life.

We call this center sexual but that doesn't mean that its activity is primarily one of genital sexuality. In our sense, sexuality is much broader, much deeper, much more comprehensive. It is an expression of elementary vitality, an expression of elementary fertility, whether it be in a spiritual, practical, artistic or energetic area.

The Sexual Center with the ordinal number 3 is part of the Warrior archetype. It is located on the polarity of action and therefore concerns behavior and movement. The sexually-centered person must, therefore, move and be active. He has to bring himself into a state of flux, to give momentum to this elementary fertility, which can extend into all areas of life. The sexually-centered person will directly behave and react from his stomach as he becomes more and more conscious of this strength. This is an enormous bundle of energies that can put much around him in motion and provides other people with vital force and basic energy. This strong vitality that's not sexually expressed but rather applied as a form of energy has a broad range, which can be directly communicated and transferred. This power not only comes into being when a person refrains from sexual activity. On the contrary, a person who's sexually-centered needs the stimulation of sexual activity or at least the fantasies tied to it, but also the physical charge of eroticism which allows him to develop fertility in the symbolic sense, which stretches far beyond biological fertility.

Sexually-centered people are, as a rule, more deeply in contact with their body and closer to their body feeling than people who are emotionally or intellectually centered. Here they are similar to the instinctively-centered and also the moving-centered persons, since all three recognize the validity of the material world as a joyful experience and know how to utilize it without making the mistake of perceiving matter as something belonging to the lower instincts, to be neglected, as the emotionally or intellectually centered people do all too easily.

If a sexually-oriented person is on a war-footing with matter (all areas of the material world, money, nourishment or his body), if he has a distorted relationship to the source of matter, regardless for what reason, his vitality will be weakened or seek channels of expression that represent emergency outlets for the potency that's trying to force its way out. Therefore, it's especially important for people with a sexual center to establish a good relationship with the material aspects of existence. They'll feel more rooted, happier, and whole if they accept and care for that which is necessary for a healthy orientation instead of denying it — their sexuality.

We've said that there is an elementary creative power in a Sexual Centering and, therefore, when it is combined with a further center as its orientation, this elementary creative power will be used in the area which is activated, whether it be intellectual or emotional, moving or instinctive.

A sexually-centered person should take into consideration his feelings of joy and pleasure in everything that he does or undertakes. He'll always be in harmony with his center if he makes his physical well-being a measuring-stick, not as a neutral state but as a noticeable feeling of joy. And the pleasure can come from centers other than the Sexual Center itself.

The physiognomy of people with a sexual center can often be recognized by an emphasis on the lower body, a protruding and inviting breadth of the hips which provides room for joyful sensations in an earthy and fiery element. The further this center (the reproductive glands) is in a standing position from the earth surface, the longer the legs, the higher is the frequency of the energy, but also the less earthy and creative. It's sublimated to the extent that it is distributed in the higher situated chakras.

The sexually-centered person is in many ways androgynous, since he/she both actively generates and passively receives. In each case a new product results from the act of energetic fertilization. He's capable of creating something from within himself since he can fertilize himself. This Sexual Center is assigned to the lower stomach (sexual chakra or hara), which is located below the navel and connected to the gonads, vas deferens, the fallopian tube.

People with such a centering like to indulge in active physical sexuality, since being sexually active and propagating are a precondition for all other forms of creativity. Carnal desire is considerably weaker for those with a sexual orientation but still very important.

This centering expresses itself in a domination by one's physical urges which can barely be controlled despite fears and limitations which may be imposed on a person and control him, especially prohibitions or taboos which he in no way wants to observe but has to. If, however, the fear disappears or is no longer fostered, the sexually-centered person can soar upwards to a physical ecstasy freed from moral limitations which will give him a physically integrated, glowing and abandoned appearance. Such a manifestation of unusual relaxation and impressive vitality is no longer captive in tense muscles and character masks. It reflects a body in which the undisturbed feelings of the joy of an infant are combined with a mature spirit.

This center is a variant of the Warrior archetype. Its plus pole can be described as productive in a material and immaterial sense. Coloured by fear, this productiveness is reduced to the minus pole of seductiveness. A sexually centered person can be seductive with words, with ideas, with political opinions, with beauty or money, with any kind of temptation including food. He lures others into doing or allowing something they didn't really want to do. Here the convincing power of the Warrior is mirrored in a negative way.

Health problems can occur in the lower abdomen, the sexual organs, the breasts or prostate. Venereal diseases are common, also inflammations, infections with candida or cramps. It is rare that someone sexually centered is frigid or impotent, but if it happens, it is disastrous. These complaints are common, though, with sexual orientations like emotional (1) + sexual (3) or intellectual (2) +sexual (3) Reaction Patterns where hightened sensitivity and receptiveness, aggressive verbal exchange and hurtful marital situations lead to a wounding of the sexual chakra.

✳✳✳

A person with a sexual (3) + moving (7) Reaction Pattern will never find true physical satisfaction if he behaves passively and waits; being doubly active he must be in continuous movement and deal with life in the sense of physical and mental motion. Both centers strengthen each other and lead to a strong need for any kind of activity including the physical-sexual, that must be satisfied before a period of peace can take place.

If a person combines a sexual center (3) with an emotional orientation (1), activity lessens and more peace, more time for softness and feelings is necessary in order to perceive pleasure. Pleasurable feelings will be expressed in warmth, emotional excitement and relaxation, not so much in movement. This person, woman or man, can be deeply hurt if ridiculed or deceived by a partner.

The sexually-centered (3) + intellectually-oriented (2) person experiences pleasurable satisfaction in creating and observing thought structures. He'll direct his creativity on ever more surprising and unusual linkages of thoughts and ideas, which until now had been isolated, in a partnership-like uniting of hitherto disparate elements in the realm of ideas. This creative, often artistic expression will give him a special, almost physical satisfaction. That which is new, unheard-of, unusual is that which satisfies him and fills him with an active, creative power. He has the best ideas in bed.

A sexually centered (3) + instinctually orientated (4) person will have little self control and looks for sexual/genital satisfaction wherever he or she can find it. Lust and procreation are the physical goals, many children often the result. Fertility is there even in later years. Permanent carnal urges can also lead to criminal acts or cruelty, to the need to buy sex for money if it isn't provided without payment or to a pleasure in pornography.

Energy 4

The Instinctive Center

− Thoughtless   Spontaneous +

Originally, incarnated human beings were in much closer contact with their Instinctive Center than they are today. It guaranteed survival through quick, life-saving reactions. And even today it immediately goes into action if true elementary dangers threaten your life.

If a situation arises in which you're very suddenly threatened with death and only have a few seconds to save yourself, your Emotional or Intellectual Center will be of little use, but your Instinctive Center certainly will, and the two active centers (Moving and Sexual) will forcibly and immediately be activated, too.

The Moving Center helps you run away. The Sexual Center is aimed at preserving the genus of Homo sapiens. That's why men often have an erection at the time of their death. But it's the Instinctive Center which dominates all others if a dangerous situation occurs. It's there not only to show you a way out if the intellect or finer feelings fail. The Instinctive Center is the area of your body in which the multitude of unarticulated information is absorbed and it converts to the psychic level what you've been exposed to on the body level. For it would be impossible for you to process with your mental or emotional powers all these influences which you're confronted with every second of your life.

The Instinctive Center, located in the area you sit upon and connected to the adrenalin-producing glands, reacts to a radiation overdose which the body senses as uncomfortable in some incomprehensible way. It reacts to unpleasant odors but also to pleasant ones. It receives vibrations and transmits these as sources of information about the mood of those who are around you and also the collective mood of those whom you can't see. So you know, for example, if there's an aggressive atmosphere in a hall even though you've just come through the door and weren't able to follow the discussion. You also know through your Instinctive Center if there's a stranger in the house, if a storm is brewing, if there's a danger of war, even if you've not been especially well-informed by the radio or newspaper.

The better the Instinctive Center functions, the more strongly a person lives according to his unreflected reactions. This can be an advantage, but also a disadvantage. For whenever an instinctively centered person is asked to explain why he has done something or arranged something, he won't be able to answer because he barely has any mental access to his own decisions. However, he'll stand by his decisions with great certainty and won't let anything or anyone dissuade him from his opinion that what he decided was right for him. But he won't be able to give a plausible reason for it. In many respects, people who have a strong emphasis on the Instinctive Center are to be envied for they often do the right thing where others only wrestle with difficulties.

Almost no one is centered here for almost everybody concerned in your western world lives from a reaction pattern in which the instinctive center is integrated as the orientation. If a person chose the instinctive chakra as his centering, he would be incapable of formulating a logical thought at all, let alone be able to move normally in society without appearing totally uncontrolled. All his actions and reactions would be completely spontaneous. Although there are indeed people who have their emphasis in their instinctive center, you won't as a rule encounter them in your daily environment. These souls prefer for once in the course of their incarnations to undertake no responsibility at all. They are often insane people who withdraw from society and its obligations and create situations in which they'll be cared for by others in some institution. For their instincts are like uncontrolled urges that don't allow them to integrate in a community or to defer any gratification, something which prevents them from learning a profession or attending school.

It's very seldom that a person who's chosen an Instinctive Center is of an advanced soul age, but it happens. As a rule the instinctively-centered people are either Infant or Child souls, although sometimes you'll find among them very old souls who want to experience unconditonal love.

You know that even a small child lives considerably more strongly from his instincts and, for example, knows exactly which food is good or healing for him, like an animal. The goal of social upbringing is to a large extent aimed at taming these instincts and replacing them with rules. We don't criticize this, we consider it an acceptable form of socialization, for it isn't meaningful for a growing person to remain completely dependent on his instincts, which corresponded mainly to a stage of development of mankind which is no longer appropriate.

However, we believe it would do everyone good to reflect a little more about the rich offerings which the instinctive center can communicate to all. As you know, the Instinctive Center corresponds to the neutral position 4, the soul archetype of the Scholar, and therefore it's not only accessible to everybody but you can all also fall back on it.

You who are reading this are probably far advanced spiritually and long very much for the development of your intituitive and inspirational abilities. We're very happy about this and we value your efforts. But we would also like to remind you that, for instance, intuition is simply a higher octave of the power of instinct. Whoever doesn't trust or care for his instincts will hardly gain access to his intuition. In the same way, inspiration is a higher octave of intuition. For there's a triad of instinct, intuition and inspiration. All three are connected by an invisible energy thread so that inspiration can only be effective if instinct is truly affirmed. Instinct is like the feet, inspiration is like the head, and intuition is like the stomach. Who wants to live without feet, who without a head, who without a stomach? Only the unison of all organs and abilities makes a person whole.

If a soul has chosen the Instinctive Center as orientation of his Reaction Pattern, he'll be spontaneous but also often quite thoughtless, and he thoughtlessly make decisions because he fears being confronted too long with the need to decide. He then withdraws quickly to his instincts—we could say too quickly—only in order to get rid of the plague of having to act, and he reacts thoughtlessly. By this negative pole we don't mean a reaction on the basis of security of instinct, but rather a rash, fear-driven impulse, a drive which also appeases the instinct but doesn't really get one any further and slows growth instead of promoting it.

Among instinctively oriented people you'll find prolific inventors, shamanic healers, tennis champions, sooth-sayers and musical infant prodigies.

For the various Reaction Patters, see Emotional, Intellectual and Sexual Centers above.

Energy 5

The Spiritual Center

– Telepathic   Inspired +

This Center possesses an ego-transcending quality. It belongs to both the expressive and the mental faculties of a human being. This quality is connected to recognition, to fulfillment through the spirit and to the spiritual energy principle. Therefore we refer to it as the Spiritual Center.

We use the term »spiritual« in a limited, narrowly defined sense. We aren't referring to the areas of belief and religiousness, the esoteric or the occult. The word here defines the sphere in which a human ratio is temporarily freed from the limits of normality. It denotes a mind which is no longer touched by the compulsions of reason and conditioned thinking, a mind which has freed itself from individual experiences and memories in order to make itself accessible by means of this sudden unusual neutrality and purity, for insights and visions which come through an energy from without oneself. This eliminates every power and voice which we describe as the »inner self« and also the so-called »higher self«, for they belong to an individual. They are not located »outside a person«.

It depends what someone in such a situation wants to receive and can receive. The plus pole of this center, »inspired«, means an unconditional spiritual openness and readiness to listen, a gracious dissolving of mental barriers. A person can't do this actively, he must let it happen. At the same time, it is, however, possible for him to influence this on the telepathic level, to create conditions with the help of his human partners, while the inspired sphere is not subject to his will. But in a non-physical dimension, there is a creative interplay with the inspirational desire of bodiless sources.

The plus pole which a person experiences as inspiration, is a feeling of being touched by the divine spirit. Momentarily one is free of all fear. As long as the Spiritual Center with the plus pole remains open (usually not very long), a person neither experiences panic, worry nor doubt. These reactions, however, can set in later as a counter-movement to the great, unconditional visionary openness once the Spiritual Center is again closed.

Inspiration means clarity, consciousness, certainty. It isn't characterized by a turmoil of emotions but is completely free from them. Precisely because of this, it is a highly conscious state that is characterized by the absence of all feelings which could judge or react to inspiration, to categorize it or ward it off. One can recognize the plus pole by the following characteristics: free of feeling, free of censoring thoughts, considerations, of any purpose, free also of reward or punishment and free of judgment. It is timeless, unfiltered, intense, filled with light, silent, unmoving, indifferent, precisely because an external, superhuman power has fully and completely been admitted.

Naturally such phenomena can only be endured by a human body for a limited time. For you, it may be both encouragement and consolation at the same time to find out that those who can endure the brightness of the spiritual center longer than only a few hours are considered enlightened. And even among »masters« there's no one who's capable of being inspired constantly with his Spiritual Center open incessantly while alive.

The inspired plus pole includes visions of worlds beyond the bodily sphere. The minus pole, »telepathic«, has a similar quality but applies to the physical and the earthly, human spheres. If the word »telepathic« is used to describe only the communication of mental data from the sources of your experience in the world, then this term is correct and appropriate. There's nothing negative in this. It's considered a minus pole only in comparison to the plus pole. By minus pole we mean: less energy, less openness, a lower frequency, less relaxation.

A state of telepathic openness can be learned if the necessary frequency level is identified and anchored in the mental system. And then such a state can be used to practice control in differing ways and means. That's why telepathic access to the spiritual center is assigned to the minus pole. For control, even in its highest refinement and apparent noblest expression, has a hint of fearful tension.

It can be proven that one is indeed speaking from the Spiritual Center (5), connected to the archetype of the Sage, if this leads to non-emotional, suprapersonal messages and information. When simultaneously you're touched by the emotional vibrations of unconditional love, the channels of the center 6 (a priestly, ecstatic energy) are also open. It might surprise you to know that both can be accessed simultaneously. We want to point out that this simultaneity can apply to all four poles of the centers 5 and 6, that's to say that the four channels open and close in such a rapid succession as is necessary for a qualified mediumistic communication.

Each of you has access to this Spiritual Center, independent of your individual Reaction Pattern, provided he overcomes his fear of contact with powers and energies beyond his human boundaries. This won't be possible before one has reached the cycle of the Young Soul. And even the Young Soul has fear when he finds out that he can be reached by other people through telepathic means, that something foreign penetrates his mind, forms his thoughts and can communicate impulses that take away the illusion of unlimited control he has over himself. And so Young Souls use telepathic abilities mainly to reach others, on controling and influencing them. The channel will be used to send rather than to receive.

If a person in this soul age, however, seeks relaxed, ego-transcending, meditative states of mind in prayer, inner composure, sexual intercourse or during socially experienced phases of trusting openness (like initiation), he can without any further effort also be inspired by another human spirit as well as by the spirits of those who are in the astral world between lives, or also by disembodied authorities of the causal world. This includes members of the individual's soul family and all people with whom one is connected in love, or sometimes in hate. Hate, too, is a strong energy and can activate telepathic powers of the »third eye«. It is connected to the pituitary gland.

In rare circumstances and in states of spiritual emergency it's possible for very Old Souls to have inspired contact with even higher frequencies and sources of godly visions. This is how Mohammed received the Koran or St. Francis heard Jesus speak to him. But we'd like to point out to you that this spiritual connection has a quality of transcendence that one can only experience if one is prepared to surrender oneself completely to it.

Energy 6

The Ecstatic Center

– Psychic   Mystical +

Ecstasy is a state of uncontrolled sensitivity. This state occurs when all personal feelings, emotions, thoughts, memories and pains disappear and a person becomes receptive for sensations which emanate from inspirational sources outside himself.

We make a significant distinction between the concepts of »feeling« and »sensation«, since sensations are free from the storms of physical excitement which prevent any distance from oneself. Feelings are, according to our definition, tied to memories while sensations are based on a pure, direct perception in a lived moment.

Ecstasy as rapture also means moving away from the entangled world of personal feelings. Ecstasy means unconditional preparedness to be loved, a groundless joy. This can only happen if nothing is being decided, planned, or wanted anymore. These sensations aren't recoverable. They can't be brought forth. They happen if you let them happen and that can't always be the case. They grasp you but you can't hold on to them.

Ecstasy stirs a person to his inner-most being without making him feel he should immediately judge or appreciate his sensations. They manifest themselves as a pure experience of being one, of unity. The rapture in the dimensions of transcendent sensation permits the experience of a suspension of time and space, not in visionary clarity and peace as in the spiritual center, but rather in an unbelievable, yet cool, turbulence. This turbulence takes place in one's inner being. It's goal is not the healing clarity but the healing confusion.

Never-experienced sensations will be felt. New types of connections will be sensed but their classification and evaluation will only be possible later, if at all. For there's no possibility of reflection during a state of ecstasy. It is impossible to think or evaluate. The word »rapture« shows an undiminished ecstatic joy in one's own ability to feel sensations. Usually, if you speak about a »mystical rapture«, without having experienced this state yourself, you imagine a period of time of complete unconsciuousness in which a person loses his identity and temporarily dissolves. Indeed, the loss of one's individuality and a kind of dissolution are characteristic features of an activated Ecstatic Center. However, they are in no way accompanied by unconsciousness. But you apply the concept »unconsciousness« basically to the mental sphere and the brain functions. Therefore, we make a distinction between a complete mental consciousness and a complete sensual consciousness, between the ability to have overwhelmingly clear visions and the ability to be enraptured and carried away by higher, limitless sensations.

A certain period of time spent in the Spiritual Center 5 allows a lightening recognition of the AllOne, while a stay in the Ecstatic Center 6 makes possible an intense direct mystical view of all unity and universal love. This especially applies to the plus pole, the mystical union, in which all barriers are broken down which have been built up because of fear of the feelings of other people and the fear of the holy terror which could be caused by touching the servants of the goldly whole.

The minus pole describes a more or less comprehensive practical sensitivity, or psychic capacity, which, however, should the situation arise, can be willfully turned on or off and which normally remains under the individual's control even if some persons who are momentarily in this center have great trouble putting limits on it. They become more psychic the more often they remain in this pole. Such a mysterious sensitivity leads, because of the fear of having to cross over into mystical spheres, of being pulled over against one's will to the limitless spaces of love, to an often painfully experienced sensitivity to all kinds of seemingly hostile influences. This, however, is unconsiously used to prevent a sudden transference to the plus pole, the mystical union.

Being psychic is not negative as such. It can be used to feel, affirm and grasp the connections among humans, between humans and nature, humans and the cosmos. Although the immense network of possibilities to consider won't be completely experienced in the minus pole, there are enough possibilities to let a person have an idea about the immense richness of universal unity and its consequences for his being.

Whenever the center 6 opens—we can no longer speak here of wilful activation—the minus pole, as a rule, first does its work. This psychic ability, with all its consequences, is perceptible by the person himself and those around him. It can't be described and expressed, but it also should be heeded here that no one, we stress this clearly, can strive or try to remain perpetually in this pole. The sixth and seventh chakras, the third eye (5) and the crown (6), need to rest most of the time to prevent insanity. We point out how necessary and important it is that the chakra be consciously and conscientiously closed beyond a certain time limit, either spontaneously or willingly through certain techniques which follow an opening, since the openness of the crown chakra, no matter in which pole, can lead to physical weakness and mental confusion. This happens because the reaction pattern chosen from the Matrix, which keeps you alive and healthy, is no longer in force. However, we ask you not to equate an increased tendency toward weakness and illness with the special sensitivity which is caused by the opening of the center 6. That would be a misunderstanding due to irresponsible handling of the Ecstatic Center.

The mystical level is like an enraptured viewing, but not with the eyes of the body, of the ecstatic truth of the unity of all things, the AllOne. It depends on the ability of the incarnated soul to endure an integration with the whole. What must be endured is the overwhelming truth which lies in the memory of the soul as well as in its vision of all that is real. It comes from the whole and goes into the whole. But it knows nothing outside of the rapture, the mystically veiled state. And when we say »knows« we're speaking neither of a notion nor theoretical idea, nor a strong desire to believe. Whoever, once in a lifetime, spends even a second in the mystical plus pole of the sixth center knows forever what he before only presaged, hoped or believed.

While in retrospect one could doubt the validity of the experienced vision, recognition and communication during a period in the spiritual center 5, in the pole of inspiration, absolutely no doubt is possible as a result of a mystical union. Its remembrance can't be wiped out. The person who's experienced it knows only one difficulty later: he can't communicate it. His ecstasy and the changes it caused can't be expressed in words and are so unique that they remain uncommunicable. Since this concerns post-verbal sensations which are similar in their intensity to pre-verbal feelings, attempts are often made to put them in a different form, whether it be poetic or musical. But the poet or composer who tries to do this will always feel he can't sufficiently convey it.

The chakra which corresponds to the center 6 is the seventh, the crown chakra. It's linked to the pineal body. Your tradition tries to portray this linkage as a non-material silver thread which originates from the chest, mouth or forehead and binds the soul to the body. This is truly an energy spiral, a very fine but very strong whirl, which can be perceived by a few psychic or visually gifted people as a silvery cord. As long as the soul is in the body, this thread is invisible. Only if it leaves the body will the energy whirl again be visible just before the soul leaves the body behind for good.

When the soul abandons the body at the end of its incarnation, not only do breath, brain function and heartbeat stop, but the very first thing that happens is that the pineal body ceases its activity. Thus it severs the tie between the soul and the body. Its function during an incarnation is tantamount to the maintenance of the ensoulment for the course of the whole incarnation. With its special ability, it maintains out-of-the-body connections and also a continuity in the communication with its godly origin.

The center 6, in conjunction with its seventh chakra, is archetypical for the Soul Role of the Priest. But since all seven Soul Roles have access to the ecstatic center at a given time, after long meditations, in prolonged states of aloneness and also in terrifying emergencies, every person, Matrix and Soul Role also has the ability to experience all the potential of this Center during the course of his incarnation cycle. The longing for a reuniting of the soul with its divine homeland exists in every human.

Energy 7

The Moving Center

– Hectic   Untiring+

An emphasis on the Moving Center associated to the solarplexus and pancreas characterizes people of great mobility. It can manifest itself in all forms of their existence: in a flexibility and swiftness of the body, in powerful movements of the mind and the emotions, but also in the desire to be on the go much of the time, to often change their apartments or their circle of friends. Mobility and motion therefore mean not only the desire and necessity of moving one's limbs through physical activity but also the need to move from one place to the other in the mental and emotional areas.

The Moving Center belongs to the level of action. Therefore people who have an emphasis here are untiringly active. It's hard for them to find peace, they're always busy, they want to do everything at once, they're prepared to change their inner or external viewpoint with a speed that, for others, is often amazing and confusing. But they don't view the constant change in location as unusual, they're used to it—it even seems to them as if they were in many places at the same time. The effortlessness with which they can concentrate on changing themes or scenes gives them a subjectively strong impression of liveliness.

And, just as the intellectually centered people long for more security of feeling and the emotionally centered wish to be able put their thoughts more clearly in order, the moving centered tries to be less unsettled and often shies from expressing his unrest in body movements. He wants to divert it elsewhere as an energy, since he fears getting into more of a mess through that restlessness which he can no longer control.

Whoever is moving centered is not always an enthusiastic sportsman. On the contrary: he can, in order not to be completely endangered by his own restless vitality, sooner behave sluggishly and wearily in order to concentrate his whole mobility on inner spheres.

Life is movement. This is especially true for this soul-personality. However, it will often happen that a moving centered child will be viewed by his parents as restless and unbearably active, although there's nothing wrong with him, and they'll curb his motor activity. He'll soon have to learn that his specific expressions of mobility and liveliness are undesired in his family. So he'll try to behave quietly—which, if he isn't successful, will turn into a nervous hyperactivity resulting in further ill-humour and punishment.

A moving person with a suppressed desire for mobility will inevitably become nervous. For the tension which makes him vital and is best diverted into visible external movements in order to flow pleasantly, is converted into inner muscular tension, and he places all his mobility on the nearby centers. He'll then appear hectic in his bustle. Everyone perceives his restlessness but he himself doesn't realize this clearly for he believes to be at one with his basic needs without realizing that his hectic mood is an expression of his fear of not being able to control his motor activity.

The moving centered person always has something planned. Boredom is for him not only unbearable, it's almost unknown. The day is much too short for him. His many activities in all areas keep him going. He seldom has a feeling of satisfaction at the end of a project, since his mind is already racing toward new tasks, his body is engaged in new movement before the old is already finished, his feelings are directed toward future delights or dangers which he goes through with great zeal to order to counter all possible eventualities with a heightened speed of reaction.

He's always prepared to act directly and to react quickly. Only a considerable fear of doing something wrong can stop him. Such a panic can bring his movements to a standstill and temporarily lame him. This paralysis will never last long but will dissolve in a mental or emotional storm before new methods of action ensue.

The moving center has its physical location in the upper abdomen, the stomach solar plexus and pancreas. And since it regulates mobility it's also responsible for the most powerful movements of the disposition—uncontrolled rage, hate and fury—which are connected to actions, but also to all feelings of fear that are kindled by violent threats, active attacks with words, accusations and insults.

If the corresponding chakra is knotted or tense, a moving-centered person who's seized by an unconscious fury or terrible anger feels completely incapable of making any kind of movement. It is like a blow or a knife in the stomach. He can temporarily neither do something nor feel something. Even his ability to think is paralyzed and only when this stiffness again dissolves is he capable of speaking. It's good for him then to move, to weep or also to shout and scream depending on what his Reaction Pattern is.

The tirelessness of a moving person is characteristic. He can actively persist in plans, the tenacity with which his body responds to always greater efforts is surprising and can be explained by the fact that his mind always keeps the whole of his being and especially the development goal in view so that a strong dynamic stirs him toward that goal. He believes he can achieve anything by simply putting his untiring energy to use, and as long as he doesn't become too hectic and thus endangers his ability to concentrate, it's possible for him to use his mobility with a dancing, playful security. Often he needs little sleep or when he sleeps, regenerates quickly recovering from his efforts in a short time.

A certain amount of grace and dignity are part of his actions if he doesn't let inner tension get the upper hand. This is due to the ordinal number 7 of this centering and the connection to the archetype of the King. Only when he falls into his negative hectic does he torment himself and others with his exaggerated activity. Then he'll want to do everything at once and to be at all places at once but doesn't find enough time anymore to really devote himself to this and to also joyfully experience the results of his thoughts, feelings and actions. Hectic agitation does not allow a person to linger while tirelessness masters the art of lingering until a natural, new movement comes forth.

When a person with a Moving Center suffers from tension not only in his mind but also in the muscular areas, it is clear that he isn't handling his natural mobility well, but lives it as a hectic, an inner urge. Then there are two possibilities of bringing him back into balance. One consists of him expressing his unrest through powerful, persevering body movements. But if hectic agitation and overwork have already brought him to the edge of exhaustion, the second possibility which would do him good would be to bring his body to a state of quiet and peace despite all resistance. The more severe the exhaustion, the longer one must rest, often for days and sometimes for weeks until the tension decreases and a natural urge to move again becomes noticeable as if by itself.

Nervous exhaustion and also overwork and its consequences are typical problems of a moving-centered person. These also include illnesses involving the movement apparatus, such as rheumatism, arthritis, spinal problems, even ulcers, inflammation of the pancreas, digestive difficulties due to eating too fast and in an unconcentrated manner, as well as headaches which occur when too much has to be taken care of at once. The brain is overloaded with all too many duties and projects or the emotional world is overburdened by all too many contacts, which the moving person happily nurtures without realizing that he will come to the limits of his load-bearing capacity at some point, even if considerably later than most other people.

He usually has many friends and acquaintances with whom he maintains diverse connections. Sometimes, the tirelessness with which he devotes himself to these relationships turns, through overstimulation, into a complete refusal to maintain contacts and to a dullness which already signals a physical overtaxing and makes a longer period of rest and abstinence necessary in order to strengthen the powers which were exhausted in the hectic movement of the mind and body.

The Moving Center 7, in contrast to the centers 5 and 6, is permanently accessible and part of the Reaction Pattern. But it's exactly his particular permanence of intensity which causes many of the difficulties connected with the center. The spiritual, ecstatic as well as the moving center have a potential of temporary transcendence. Therefore, a moving person also tends to overtax or overstimulate himself. He doesn't want to realize his limits. He always borders on the brink of exhaustion. Since he finds his joy in tireless inner or outer movement, in actions and emotional or mental activity, he seeks a corresponding amount of excitement and finds it in the unusual. The adventurous, the unconventional, the exciting await him. The moving person looks for tension. The greater the tension, the more intense is his feeling of being alive. But he doesn't realize that he can only endure intensity of such a high degree if he also allows himself periods of absolute withdrawal, times during which nothing especially intense happens so that he can afterwards again move in higher regions of intensely exciting mobility.

A Moving Center is basically an expression of the richly vibrating dynamic of a person. But it also contributes significantly in giving the movement of the soul a new centrifugal force in its subtle growth. A person who wants some drama in a particular incarnation or who wants to set fixed patterns of former lives in motion, often chooses a motor center ing. It guarantees that nothing will ever really get stuck in the course of his life. His tirelessness or hectic agitation will force him forward, won't let him rest in his search for the new, the different, and the orientation of his Reaction Pattern shows the areas where he aims for deep renewal and change.

So a Moving Center, with the ordinal number 7 and the basic energy of the King's soul role, is an advantage for all who have been concerned with a certain theme over many lives and finally want to come to a conclusion that's freed from decrepit structures and rigid ways of behavior. The liveliness and dynamic temperament of a person with a Moving Center leads him to find people and to choose countries corresponding to his soul's goals. He's mobile and moves others. His contribution lies is his ability to cross over borders, both his own and those of others.

***

We've already indicated that the Reaction Pattern influences the type of motor activity, and therefore it's necessary to take into consideration the individual orientation of the moving-centered person. The moving (7) + intellectual (2) pattern shows especially the mobility of all the comprehensive powers, the ability in a fraction of a second to understand even that which is contradictory, to draw conclusions, to combine, to respond to others' thoughts, to quickly produce an overview. A moving-intellectual person also has the ability to receive the thoughts and moods and motivation of others without them being verbally expressed and to combine them with his own with lightening speed. The mobility and rapidity of his reactions distinguish him from the intellectually-centered, who remains mostly in the heights and depths of thought but who doesn't, however, concentrate on the breadth and the swift capacity to grasp and combine the most different things.

The moving-intellectual person is not only able to cope with several mental projects at the same time, but also to store many separate thoughts in his consciousness and to keep them in view. His thought processes take place on various levels at once, and he loves to jump back and forth between these levels, a process that makes him very happy, but which, however, makes people who aren't moving-centered uneasy and confused since they never know from which of the many mental layers the next answer or following argument will emerge.

A moving-intellectual person needs to move his body in order to fertilize himself within his world of thoughts. The best ideas, the most creative notions will emerge not when he rests but when he moves and apparently is busy with this movement, while his mind is following another movement and can make leaps in the thought process which wouldn't have been possible even over a long period of reflection. His ideas often have ingenious components that are based on the fact that adventurous, even daredevil ideas put his intellect in motion and in such a way shift him into the ecstasies of fantasy, which only need to be a little transformed in order to take concrete shape and become feasible.

The moving (7) + emotional (1) Reaction Pattern, in contrast, seeks the great, often unsettling, not seldom dramatic movement in the world of sensations. This type of person is characterized by inner revolutions, extreme variations, the most rapid fluctuation between elation and depression, the changeability of ideas accompanied at the same time with a sensation of continuity, and also a constant feeling of unease, of not being at the right place, of not finding the right thing—a feeling of being alive which is paired with a chronic deficiency of calmness. This is also a hectic, nervous person, but for other reasons. Emotional problems are his main concern.

His Reaction Pattern is connected to drama, fateful events, abrupt change in the life history, the deep, existential uncertainty followed by the highest inner certainty of being protected by existence. A moving-emotional person feels driven and shaken, abandoned and at the mercy of the world and it's difficult for him to understand how much he contributes with the minus pole of his Matrix elements to the shaping and interpretation of his fate. On the other hand, he's capable of maintaining tireless friendships and love relationships. He is also an untiring worker if the subject gives him sufficient emotional satisfaction. His sensibility is marked by the ability to very quickly catch the emotional signals of others and to tune in to them. He also possesses an extremely fine sense of the possibilities of motivating people, encouraging them to undertake a guided tour in the area of feelings, which is convincing and, in a restrained way, charismatic. And he has a gift of moving people to tears, with a poem, a piece of music, a novel or even a birthday cake.

A Moving Center combined with an emotional orientation transfers people who are receptive to it into a movement of feeling, which causes an unforgettable feeling of being touched and experiencing deep change. Movement is contagious and so a moving-emotional person is capable of rousing not only individuals but large groups of people and to positively shake them up.

Physical movement is also of considerable significance for this reaction pattern, however the moving-emotional person often shies from an excessive activation of his feelings, which is invariably accompanied by powerful body motion. He's afraid of losing control of them by bursting into tears and, through the acceleration of his metabolism and breathing, again reaching the point where everything that he had just brought to a peaceful state would again be stirred up. However, he shouldn't avoid altogether a regular airing of his emotions. The increased intake of oxygen in his blood which results from physical activities, even if it can only be briefly endured, serves him better than contemplation of, or the waltzing back and forth between, his sensations.

The moving (7) + sexual (3) Reaction Pattern describes the most active people among all the archetypes, not only in work or sports, but also in sexual exchanges. They tirelessly seek erotic tension and relaxation, have the need to constantly seek stimulation in the most differing ways and suffer because social norms often place severe sanctions on such an active erotic-sexual life, a style of life which would do them good. The disapproval which they see themselves subjected to causes them to suppress in a harmful way their urge to quickly change partners or to engage in an intense sexual life. They feel obliged to curb their basic energy, but in doing so destroy their own wonderful individual creativity and vitality. No one appears as rigid and cold and controlled as a moving-sexual person who, for many social or personal reasons, denies his Reaction Pattern. And so it can easily happen that his needs turn around and seek outlets which bring even greater disapproval from society.

This type of person appears especially restless but also extremely seductive and enchanting. He has a powerful force of attraction, an aura of total interest in his fellow-men. The moving-sexually centered people don't concentrate as most of the other centers mainly on an intellectual or emotional exchange, but bring instead their entire body into play. They love to touch and be touched, which always has an air of the erotic, without insisting on direct sexual fulfillment. Their company is exciting since their energy is capable of putting into movement all physical juices, all gland functions. They are often very fond of beauty and are aesthetically and artistically talented. Their eyes, their heart, their body revel in the magnificence of creation in all forms and colors. They appear full-blooded, sensuous and temperamental. Moving-sexual people are strong personalities, who prefer to laugh at convention and aim with great immediacy for the satisfaction of their desires.

Among the moving (7) + instinctive (4) Reaction Patterns one can find the most admirable sportsmen, the most tireless factory workers and handicraftsmen, the most patient, persistent people who aren't afraid of physical activity and who achieve a satisfaction in their work through their hands that most people don't have in this elementary way. A moving-instinctive person needs a profession which keeps him in continuous movement, whether it's body movement or passively being moved. This could be a dance instructor or a ballet dancer, a crane operator, truck driver, owner of a racing track or long-distance runner. Every movement comes natural, little thinking is needed to produce a harmonious flow, all becomes one.

The joy of movement per se characterizes the moving-instinctive person. However, their motor reactions are often so fast and steered by instinct that they feel like immediately striking back whenever they think their feelings or intellect have been wounded. Since they react instinctively, and only think or feel later, and the movement happens so swiftly, they can no longer brake their reactions. A moving-instinctive person quickly approaches another person or runs away from someone, depending on whether he feels drawn to the person or driven away by antipathy. He tends to warmly embrace his fellowmen or race toward them, but also can just as well turn his back and head for the door if his motor reaction demands this.

Soul Ages

(5)

Old Soul

(2)

Child Soul

Expression Level

(6)

Transpersonal Soul

(1)

Infant Soul

Inspiration Level

(7)

Transliminal Soul

(3)

Young Soul

Action Level

(4)

Mature Soul

Assimilation Level

VII The Seven Soul Ages

You are human beings. We speak to you as human beings. Your soul has once again reincarnated. It isn't for the first time present in a human body. Every time incarnation happens not only does a plan for another life materialize in a physical form, but your soul moves toward a new level of insight along its path of development.

We refer to the five Soul Cycles in an incarnated body when we describe the span of the complete incarnation path of a human soul. We also describe these five soul cycles according to your experience in analogy to the development which a human body experiences from his birth to his natural death. However, just as after the physical death there are disembodied forms of existence for every human, which are open to him and to which he is entitled, these five Soul Cycles are complemented by two further Soul Manifestations. These draw their characteristics from an interplay between the embodied and disembodied dimensions.

The five incarnated soul cycles are:

– the Infant Soul (Energy 1)
– the Child Soul   (Energy 2)
– the Young Soul   (Energy 3)
– the Mature Soul (Energy 4)
– the Old Soul   (Energy 5)

The five cycles correspond to a great extent—in their requirements and results—to what a human being experiences during his life as long as he reaches the age of seventy or eighty. As we have already intimated, in addition to these, there are two other forms of a soul occupied body—and we state this here explicitly—which don't belong to an individual soul's plan of development: the Transpersonal Soul with the ordinal energy number 6 and the Transliminal Soul with the energy number 7.

Speaking about the individual soul ages, there is nothing more important or more essential than to emphatically and lovingly point out to you that an Old Soul is no better and, in a qualitative respect, not any further along than a Young Soul, just as a seventy-year-old is, of course, not »better« than a twenty-year-old person. We stress this fact because we realize how extremely difficult it is for you to deal with the aspects of Soul Growth and the themes of the non-material world, and in view of all the efforts and work you have invested in your spiritual development, to renounce the arrogant fruits of self-exploration and self-praise and to free yourself from the deceptive feeling of elation over spiritual advancement and the wishful notion of having already reached your goal. We tell you this in order to soothe your ambition. Every individual is in exactly the right place regardless of which Soul Cycle and level of soul development he is in. There is neither the possibility of intentionally skipping an individual learning and growth phase nor of stepping backward as punishment for spiritual inertia or so-called bad deeds.

Each one of you—in your own self-determined rhythm, in your own individual time, according to the requirements of your soul—will reach the end of the fifth or Old Soul cycle, a little bit earlier or a little bit later than other members of your Soul Family. Each soul was at one time an Infant Soul and each without exception will become an Old Soul. Therefore, guard against hidden pride over your natural advancement along the path of knowledge and hidden contempt for those who are advancing more slowly along this path for this is only because they started out on the path later than you did.

The last great tide of incarnated souls on your planet, who occupied a body for the first time to reach their goals, inundated your planet in the seventeenth century according to your time. Before that there were several global waves of dispersion of souls from the astral world who shaped your soul development, your culture and your religions. This took place at a rhythm of a good 2000 years, beginning approximately from 6500 years before Christ and then some 4300, 2600 and 500 years before your time. Of course prior to this there were other waves of incarnation.

There are only a very few Old Souls left over from the first of the above-mentioned tides of incarnation. Some of these have undertaken great and important responsiblities. Even though they are not always publicly acknowledged, these souls steer the fate of large groups of souls with an experienced hand. Souls who have now reached the level of Mature and Old Souls came to a large extent from the second tide. Souls who at the present time are Young Souls first began their incarnation some 2500 years ago. Most of you who are reading this and absorbing our information belong to the second tide of incarnation we mentioned. This explains why the large majority of those who are now listening to us and understand us are late Young, Mature and Old Souls, but not Infant or Child Souls.

The number of distributed Soul fragments of larger units as Soul families or Soul Tribes varied greatly each time since life on earth depends on the necessary nourishment, the protection which is sought and given, and the climatic conditions. Therefore, you should not be surprised by the fact that there is a global population explosion at your time. For increasing technological advancements provide a great deal of nourishment and protection for increasing numbers of souls who choose to manifest themselves in comparatively positive historical conditions. Since the seventeenth century there has not been any further dispersion of souls.

We assure you, however, that all souls which are now in the Infant or Child-cycle will find, in one way or another, possibilities of existence on your planet. There is no reason to fear. Human consciousness has access to the great evolutionary process of the cosmos. No one will be prevented from developing their soul. Of course these fragments will not be able and will not even want to experience the same things you have. They have the right to create their own learning stages.

The period of incarnations from the first to the last, with its five bodily cycles, lasts, according to your time scheme, approximatively ten thousand years. Sometimes it is longer, sometimes less. It encompasses roughly one hundred incarnations and thirty five well-defined stages of development. The intensity with which you realize your Soul Role in conjunction with a hundred different soul patterns or MATRICES, combined with the particular characteristics of the path which is pursued, can speed up or delay the course of events. However, acceleration—we would like to insist on this fact—is not a positive quality just as delay or deceleration is not a disadvantage. In any case, the appropriate level of vibration in the physical-astral world will only then be achieved when all members of your Soul Family have completed all their physical incarnations.

Therefore, it is not only the individual soul which is responsible for its development but also the structure of your Soul Family and the possibilities that as an entity it finds on your planet in order to fulfill its responsibilities and to help you fulfill yours. The individual soul can develop, grow, gain new knowledge and widen its consciousness, but if the temporary conditions of the whole Soul Family prevent the achievement of its collective purpose, the fragment will wait with a new life until a better opportunity presents itself. This period of waiting can take place during a physical incarnation, but more frequently takes place in between incarnations, in the regions of the astral world which are freed from time and space.

A. The Five Soul Cycles in the Body

Energy I

The Infant Soul

When a soul for the very first time chooses a body and manifests itself in it, it feels exactly as does a human infant in the first weeks and months of its life: so sensitive, so defenceless, so dependent on support, contact and a close community. This is a cycle with the archetypical energy quality of the Helper/Healer. Its principle is supporting.

The soul manifesting itself in a body for the first time is like an infant, overwhelmed by sensations that only a body knows and which were unknown to the soul while it existed in the incorporal regions. There are the feelings of warmth and cold, of pleasure and pain, of light and darkness, of contact and non-contact, of hunger and thirst, of the functions of elimination. For the first time growth occurs in a material form, and all this is frightening, confusing and disturbing. Therefore, an Infant Soul incarnates whenever possible under circumstances and in human societies which fulfill two requirements. The first is the possibility of leaving the body again without causing a great deal of fuss and without having too many feelings of fear and horror connected with it. The second requirement is the possibility of leading a life which finds its forms of expression in a secure social and, above all, close physical society. Both of these conditions can be found on earth in some countries and in human groups which you, who are reading this, usually describe as »primitive.« But this primitiveness, which we would prefer to see regarded as a neutral characteristic of quality, fulfills to a great degree the desire and needs of an Infant Soul and therefore deserves neither contempt nor pity. Imagine how life-saving in a psychological sense the custom is of many mothers in primitive tribes to not let their infant out of their sight for two to three years or to carry the baby close to their body so that it senses the safe and comforting nearness of the mother. The Infant Soul's wish to be held, carried and nourished at all times is of immense importance.

This soul can further develop only when the worst threats to its new form of existence have been averted. We would like to say at the same time, however, that another requirement is fulfilled in just this primitive society, namely the immediate proximity of death, which can be caused by warfare, sickness, drought, hunger and a general widespread infant mortality rate. In order to want to incarnate at all, an Infant Soul needs a type of safeguard which allows it to retreat at any time. It won't often take advantage of this but it helps it to set out on its new, fearful and unknown path.

The very first humanoid incarnations on your planet began more than three hundred thousand years ago. They had the task of exploring the possibility of soul development on your planet earth. Groups of individuals belonging no longer to primates of the ancient stamp arose in various places on your planet. These humans were gifted with a new variant of ensoulment (the Matrix soul you all have now). These pioneer souls lived on the Planet Earth for several thousands of years. After finishing their soul cycles, they went on to the causal planes of consciousness providing courage and information about the possibilities and dangers of incarnation on your planet to those who still hadn't tried to incarnate but were willing to try.

The beginning of the larger waves of incarnations was about a hundred thousand years ago. At this time there were enough Soul Families who had completed their earthly cycle and had advanced to the Causal World of consciousness that they could watch over a considerably larger number of newly-incarnating souls. Besides, the individual incorporated existence was at that time relatively brief. Life expectancy was limited. The cycles were more quickly passed through so that an accelerated exchange of Soul Families could take place.

However, even at that time solitary groups of incarnated souls formed racially and culturally isolated units which seldom mingled with others. That stage of possiblities was only reached later when it could be ensured that what was learned in one area could be valid in another. Ways of communal life, survival techniques, possibilities of overcoming fear, the channeling of feelings, the rituals and expressions of creati-vity were learned on the cultural-social and on the soul level.

When someone for several hundreds or even thousands of years has incarnated in the Pyrenees, at the beginning of another life, he cannot simply choose a life in the Euphrates or in Africa since what he (or his soul) has learned in the woody mountains hasn't prepared him for such a change. To the degree, however, that individual soul groups find their inner steadfastness, they would also be able to choose a life here or a life there, or one life here and twenty lives there. But even this was possible, or would appeal, only to a few especially courageous, accelerating soul fragments.

However, in no way are Infant Souls found only in the early period of human tribal development or in technically and medically underdeveloped countries. In your days, they are also found, although to a smaller extent, in societies of industrial nations, above all where you see a person who will be entirely dependent on help—not only in his early years but even in advanced adulthood. Sometimes this may be due to physical or mental impairment. However, one should not assume automatically that a person handicapped from birth has an Infant Soul. For an Old Soul also often chooses this form of existence in order to gain a particular experience in dealing with dependency and helplessness.

However, many of those who, during the course of their lives, must be cared for are Infant Souls who are unwilling to immediately leave the bodily existence they have just chosen. For this must almost inevitably happen when such souls are born crippled, brain-damaged or severely handicapped in a primitive society. If, therefore, an Infant Soul gathers its courage to finally

incarnate and also chooses the Mode of Perseverance or the goal of Acceleration or has the Soul Role of a Warrior, it will prefer to incarnate where
there is sufficient medical help and knowledge to assure that it will reach
the age of thirty, forty or even fifty. For when an Infant Soul has reached
more than half of the average life span, it becomes accustomed more easily
to the requirements of the body and therefore needs fewer individual lives
in the cycle than if it must make several attempts to adjust to a body at all
and then to have to leave the body in the first year of life or before reaching
the tenth year.

The Infant Soul shrinks from the fact that it is now separated from the
whole, is physically separated also from the siblings of its Soul Family, is a
lone individual and must live divided from others because of its flesh. The
incarnated Infant Soul feels abandoned and lost and therefore grasps at every
opportunity to overcome this feeling or to deny it. It feels most comfortable
when it has as much bodily contact as possible. It finds it unbearable to sleep
in a room alone, it seeks the nearness of animals and plants, since it hasn't
lost completely the memory of being one with all the entirety of manifestations and phenomena.

The Infant Soul needs the context of communal action and responsibility since as an individual it neither wants nor is in a position to follow independent impulses or to bear responsibility for its own actions. Everything
which separates it from its group, family or tribe, causes such unbearable fear
that it prefers not to spend even a minute alone in its life. Physical separation
happens only when the Infant Soul is infringing a taboo. In this case death is
the unavoidable consequence, for the Infant Soul isn't capable of existing apart
from others, feeding or protecting itself. The relationship to the racial or tribal
customs and rituals and the protection they offer is so powerful that an
Infant Soul cannot survive in isolation.

It's as if it were connected to the AllOne by an umbilical cord—however this umbilical cord is already dead. This same broken connection can

also be observed in the Infant Soul's relationship to the divinity, as it understands it. For the Infant Soul the divine is present everywhere at all times, not as a manifestation of love, however, but as a fear-provoking and horrifying authority whom one must mollify. The Infant Soul has forgotten that it chose to manifest itself in human form. It feels rejected, it feels punished by the fact that it must exist in a helpless, vulnerable body, instead of weightlessly and effortlessly gliding in the realms of the Astral World. It hardly remembers that it is a fragment of the whole and part of the godly spirit. It cannot and may not recall what it has left behind for it must focus its attention on its duties and plans as an ensouled human.

The godly power is sensed as omnipresent, but also as punishing and malicious. Therefore, the Infant Soul can do nothing but appease this supposedly revengeful, adverse authority with blood offerings and food, and to perceive the forces of the invisible as a mirror reflection of its own fears and threats, as something similar and yet different. It sacrifices the bodies of animals in place of its own. That's why there are, at this stage, so many symbols of the godly, the cult figures, the totem, the stone statues and the frightening sacrifices of live animals and blood, for food and drink as well as the protection of a cave or hut are precious things to be sacrificed to the gods.

Fear and helplessness determine the first life of a newly incarnated soul. This fear, this helplessness are reflected in its facial expression and, above all, in its eyes. The eyes are either wide open, and usually filled with a dark horror, or squinted, since a frightened soul believes, through a fundamental distrust, that it must now protect itself from life through a defensive stance. This occurs because an Infant Soul doesn't test life as such, but only tries to prevent the impressions of the hostile world from reaching him.

He believes that when he closes his eyes to all that threatens him, he can conquer his fear. That's why the eyes are often infected and this leads to either an extreme deterioration of sight or to blindness. In this event, two things are achieved: an official recognition of the state of helplessness and the impossibility of perceiving reality with one's own eyesight.

A third fact is of great significance. For although an Infant Soul is dependent to a life-saving degree on contact, it prefers to experience this contact with closed eyes or in the dark. What disturbs it most of all is eye contact with its fellow human beings because this contact scares it to death, reminding it of that unquestionable contact between bodiless souls which has been lost. The Infant Soul becomes aggressive when it, however unconsciously, remembers the security of the Astral World left behind. It does not want to be reminded of the indivisibilty which lies behind it. Such a soul views eye contact which lasts longer than a split second as a reason for fear and hatred. It is either avoided completely or regarded as »the evil eye«.

The Infant Soul isn't interested in politics. It's unimaginable that it could affect the fate of its group, its people or the whole earth. It's impossible for the Infant Soul to desire something beyond its immediate needs or to look beyond its horizon. It feels just as helpless toward someone who determines its daily routine or professional fate as it does toward a deity. It no longer feels a part of the whole but is also not aware of itself as a member of another society or a group, which represents certain matters or seeks change. But despite this it is precisely because the Infant Soul is so unbelievably dependent on the leadership and companionship of other souls that it is also dependent in the area of social and cultural connections. It allows itself to be shoved here and there and to obey without developing its own opinion. It also doesn't understand for which purpose it is being used because it chooses not to recognize the overall causes and implications.

Being an Infant Soul is a form of life which is greatly satisfied when it doesn't have to do anything more than concern itself with its physical survival and procreation. It doesn't strive for anything more. It is prepared to work as long as its requirements for helplessness and dependency are allowed, but it relies passively on the support of the family, the tribe or state as soon as its survival and needs are threatened. It's difficult for the Infant Soul to aid someone else but it expects everyone to help it.

In this stage of soul development the body needs a great deal of sleep, since the person can only gain access to out-of-the-body dimensions in an unconscious state. During sleep the Infant Soul finds the sympathy and security it needs in life but often does not find. Its sexuality is tied to indiscriminate and repeated satisfaction and is aimed at having as many descendants as possible since the Infant Soul is not happy being alone. The assurance of having a large number of relatives and dependants gives it the certainty of never being lonely and also of being cared and provided for in old age. This soul is truly happy during its very first incarnations when it can eat with its closest relatives and then lie down to sleep without parting from the warmth and care of others. Nothing is more rewarding for it than to have its basic needs of nourishment, security and sexual satisfaction met as often as possible. Then it doesn't feel threatened and it harms no one. But, despite this, the Infant Soul senses that in order to fulfill its obligations in the entire incarnation cycle it cannot reside much longer in this state of simple blessedness. After some fifteen lives it prepares itself to depart the confinements of dependent security and to move toward the stage of the Child Soul which will lead it from the feeling of helplessness which it had until now thankfully enjoyed to an exploration of the physical world.

Energy 2

The Child Soul

The Child Soul stage marks a segment of soul development which is characterized by ambivalence and a conflict between a painful dependency on one hand and a desire for independence on the other. This is a cycle with the archetypical energy quality of the Artist. Its principle is inventing.

The Child Soul senses very clearly its curiosity, its need to approach the unknown and therefore to accept separation from a primal group and its security. As soon as this curiosity and this separation reaches a critical point in which the detachment causes fear, the Child Soul feels guilt over its desire for independence and returns to the bosom of the social community in order to assure both itself and others that it is still prepared to regard dependency as something good and beautiful. It admits remorsefully that it was presumptuous to seek adventure, to place oneself in danger or undergo risks which could have no other consequence than to distance oneself from the security which it hopes forever to experience if it doesn't separate itself from others.

And yet it wants to separate and must separate itself from other individuals. The phase of bodily existence to which this section of soul development is dedicated leads further and further to an ever greater distancing from the collective. This is a frightening experience on the one hand, but on the other, is so enticing that it seems increasingly impossible to forgo excursions into the realms of independence.

All lives in the cycle of the Child Soul serve to experience dissolution while at the same time relying on the still important guarantee of returning to security. All energies are invested in the service of a growing independence and to become reconciled to the fact that the fragmentation of the soul family, the original soul entity, has indeed taken place. The Infant Soul could not and did not want to acknowledge this fact. The Child Soul, however, senses its truth and gradually finds happiness and even a desire to be more isolated.

But just as a child who makes its first flights into independent experience must make sure he has the possibility of running back to his father's hand or his mother's skirt-hem, so the Child Soul is dependent in the first life of this cycle on the social community as a constant background. We refer here not only to the fellow beings but also the community of those souls who are in the same development stage and who have the same needs, so that there is suitable harmony and a possibility of refuge.

The Child Soul is immensely curious. It wants to cautiously explore the world and the »other« person. It wants to find out what happens when it »lets go«, and it receives its very first answers. But at the same time these answers evoke distress for they bring pain and hopelessness along with the first understanding of fragmentation. It realizes that it would like to return to the whole but separation is irrevocable.

Now the soul begins to realize that it can only go forward, and since the pain caused by the longing for a return to the original security of the Astral Plane is unbearable, it vows not to look back anymore. Therefore it voluntarily detaches itself from this secret desire. This appears to be a voluntary act but is only an illusion; nevertheless the Child Soul insists that from now on it makes its own decisions.

What is new is the realization that it can either accept its own guilt or place blame on others. Whether it chooses one way or the other depends on how its MATRIX is structured. The choice to either become a victim or create one appears for the first time in this soul development stage. At this stage the first karmic ties are also created. While the Infant Soul sacrifices animals in order to appease its fear and its subconscious feelings of guilt towards the gods, the Child Soul is now prepared to sacrifice itself or other humans. If it prefers to let others atone for its fears—and this is unavoidable during the course of this development cycle—it means at the same time that others are prepared to be victims. In such a way karmic connections are made which, at a later stage, usually in the Mature or Old Soul cycles, will be resolved.

In order to profitably pass through this cycle as part of its evolution, the Child Soul needs the possibility of dealing with guilt. However, since it can't understand its own motivations nor its own pain because it still lacks deliberateness and self-distance, it pursues a pattern of punishment and reward and thus punishes others in order to feel better, even if they haven't comitted a crime. It doesn't leave the punishment up to a higher authority since it doesn't sense the divine any longer as a presence to whom it can turn in order to overcome its difficulties. It must, therefore, seize the weapons, whether they be spiritual or material, in order to complete what it views as necessary according to its present viewpoint. It kills in order to survive, not because of moral reasons, not because of a desire to achieve a victory for an ideal but because it thereby creates room for its own needs. These can be described as exploration and active discovery.

The Child Soul is neither in a position nor ready to take responsibility for what it must do in order to assert itself and to develop independence. Responsibility is a concept which it can only understand in the material sense. Just as a farmer feels responsible for his cow because it serves him and feeds him, and disappears from his consciousness when he isn't milking it or has sold it, so does a Child Soul regard its environment and fellow men as servants of its needs and takes responsibility for them only to the extent that they fulfill a certain function in respect to the achievement of its own desires. The attitude of the Child Soul toward social forms and politics is marked by a basic, helpless resentment. If something bothers or harms the Child Soul, it feels that »others« or »those on top« are to blame.

The Infant Soul has no impact on events. The Child Soul, in contrast, complains and rebels without making a connection to the consequences or to a changed way of behavior. The Child Soul, therefore, never seeks to change anything itself. It only calls on those it believes responsible to do something, the »parent figures«. It doesn't realize that great changes ensue from small changes. When events don't occur as it wishes, others are always responsible. It's not yet able to take responsibility for the entire situation.

However, toward the end of this development cycle, the soul changes its perspective and the Child Soul begins to realize that it can make a contribution to the shaping of its own life. Now it develops a new desire. It not only rejects all that is expected of it but makes its own new suggestions for changes. It also develops ideals and can now imagine what the world would be like if only it wasn't the way it is. Its desires are now directed toward a perfection which it views as an unbridgeable contrast to what it perceives. It asks and prays often to the gods in order to express its hope for a change in present life conditions. But it's still only the gods who could really improve the Child Soul's lot.

The religiousness of the Child-Soul is directed at a variety of godly figures. The devil or other evil forces are also represented by a number of images. The Child Soul creates a pantheon of authorities to whom it can turn and by whom it can be ruled. Heaven and temple are filled with images and statues which contribute to both reassurance and confusion. The reassurance results from the fact that the Child Soul can turn with its wishes to a suitable god-similar but also human-like carved figure. The confusion is brought about by the unanswered question of whether the saint, the individual deity or the manifestation of the Buddha really hear the wishes and the pleading. It remains doubtful if the worshiped image takes the frightened soul seriously or remains silent, immoveable and merciless.

If the prayers go unanswered, it blames itself partly for this and feels called on to take increasing measures of subjugation or pacification. The deity or the saintly image should be forced to do what the Child Soul doesn't dare do. And it will persist in this until it reaches the stage of the Young Soul who, in counter-movement, tries to achieve everything alone without depending on anyone else's help.

The Child Soul plays happily with life and the possibilities which form its existence. It moves preferably in the regions of »if« and »what would be if«. The important thing is to experiment without taking too great a risk or having to overcome the consequences. It reaches out but also needs the possibility of being able to retreat at anytime. Its desires and fantasies are overwhelming but it makes few attempts to translate these into reality. It often suffices for the Child Soul to explore with its thoughts the potential of what it regards as worth striving for. It also experiments with relationships, not because of ill-intention or a lack of love but because of the need to not tie itself down. It thinks nothing of having a brief relationship and then to abandon that person, regardless of whether this be a spouse, friend or child.

The Child Soul cannot concentrate for very long on the same strand of its development. Just like a young kitten, which doesn't know what to do with a mouse which it has observed and then caught, the Child Soul encounters its experiences, lets them roll here and there, observes them with curiosity and then releases them when its curiosity is satisfied.

This behavior also marks the sexuality of Child Souls. Fantasies play a great role but seldom are these shared with a partner. They are limited to »what if, when«, to playfulness and an infantile retreat. Fear determines the Child Soul's sex life. These persons are very jealous. The fear of too much responsibility results in the fact that fewer descendants than during the first cycle are procreated and born. This doesn't mean that there is a desire to display more responsibility for fewer people but rather there is a wish not to feel overwhelmed by duties. The Child Soul is now ready and feels called on to take limited self-protective precautions in order not to lose its still unstable individuality. It is prepared to make the first deliberate restrictions on itself. The »other« is understood as another person, however it is viewed as strange and fundamentally incomprehensible.

Since the Child Soul has almost no hope of sharing its insecure inner life with other people, it refrains from showing its emotions so that only the results or forms of expressions of already processed or supressed emotions are visible to the outside world.

The physical health of a person with a Child Soul is generally robust and sound. It is only affected by apparently accidental, fateful events, through the influence of others, accidents, imprisonment, natural disasters, epidemic infections or incorrect medical treatment. The Child Soul is convinced that nothing can happen to its body if it is cautious enough both in watching over it as well as instinctively avoiding dangers. And since it is convinced that, through the force of its inner strength, it is invulnerable or even immortal, it unconsciouly rules out anything that would enable it to experience the unpredictable or incomprehensible. If something terrible happens, it is simply the victim and can do nothing to prevent this.

There is a characteristic innocence and often also a vulnerability in the eyes of Child Souls that is connected to their feeling of being a victim. The Child Soul transmits two messages: »No one can harm me.« and »You can't do this to me!« And its fellow men react in the same way to these communications. They want to protect a person with a Child Soul but are also repeatedly irritated by the innocence and defencelessness to such an extent that they strike out at it without consciously wanting to do so. This confirms the Child Soul's attitude that it is pure and innocent and that evil is only found in the external world.

A soul needs between fifteen and twenty incarnations in order to experience and integrate all that is necessary in this cycle. Finally, the soul is prepared to accept responsibility for itself and others. It discovers through various kinds of painful experiences that life is not just a game. It begins to view the shaping of its life as a part of its own responsibility. It will soon no longer be satisfied to passively accept its fate. It prepares itself for a phase of great activity and self-determination which the long cycle of the Young Soul will provide.

Energy 3

The Young Soul

If you view the approximately one hundred lives, the average time period of an incarnation cycle, as equivalent to eighty, ninety and more years of a human life, the Young Soul cycle lasts appoximately from the fifteenth to the thirty-fifth year. This is a cycle with the archetypical energy quality of the Warrior. Its principle is fighting—for self-assertion, for material success, for the conquest of the world.

The Young Soul is no longer a »child«. It's also not mature. But it will indeed grow during the Young Soul cycle. Growth and maturity, however, are two different things. Following the stage of the Infant Soul and the Child Soul a period of corporeal existence begins which lasts relatively long and therefore provides much space for development. This cycle lasts so many lives because the Young Soul is laying the basis for its further development during this period. This basis consists of a provisional orientation, in the development of a value system, in the testing of one's strength, in an examination of the world, in the fulfillment of material desires and in the schooling of intellectual powers.

The words I, me, myself are the most important during this cycle.

Before the ego can start dissolving during the Mature Cycle, it must be thoroughly affirmed. To older souls, Young Souls may appear to be selfish, but that's right for them. Self-assertion in every respect is the main concern during this Cycle. The many lives are used to explore the connection between oneself and the world, to sound out how far one's individual possibilities reach, and what is demanded and needed to bring oneself and the world under control. Just as in a fairy-tale the young hero leaves his mother and father, ventures out into the world to make his own mistakes and achieves success, the Young Soul also leaves the relative security of the Child Soul Age, overcomes his secret desire for dependency, becomes independent, takes up a wandering-stick and conquers the world. It seeks adventure and is prepared to stumble and fail and to face all kinds of dangers in order to satisfy its desire for adventure. This doesn't mean that the Young Soul is really aware of all the dangers and adversities. It considers these possible but tries, at least at the beginning of this cycle, to ignore them since otherwise it wouldn't have the courage to face them. Therefore, the Young Soul is filled with an adolescent naivety in the first part of this cycle. At the same time this protects it from a number of difficulties and also intimates to it that what it encounters may be unpleasant but isn't really all that bad and one can easily recover from it.

The Young Soul strives for visible, external success. As in a fairy-tale, it seeks to return home victorious and to present to its parents a triumph over that against which they had warned it. So the Young Soul is a brave dragon-slayer, a person who's prepared to pluck fruit from the tree of life and also to eat it in order to achieve wealth and power. We refer here specifically to wealth and power and not to affluence and influence. Affluence and influence are terms which are more appropriately applied to the Mature Soul. The Young Soul is not content with affluence. Its dream is to get fabulously rich. Determined to go to the limits of what can be achieved and, if possible, to surpass those limits, it finds it enticing to exercise power. It wants to act and move, to actively decide its life and doesn't refrain from just as actively intervening in the fate of others when it has the chance.

You know from all the different aspects of the MATRIX that everything that exists can be used in a positive or negative way. This applies also to wealth and power. The Young Soul in no way wants to do anything bad or misuse achievements. Quite the contrary, it seeks to go through life without accumulating any guilt. It's exactly this desire which shows its naivety, since now it will and must experience the fact that it will innocently accumulate blame, that it will find itself in circumstances in which making a choice is inevitable, and that karmic ties are unavoidable.

Despite the fact that the Young Soul wants the best, it will make the worst mistakes since it lacks the experience, the wisdom, the introspection and the composure which will become more and more accessible in the Mature and Old cycles. The cycle of the Young Soul is, therefore, part of a development where it is necessary to come into contact with injustice, abuse of one's rights, cruelty, egotistic behavior, dastardliness and fanaticism. It also means that the greatest number of karmic ties are made during this period. The commitments which the soul makes through karmic behavior are necessary for they are a precondition for insight into the laws governing the whole and the growth of the capacity for love. This is a time of turbulence, of rise and fall, of great contrasts. All borders will be passed through, not only in the area of action but also in the passivity of suffering. Not only will suffering and punishment be tested, but also the first conscious acts of either love or unkindness.

The Infant Soul and the Child Soul do much which is loving or unloving, but they aren't conscious of it. It can be said that they know not what they do. Young Souls, in contrast, begin to realize that their actions have consequences, both in the good and bad sense. They cannot however see the extent of the consequences and try to close their eyes. But the first feelings of security begin to fade. Since the Young Soul views itself as omnipotent and in fact achieves great things in conquering its own world, it cannot and will not realize that it will one day have to take responsibility for what it has done. And since these ultimate consequences are denied, the ideas of guilt, punishment, sin and atonement play such a great role in the thoughts, ethics and morals of the Young Soul. Since it isn't capable of envisioning a reconciliation in a later soul cycle, it assures that all punishment occurs in this cycle. It issues strict laws and honors religious priniciples which, like an unrelenting judge, punish every indiscretion on earth, in the hereafter, or on the part of the Gods with great atonements. In this cycle, punishment must be experienced personally, through bodily pain, death, torture, the dismemberment of bodily parts, severe dungeons, or the eternal fire of hell.

The Young Soul still can't forgive itself for not being perfect—as a mother, house-wife, salesman or artisan. No mistake is allowed. Should one occur, it is punished with draconian measures. Young Souls are very strict with other people. They feel the need to keep distant from all those who would remind them of their imperfections. If they attain power and wealth, they associate only with their peers. They prefer not to see that other people are worse off, hungry or cold, sick or unhappy. All this would be too threatening and cast doubt on the belief that one has been rewarded by a godly authority for one's honesty and legally correct behavior. A Young Soul assumes that those who are doing poorly are not only responsible for their fate but are justly being punished on earth and in the hereafter for their sins.

This makes it easy for Young Souls to differentiate between good and evil. Now is the time to tie karmic bonds as a preparation for later development of love in dissolving them. The Warrior-like quality of this cycle seems to justify wars, crimes, reckless acts to one's own advantage. Young Souls are filled with a spirit of fighting and winning. And so they plunge into the depths if their luck is suddenly no longer fair, if they become sick or are betrayed. Then they feel battered by fate, punished by life even if they don't know why. They transfer their feelings of guilt and self-hatred to others who are weaker, who serve as scapegoats for the difficulties which the Young Soul is experiencing.

This cycle lasts a long time and has a tendency to last longer and to take more lifetimes than it should. For, just as many people on your earth want to stay young as long as possible, to remain at the heights of success as long as possible, to gain ever more riches, so do people develop the need to cling to those values in the Young Cycle for as long as possible. The Mature cycle can only begin after a soul or also a person realizes that the achievements which at one time seemed worth striving for no longer seem so beneficial; when a soul begins to question external fortune and no longer feels an overwhelming desire to pursue it. As long as the general value system of your society places youth, success, wealth and health above everything, the majority of souls will not be able to separate themselves from the Young Soul cycle even though sometimes it has lasted more than long enough.

A soul in this stage of development wants nothing so much as a valid confirmation of its existence. Infant and Child Souls exist but neither doubt nor are conscious of their existence. A Young Soul gradually experiences a greater distance from itself and for the first time poses the question: »Who am I? Why am I here?« And: »Do I even exist?« Therefore it relies to a greater degree on reflection and confirmation, so to say, as proof of its existence. It seeks reflection and confirmation through external factors, since these seem the most accessible and conclusive. It only knows itself when it views itself through the eyes of others. It's all the same if this is a shoe polisher, who places great pride in the gleam of a stranger's shoes and who depends on the praise of a satisfied customer for his identity, or if this is a politician who measures his worth according to the number of votes he receives or on his reputation in his party: It's the exterior radiance and the resonance which serve to bolster the feeling of self-worth of the Young Soul, and this radiance must be constantly maintained by energetic polishing.

This is reflected in the concept of »self-image«. The popular folk-singer, the evangelist, the leader of a youth gang or the best student in the class all polish their self-image. They depend on the constructive, confirming admiration of their environment and this admiration should also be physically manifested since material assets and self-worth are, in the view of the Young Soul, directly connected.

A Young Soul, therefore, needs its fellow men in order to constantly be assured of its own existence. It does this sometimes even if it tries in fearful pride to free itself from all ties in order to find out if it can exist without the sustenance of confirmation. The rejection of praise, the exaggerated need for transgression and the desire for unconditional autonomy show the need which lies behind the desire not to be dependent on anyone. The Young Soul places a great deal of value on progress, improvement and advancement. Its path can't be compared to a level street but rather to steep stairs or to a ladder. It finds climbing laborious but is very proud and satisfied with the overcoming of each tribulation. It directs its attention more on the next higher step than on the one it is presently on. Here progress always means »more«: more fame, success, recognition and confirmation. And since a Youg Soul's eyes are constantly focused on the heights, it suffers from feelings of envy that never abate as long as there are social steps to be climbed.

A Young Soul is still hardly aware of its worth as a unique individual, and therefore constantly compares to others to define itself. And in order to not come up short in these comparisons—for there are always people who have more and who make more of an impression—the Young Soul uses contempt as self-protection and either secretly or openly belittles neighbors who have a bigger farm, a more expensive car or a more beautiful wife in order not to have to constantly feel humiliated by these comparisons.

Since Young Souls have such a strong inner drive spurring them on to act and giving it the strength to achieve something, they do indeed accomplish great and impressive things. Actively directing one's own fate and the fate of those who trust is a highly responsible act in the creation of communal ties, in the family and management, in trade and politics. Much of what has been done to make life in many countries of the world safer and more comfortable is due to the beneficial efforts of Young Souls. Progress and discipline is written on their banner, and they profit from their desire to create a better world. They are the ones who spend money on road systems and see to it that clean water runs from the taps. Research in medicine and pharmacology is mostly due to them. Mature and Old Souls ought to be grateful to them.

Young Souls insist on their right to allegiance and pedantically differentiate between friend and enemy. A friend can expect a great deal of goodness. An enemy will experience undiminished enmity but will always know where he stands. A Young Soul needs and creates clarity. It's happiest when its interests are clear, when it knows exactly who belongs where, whom one can depend on, what has to be done next, and for what purpose. The classic fantasy of a Young Soul is a dish-washer becoming a millionaire, or a garbage man married to a princess. Life, as viewed by a Young Soul, has all possibilities open. There's a direct creativity which lies in this marvelous dynamic, which is based on an elementary inventiveness. It's elementary because it serves the victorious survival, the triumphal achievement. The Young Soul is inspired by the thought: »I'm going to show you!«

This thought mobilizes all available energies and strengthens the willpower. Hope never ceases for an improvement in a situation, for final satisfaction and of reaching the top of the ladder to success. And if life doesn't fulfill these high expectations to the extent that the Young Soul hopes, so that the ideals as such ought to be questioned, the Young Soul prefers to place all hopes in being successful in the beyond. There, after death, everything will certainly be attained that had been hoped for on earth: fame and glory, gold-filled splendour, perpetual good-health and magnificence as well as satisfaction of all the sensual desires which, for some inexplicable reason, failed to be satisfied during its bodily existence.

The sexual inclination of Young Souls, which in a strong physical body strives for immediate satisfaction, is accompanied by a basic belief that there is never enough of it. Therefore, Young Souls need a great many sexual contacts or many different partners. The Warrior-like determination to make conquests, the striving for confirmation causes the Young Soul to especially desire people who refuse or withdraw from it since its inner dynamic is excited by not attaining that which it wants immediately and this releases an enormous urge for seduction. Once married, they want to show off with a beautiful wife, be proud of a rich husband. Children are creatures either to be boasted about or to be ashamed of. If possible, they are supposed to be more handsome and more successful than their parents. If not, they are sometimes denied or even disowned.

The desire to conquer and possess a partner as such cannot be suppressed and if one's punished for this, as happens in Puritan societies, sexual fantasies and deviations serve as a valve. Rape may be the consequence. Fantasies deal with the themes of conquest, humiliation, force and triumph, for the Young Soul seeks to struggle in all areas of its life for something which it views as worthwhile (like virginity) and nothing makes it unhappier than temporary contentment.

Since in this cycle souls feel restless and also basically insecure, they constantly seek security. And they find security in property, in accumulating money which mustn't be spent, in inviolable marriage- and family relationships, and in religious contexts which provide a dogmatically-validated treasure of guidelines which Young Souls can follow. They want to know what is allowed and what is sanctioned, they need laws and regulations which stipulate what is right and what is wrong, and they want to be able to rely at any time on what is customary.

The more religious customs are filled with precepts, prohibitions and taboos, the more they meet the needs of the Young Soul. This soul can calm its unrest in the spiritual area when it is clear at all times what is allowed and desireable and what is sinful and therefore punishable. While the Infant and Child Souls prefer nature religions or shaman cults in which there are magic rituals and animal sacrifices, dance and smoke ceremonies, bodily ecstasies and many different deities who can be clearly indentified as good and evil, holy or unholy, the Young Soul tends, because of its need for security, to prefer monotheistic religions in which a strict father- or mother-like Godhead watches over everything, all-seeing and unforgiving. Then the Young Soul can decide on pacifing it or to go against its rules.

The eyes of Young Souls are often beautiful but not very soulful. A certain distrust and wariness is in their look. They are checking the world for potential enemies. Eye contact becomes more interesting than it was for the fearful Child Soul but has the function to control, punish or dominate more than to actually encounter the depth of another person, although this also happens more frequently now when the situation allows trust and confidence.

The setting of clear limits and succinct definitions doesn't entirely remove the Young Soul's doubts over its good behaviour, for there is always something which is incomprehensible and therefore unsettling, whether it be an expression of mercy or a form of arbitrary punishment. The deity, which sees all and directs all, is in its way unpredictable since it's been attributed a will and a power which the Young Soul finds extremely confusing and which it feels helplessly at the mercy of. No matter how carefully it tries not to go against the divine commandments, it is always aware that one careless false step is enough to cause eternal damnation. The Young Soul's reaction sometimes is: »Ok, if that's the way it's going to be, I might as well earn it!« and to disobey the rules so rigorously that it doesn't even allow something as dangerous as pity and forgiveness to enter into its considerations. It still doesn't have access to the karmic laws of compensation.

Since Young Souls live life on a material and physical level, they like to believe everything ends when the body dies. Why should one try to be good if this isn't perhaps recognized by God? Recognition and confirmation are of greatest significance here. If a Young Soul can't maintain its belief in the hereafter in a religiously dogmatic sense, as a Christian heaven or Elysian Fields, hell and purgatory, it doesn't feel inclined to observe the rules. Quite the contrary, it wants to find out if what was promised is really true and it can only do this by making a robust spot-check, despite all the fear of hell. Here it's also clear that security and insecurity are two aspects of the same need. The Young Soul longs for validity and complete protection. It wants to depend one hundred percent on all promises, also those of the priests. It must go against the laws in order to find out if they're valid. In such a way the Young Soul opens itself up to powerful uncertainties which in turn lead to an increased need for security.

Autonomy in all areas of existence is what the Young Soul is aiming at and this includes autonomy from divine guidance and influence. The most fervent, almost militant atheists are therefore found towards the end of this Young Cycle. The feeling behind this attitude is: »I don't want to rely on anybody. Nobody must interfere with me. It's my life. What do I need a God for?«

Nevertheless, the observance of meaningful and security-enforcing rituals creates great satisfaction and provides the framework of comfort it seeks. Social rituals within the family such as a weekly barbecue, in religion such as singing together, as well as in business-life (drinking with the colleagues), at the stock market, during the course of daily routine, in attire, body-care and nourishment (the latest fashion), determine its life and provide security. »I'll do what everbody else does!« Related to the Warrior energy of this cycle, comradeship and group feeling are most important. Young Souls need security and seek it in the form of behavior since they can only seldom find security within themselves. Rituals provide the protection of society and the possibility of defining oneself as a member of a family, group, tribe, people or nation. The definition of one's own identity still depends on the norms of society. Security comes from without. No other security is sought. The work which a Young Soul puts into the construction and main-tainance of its world creates contentment, and if this world for some reason collapses, it will begin immediately to rebuild it. The Young Soul likes to work hard with Warrior-like discipline and vitality. Work gives it the assurance that it can determine the course of its existence and this realization will always make it happy. It deals, therefore, more easily than the Mature Soul with the blows of fate, recovers from them, interprets them as challenges, rolls up its arm-sleeves and begins anew.

Young Souls will never give up and, until their last breath, they will never doubt in the power of luck. And, since they strive for earthly happiness by achievement, they take credit for all their accomplishments and successes or are prepared to recognize their own mistakes and to pay for them. They're proud of everything they have achieved. Fate, the twisting path of life, the power of subconscious motivations as well as the soul's own plans are not taken into consideration. Doubts will be pushed aside or ignored so that only one's own achievement remains in the conscious mind as a glowing bril-liance. But this also results in the Young Soul being able to reach states of contentment that are unique and won't be enjoyed by later Soul Cycles. It celebrates its great self-confidence in ecstasy over its mastery of life, and will enjoy this until it crosses over the threshhold of the Mature Soul Cycle.

Energy 4

The Mature Soul

Mature Souls discover a new world. While the cycles of the Infant Soul, the Child Soul and the Young Soul were devoted to exploring and integrating the external requirements and possibilities of physical life, the Mature Soul encounters layers of reality which, until this time, were unknown to it and which couldn't have interested it. This is a cycle with the archetypical energy quality of the Scholar. Its principle is therefore learning and teaching.

The formerly vague notion of possessing a psyche and a soul becomes a tangible reality. The Mature Soul experiences this admittedly in a fundamental conflict but also in an incesssant dialogue between its external and internal life. We've said that the Mature Soul discovers a new world. It's like a person who with diving equipment is swept away in the tide of the sea and, to his immeasurable astonishment, but also with a certain degree of uneasiness, for the first time gets a glance at the fantastic, colorful, many varied forms of the underwater world. There's much which makes him curious but also much that frightens him. He doesn't know how to categorize all the strange discoveries, he fears the unknown. He doesn't sense where dangers are and where he can feel safe. He wants to go deeper but still doesn't know all the requirements and laws which are valid in the realm of the deep, the area of secret, unexplored inner life which he's entered.

And, as the diver must return repeatedly to the surface for air, to fill his oxygen tank or to avoid spending too long in the pressure of the depths, the person who's reached the stage of the Mature Soul must learn to approach carefully the exploration of conditions in his newly-won dimension. He must not near the depths of his inner reality unprepared. At the beginning of this cycle, he assures carefully that he remains mainly in the sphere of external reality, with which he became so well-acquainted during the first three long Soul-Cycles. They are at his disposal, he can handle them, and he masters them to the extent that they can be mastered.

The Mature Soul begins to recognize problems everywhere, even in areas where there previously didn't appear to be any difficulties. The Young Soul was constantly ready to deny or to forcefully resolve all conflicts, problems and difficulties. Everything seemed feasible and solvable and it ignored anything which might block it since it didn't want to deal with something which might shake its faith in its own powers. The Mature Soul can handle its fear of problems a bit better and therefore also encounters more problems. And since it begins to look inwards rather than outwards, it now discovers abysses and dark zones which until now had not been visible to it. What is surfacing can no longer be ignored and, with increasing courage, Mature Souls shape their lives in such a way that the problematic nature of relationships, work, property, health and success can play an ever greater role.

And the more often a Mature Soul examines itself and the powers of its existence, the more painful becomes the examination of its identity. It plunges into the depths, the mysteries of its psyche and resurfaces again in order to become better acquainted with itself and with life. It discovers the deep insecurity which lies in the question »Who am I?« But it also hears new answers which give it at least temporary consolation and a certainty that it exists as an individual irrespective of the confirmation of other people, social norms, a nation or race.

With the growing awareness of itself, the Mature Soul recognizes the predominant connections on the bodily, psychological, intellectual and spiritual level. It no longer seeks as a matter of course those who are exactly like it, but approaches people who, through their different nature, provoke a desire for growth. A difference in the world-view, lifestyle or shape of relationships no longer is viewed by the Mature Soul as threatening an eternal order or deserving of contempt. The person with a Mature Soul seeks new ties and feels a new closeness. But it's not only the exploration of people in their many colorful, varied forms which satisfies the soul in this cycle. Its relationship to nature now contains new aspects. Exploration becomes more interesting than exploitation. The world of physical, chemical, biological or geological phenomena now commands its respect. It begins to explore the connections between the microcosmos and the macrocosmos since it looks beyond what is immediately perceptible. It gradually realizes that a spiritual power might possibly unite all phenomena of existence and can now also view its own being as a meaningful particle of all existence.

The Young Soul realized itself mainly through its actions. The Mature Soul views action as a necessity, however not meaningful of itself. Reflection becomes more attractive. Introspection and contemplation happen more and more often, quite naturally. And as the Mature Soul wanders through all areas of its being, both the visible and invisibile, in search of purpose, it will doubt being able to find this purpose. Younger Souls were not plagued by doubt. Now life is taken much more seriously than before, it almost presents an unsolvable problem. Mature Souls will be aware of the hardships of life in a different way than the Young Soul. Namely, they understand now that suffering, hopelessness and torment are not only unpleasant phenomena, not necessarily something which is caused by sinful behavior, but are intrinsic parts of life and experience.

It is not easy for Mature Souls to deal with the dark side of human nature which they acknowledge in others and in themselves. But during this cycle they will experience more of it than in the previous or future cycles. Through suffering one gains understanding for the suffering of its fellow men. Therefore, the Mature Soul often chooses activities which bring it into contact with those who are faring badly: the poor, the sick, the unfortunate and the despairing, those who have suffered losses or who are disadvantaged. In such a way souls in this Cycle learn much about the problems of life without having to personally experience them in every incarnation.

The world-outlook changes. It's no longer external success which is the lodestar for all desires and actions, but rather an inner satisfaction over one's own esteem for what has been accomplished. Ethics and morals become more personal, and also the artistic expression, no matter how at odds with itself and tormented it might seem, no longer pays tribute to the mass but mirrors the awareness of the defectiveness, the naked humanity, the transience of all human life.

At this time responsibility will be assumed to an extent which was still unknown to the Young Soul and which will later again be abdicated by the Old Soul. While the Young Soul willingly took over duties in the shaping of the world, the Mature Soul prefers to take on social burdens. It looks after the well-being of the community, and not of the richest or most successful, but rather of those who are unable to care for themselves. Responsibilities also play a significant role in the psychological area. Since the Mature Soul shows great readiness to observe its wishes and desires and is for the first time painfully aware of its weaknesses, it knows better what is possible and what is not. It often happens, however, that this preparedness to assume responsibility turns into an exaggeration which stems from the reluctance of allowing others to be called to account. And then when something happens which wasn't planned, the Mature Soul blames itself more than it should for its failure. It suffers from self-recrimination and depression because it doesn't realize that it tried to assume too much and that other people also ought to fulfill their duties. It yearns for a social and moral righteousness which it had during the last soul cycle but can't find in this new sphere of existence. From now on, it will only be able to find safety if it explores the inner core of its being and anchors it in the harbor of its identity.

It's not easy to master this cycle of soul development which presents an acid test for the soul who seeks to integrate the experiences of the first three cycles. It's a phase of great inner challenges continuing through many lives. In general, a soul needs approximately twenty-five incarnations in order to grow to full maturity.

These incarnations are also marked by the fact that now the first karmic debts from earlier incarnations are recognized. The soul gradually begins through corresponding conscious actions and adjustments to resolve them. Whatever had caused pain at one time will be rectified as much as possible. The Mature Soul's capacity for love will grow step by step through the gradual recognition and resolution of these karmic debts incurred during the late Child and the whole Young Soul cycle. Since the Mature Soul no longer lives mainly surrounded by the security systems of the groups it belongs to but is more and more in contact with its own individuality and that of others, it is extremely thankful for every meeting with an incarnated soul whom it knew from an earlier incarnation, whether it be the result of good or bad experiences. The Mature Soul still will not recognize in every case the trusted vibrations, but toward the end of this cycle there will be more instances of soul recognition. Even if such meetings are not experienced consciously, they're still valid and will occur more frequently in this cycle than in the previous one. And the Mature Soul experiences this with a previously unknown intensity.

It's basically prepared for happiness and suffering to the same degree, to measure the limits and to accept them when they are reached. Almost every incarnation is devoted to resolving at least one or even more karmic ties. The Mature Soul in such a way always approaches the point where it wants to be good and loving, forgiving and giving at all times, but doesn't succeed since it's so needy in its sensitivity and its concerns about the limits of its love.

We've said that the Mature Soul no longer seeks its well-being in external success, in riches and fame and in mastering the challenges of the external world but rather turns inwards in order to realize that the search for its individual truth and authentic personality includes dimensions which so far have been unexplored. This doesn't imply, however, that such a turn to the depths of one's own psyche means that the Mature Soul happily forgoes security, prosperity and comfort. On the contrary, it needs security in its external life in order to devote attention to its inner life. And since it's prepared to seriously take on great responsibilities, it often occupies influential social positions which enables it to possess property and money. In contrast to the Young Soul, however, the Mature Soul no longer immediately identifies itself with what it has achieved or accumulated. A certain degree of recognition and affluence suffices. It can truly enjoy what it has but it can just as well make do with less.

It knows that the material framework of its bodily existence is only a frame and not a goal, purpose or content itself. And since it no longer depends upon material success and wealth for its entire existence, including the psychological, it can freely disperse what belongs to it or what it acquires during a life time. Mature Souls are often generous when in their MATRIX an Archetype such as Greed doesn't interfere. And it will give away much of what it possesses in order to acquire non-material wealth: knowledge, experience, recognition and impressions.

We don't mean to imply here that all Mature Souls are prosperous. We speak here of a relative prosperity which is dependent on the social-cultural context into which a Mature Soul is born. But since it's necessary for its learning process to understand that its psychological and mental existence follows laws other than the world of acquisition and material security, it is necessary for it to personally experience the contrast between both spheres, the inner and outer. It therefore often happens that a Mature Soul is born to parents who assure that the childhood is materially-secure but that he later must experience losing everything and realizing that nothing remains except the knowledge that its own humanity remains unblemished. Or a person may grow up in impoverished circumstances and later achieve the long-desired prosperity. He must realize at the same time that he's thankful for such a life but can't deny the fact that all of this prosperity is only a way to a goal, not the goal itself. No one knows better than the Mature Soul that money doesn't make one happy. For it experiences this in its environment where often the opposite is true.

Therefore, a person in the stage of the Mature Soul is thankful for every moment of happiness. It enjoys these hours or periods more intensely than a Young Soul or an Old Soul, for the Young Soul always believes that happiness lies in the foreseeable future and is a reward due to his own discipline or will power. And an Old Soul longs so much for a happiness that is not of this world that it is seldom satisfied with the joys of the moment. Only the Mature Soul consciously experiences times of quiet and happy contemplation during the course of its many incarnations.

It needs family and friends in order to sense this happiness. But even when surrounded by many of its beloved friends, it will always feel a bit isolated since its needs on the soul level—and often also on the level of the psyche—are different from those of most loved ones. In his eyes, they are somewhat superficial and don't see what's really important. It tries so hard to feel with greater awareness and to act with greater consciousness than they do in their earlier stages of Soul Development that a certain loneliness is the natural result. It places great worth on the education of its descendants, on the intellectual advancement of students, on the impression people make on mankind in general. But emotional education seems even more important. Mature Souls are found in all areas of human life as teachers, educators, artists, scientists and politicians, as doctors and priests, as craftsmen and technicians but also as social workers, nurses, therapists. They don't rely only on their deeds but also want make an imprint on their fellow-men through their loving influence. The most important thing for a Mature Soul is the insight which is achieved through some change.

A person with a Mature Soul is religious in his own individual way. Since he's no longer directly guided by the collective of a church or creed, he seeks his own path of knowledge in his religious ties. A monotheistic or atheistic belief, which is seldom militant, offers the best possibility of finding a resonance of the godly principle within himself. He discovers his own unmistakeable form of contact and worship. If he belongs to a particular faith, he'll always seriously try to find the personal or spiritual truth behind dogmas and belief systems. Doubt and longing rule him to same degree. No one poses as many questions as the Mature Soul. And no one so seldom finds a satisfactory answer. Faith and the very existence of a divine power become a problem to be discussed and investigated. The search, the doubt and the despair of not finding the answer oftens leads a such a person to say: »I don't believe in anything anymore.«

But it is precisely in this formulation that the characteristic structure of awareness arises in this period of spiritual awakening. For the Mature Soul has left behind what in the stage of the Young Soul provided promise and security. The new state is characterized by the fact that steadfastness, consolation and security can no longer be found exclusively in traditional communal belief systems or in institutionally prescribed ethical guidelines. A Mature Soul can no longer act without questioning his actions and motivations. It can no longer think without thinking about its thoughts. It has reached a stage where his own self is no longer self-evident.

Health is now less sound than it was during the Young Soul Cycle, so full of vitality, since the Mature Soul wants to start experiencing the transience and fragility of physical existence. During this cycle painful illnesses, handicaps, and accidents which have serious consequences will be encountered in order to explore the limits of one's own identification with the body. Protracted suffering serves to explore whether the inner-achieved stability will stand the test of a threat to the body.

Pains and problems are an important theme in this cycle, and this applies to both the psyche and the body. Since a person with a Mature Soul from now on is prepared to assume responsibility for his body, he realizes for the first time that he can do something for his well-being himself and feels called upon to make sacrifices in order to preserve his health. He can no longer overtax himself as much as does the Young Soul who sees the body as a machine and the doctor as a technician whose duty it is to keep it running. His energy structures become more refined, he needs a different kind of nourishment, more peace, more rest, more protection. He's more susceptible to external influences and also more sensitive to poisonous substances which assault his body.

But it must be mentioned that a person with a Mature Soul is often so dismayed by the many problems in its life that he will employ all possible poisonous antidotes, and especially those which promise to make the torments of his life forgettable. Among these are stimulants as well as all tablets and drugs which bring about sleep, forgetfulness or a changed state of consciousness. It's important to note here that most illegal drugs create a psychic perception in areas which will be naturally accessible only later in the Old Soul Cycle. The longing for increased consciousness, just as the fear of a premature altered state of consciousness is, though, already very great in the Mature Cycle.

Since everyday-life can be viewed as unbearably exhausting, many Mature Souls try to deny it or reject it as boring. They often choose to escape the dilemma by giving it up. They don't even try to understand and master daily life. In this cycle souls explore manic-depressiveness or schizophrenia. It isn't necessary for every soul to experience this »being out of one's mind« in the Mature Soul cycle. This experience can also take place during the Infant Soul cycle or the very last incarnations. But since mental illness and handicap is an essential experience for the total development of all souls, it must find a place in one of the development cycles.

We would like to stress that people with a Mature Soul are almost always extremely courageous individuals who pursue their spiritual goal, who confront the difficulties of their existence with great seriousness and overcome them. These include themes such as chronic illnesses or an early separation from one's parents, loss of one's native land, unjust sentences and loss of freedom, a sudden loss of one's beloved mate, a bitter quarrel with one's twin soul, all types of difficult karmic ties, life in a strange foreign culture, marriage to a person of another race, a loss of property, an unexpected acquisition of wealth, artistic expressiveness which is not immediately validated. Also included are the sacrifice of oneself in caring for a relative, giving birth to, and caring for, a handicapped child, the escape from the traditions and conventions of the family, also in a professional sense, as well as the themes of being blamed for something when one is innocent, unintentional arson, causing death by negligence in traffic or war, and serving faithfully an unjust master. It can be said that almost every incarnation in this cycle is tied to an accepting understanding of these frightening life situations. But people in the Mature Soul cycle often die peacefully after a fulfilled, turbulent life. The term fulfillment shouldn't be understood as a characteristic of a constantly harmonious, happy, almost uneventful existence. Wisdom and the ability to love grow steadily with the recognition and mastery of problems.

The limitations and fears of earlier cycles disappear. A Mature Soul seldom creates new karma. On the contrary, it works persistently to understand the soul's past and to affirm it. The Mature Soul loves deeply and enduringly. It is prepared to make sacrifices for its love. Spending a whole life with a person, whether it be a spouse, parent or child, and not to take this relationship for granted but rather to confront its problems, fill it with love, meaningfulness and deliberateness, is one of the themes of this cycle. Mature Souls are very loyal, reliable and constant. It can happen, though, that a Mature Soul seeks a certain other soul as a partner because that was promised in between lives and therefore must change mates several times before it meets the person with whom it was intended to be.

Sexuality serves to a greater extent than before to really come close to another person, to open oneself, to sense and reveal one's own vulnerability. It will also be used to attract partners with whom one already had relationships in earlier lives. Children who result from such relationships are often soul siblings or trusted souls who reached agreement between lives or declared themselves ready in the Astral World to help the future parents in some type of important development tasks.

Since people in this Soul Cycle have shed many tears in order to free themselves from fear and oppressive feelings, their eyes are usually clear, self-critical, knowing and kind. They always convey the impression that the person is looking for something, peering into the distance or into the depth of a person. From time to time they almost appear to have a metallic brilliance. Their glance bores deeply but the eye muscles are seldom relaxed, and eye contact can't be endured for very long since it only takes a fraction of a second for a Mature Soul to gain access to the soul of another person. Even if its human heart can't constantly be filled with affection, there are many hours in every life in this cycle in which the eyes of such a person radiate with the softness of love.

Energy 5

The Old Soul

The Cycle of the Old Soul is dedicated to a theme which can be described by the words loneliness and attachment. While all the previous cycles served the gradual dissolution from the collective and were aimed at increasing individualization, freedom and awareness of the soul, the self-awareness now reaches its highest point in the body. The soul realizes irrevocably its fragmentation. Painful knowlege about the loss of unity with the Whole (of the Soul Family) creates an irresistable longing for reunion. This is a cycle with the archetypical energy of the Sage. Its principle is communication.

At the beginning of this cycle one tries to deny this knowledge of its fragmentation, to cover it up, but it's no longer possible to close one's eyes to the essential truth. And this essential truth means: An Old Soul is very much alone while in the body. It's alone, first of all, because there are only a few people in its immediate surroundings who also have Old Souls and who can share the experiences, the blessings and the pains of this stage. That's why a person with an Old Soul encounters misunderstanding, estrangement and distance in its environment from the moment of his birth. It needs all its strength in this stage to maintain contact with its inner self, the only thing which seems to provide an anchoring.

It would be a shame, however, if it sought to avoid contact with the life it chose to live. For an Old Soul must never forget that it chose the present incarnation just as it is, that it is an important matter to be at this place, under exactly these circumstances and to deal with this. Otherwise it wouldn't be here. But there's also something new, something different which characterizes the Cycle of the Old Soul, and that is the sense and real experience of an increasing closeness not on the physical level, but on the level of consciousness to the Astral and also the Causal World. This closeness can and will only occur when fragmentation is truly recognized and accepted. It results from a new orientation. It grips the conscious and the unconscious in a way that was previously unknown, and manifests itself in a telepathic, visionary and spiritual preparedness to make contact with forces which can't directly relate to everyday consciousness.

These are in the first place all those who exhibit a close soul relationship to the individual fragment. This includes soul siblings but also authorities who extend beyond the realm of one's own soul family like guides. The inner or higher self also plays an important role. The ability increases to perceive higher levels of consciousness, either intuitively or inspirationally, and to learn from transpersonal entities.

An Old Soul senses the desire everywhere to unite with its Soul Family, which, on the physical level, it left an endlessly long time ago. It tries to do this with all the ways and means at its disposal. This occurs in every moment of peace, during each meditation, during sleep and dream, during ecstatic sexual contact, in all hours in which the heart expands and the eyes become moist. Since the soul realizes in this stage that it is utterly alone and that, at the same time, it is not alone, it calls out to those who belong to it always. And in such a way realms become accessible which in the course of the Mature Cycle had begun opening up but which now become an experienced reality.

For this reason, the Old Soul at the beginning of this Cycle experiences a new feeling of insecurity. Its emotions are marked by contradictions. It's completely alone but yet not alone. It feels abandoned by people who ought to be there like relatives and school friends, it often has no sexual partner or spouse, rarely gives birth to children, and yet receives love and friendship, warmth and closeness from individual souls and soul entities who aren't on the physical level. But also in the physical world the Old Soul experiences a special, hitherto unknown love for a smaller number of other Old Souls, a love which is no longer dependent on whether two people belong together, are »suitable« or understand each other or are willing to spend their daily lives together.

Compared to the previous Cycles the Old Soul experiences a new conflict. It possesses a body and is clearly a person who's governed by the laws of the physical world. But it feels estranged from these laws of nature and doesn't really know where it actually belongs. How can it feel at home on earth when its soul senses more definitively companionship, love and nearness in other spheres? Should it be here or there? Does it want to be here or there?

Its body will now be afflicted by various states of weakness. It isn't sick and it isn't well. It is extremely sensitive and constantly tends to withdraw from the burdens of bodily existence. Life with its daily necessities, such as eating, drinking and sleeping, earning a living, the necessity for relationships, the desire for nearness and confirmation, often appears tedious and exhausting. The Old Soul tends to neglect these matters or to withdraw in some way from them. It seeks as great a distance as possible from daily reality.

Sometimes it despises or belittles those who pursue the sensual pleasures of life. It seeks to exist without material needs, a state of being which would correspond much more to a disembodied state. But an Old Soul must in every hour of its life realize that it isn't possible to both live life and at the same time reject life. Therein lies the greatest difficulty which characterizes the Old Soul cycle. These last incarnations must be consciously lived and experienced. They must be affirmed and enjoyed, not simply endured, in order to proceed through the various necessary steps of love and understanding which will complete the whole circle of incarnations. The challenge for the Old Soul consists, therefore, in truly living in the here and now and, at the same time, allowing its consciousness to reach out beyond the barriers of physical existence.

Old Souls are basically tired of fighting for their material existence and basic daily needs in the real world. They've done so much and experienced so much. So much lies behind them that they would prefer to withdraw into a little corner, be nourished and cared for, in order not to have to do what has become so burdensome to them. They would like to find some way of life which provides for them, to receive a pension, to have some inherited income or to find some person who would take them under his wings and free them from the troublesome duty of caring for themselves materially. They happily occupy insignificant and dependent positions and indulge in an inclination to muddle through life without the tension and attention they needed in earlier existences, without the feeling that they must be famous and recognized, without the desire to achieve yet more great things.

They are more than Younger Souls impelled to check things, not to take things at face-value, but to put everything to a test, to see whether they are also actually right for themselves and not only for the majority of people. Old Souls are no longer »normal«. Normal food, normal behavior, normal efforts and exertions are too much for them. This leads to painful comparison and to the general impression of being something like a freak.

With few exceptions, they have difficulty in getting along with authorities and rules, with work requirements and social customs which seek to set limits on their unusual personality. On the other hand, Old Souls also need guidelines but they must have the freedom to either accept or reject them according to their momentary needs.

We've said that Old Souls cast their glance in distant dimensions. They often look more than they see, and they appear to observe in the phenomena of life not only the visible but also transcendental or symbolic aspects. They constantly watch their reality in connection with other realities and this means that they see associations between apparently separate manifestations which aren't generally recognized as valid. Old Souls sometimes have access to shamanistic or kabalistic knowledge. But in contrast to Young and Mature Souls, who are fascinated by purely intellectual parallels such as ethnology, Old Souls sense the whole interweaved spiritual reference frame as an energy phenomenon which can be experienced.

Energy in its multi-facetted manifestations plays a commanding role in the life of a person with an Old Soul. The refinement of a person's energy system on the physical and psychological level makes him more accessible to non-human vibrations that can be received over newly-achieved inner frequencies. He will, of course, also be more sensitive to energies which cross or disturb him.

But since, on a certain level, everything is energy, the bodies of Old Souls can find their place in this spectrum of vibrations. It will be possible for them to better perceive the different frequencies of their own energy and to play with them, to change them and to use them. They can do this in meditation, or in observing their dreams, in deep relaxation in which they recognize their individual vibrations and those of their fellow-men, in which they travel to astral regions and use the fine-grained connections which can help heal the body like homoeopathy or Bach flowers. They can use their own energy to reflect and understand various afflictions of others and to donate it freely knowing it is a divine gift.

Therefore, in the event of physical illness, it's good for an Old Soul to choose a gentle treatment. This differs significantly from the first three development cycles where the body is stronger and less vulnerable. However, it's also advisable even for the Mature Soul to find more gentle methods of medical treatment since it's equally susceptible to poisonous substances.

This sensibility toward unpleasant or harmful substances increases significantly in the Old Soul stage. No one suffers as much from dirt, noise and bad aromas, no one is tormented more with supposedly harmless fumes or influences, never are there as many difficulties in maintaining a sound immune system as in this cycle. For the body of an Old Soul becomes increasingly permeable. Since it's nearing the final dissolution of its physical existence, already several incarnations before its last life it experiences a perviousness and transparency, which at the same time becomes a filter absorbing everything and then again expelling the agreable or disagreable energies which flow through it.

But if a soul in this late stage attempts with all means to defend itself against unpleasant or harmful influences of the physical world in which it finds itself and has chosen to be, it doesn't really do itself any favor. It's more important for Old Souls to learn to allow the undesirable to flow through it and to call on the spirit with its overwhelming potential for help to filter and cast out the poison and undesirable energy. Otherwise it will have to keep everyone and everything distant from itself. That wouldn't do it any good. It would be regrettable to avoid contact with the life it had chosen out of pure fear of the pain it might involve. For an Old Soul must never forget that it chose the present incarnation—just the way it is. It was a choice to be in this place, to live under these circumstances, and to deal with this. An Old Soul should also remember that it undertook, or can undertake, within its physical-spiritual context, measures which can help make its life more bearable. At the same time we don't want to conceal the fact that an Old Soul, because of its many sensibilities, will suffer and that these sensibilities are necessary conditions for an increased mental and spiritual sensitivity. We don't want to imply here that Old Souls automatically possess a clairvoyant ability or visionary imagination. But much which has been concealed in darkness will now be recognized and revealed.

Intuition and inspiration will be utilized in order to achieve the necessary steps which the incorporated existence strives for with great precision. The few lives of the Old Soul offer in an especially condensed sequence an abundance of experiences and developments which, because of reasons of completeness, must still be mastered. In addition, one must encounter the most important members of the Soul Family who are presently incarnated, or in some way establish contact with them, whether it be telepathically or in person. Since most people follow until their last life their own intuition and the instructions of their higher self, although this is seldom consciously realized, contact to their various soul siblings and also to the most important soul companions who in previous lives played an important role, takes place on a half-conscious or subconscious level. And it is no way vitally essential to experience consciousness in the complete, comprehensive sense of enlightenment in order to absolve the last incarnation. Every soul, no matter which path it chooses, arrives at its goal.

The very last karmic ties near resolution. The older a soul becomes, and the closer it approaches its last incarnation, the more it will encounter old, familiar and beloved companions. These contacts precede the great happiness of reunion with the Soul Family which can only take place when all individual members of this family have completed their travels through all their lives.

The transcendental dimension, which now becomes accessible to the Old Soul, and the transpersonal energy field which arises around it, create an expression in its eyes which can truly be described as soulful and which carries with it an ability to make an especially deep eye-contact. The Old Soul can find its way back to a guilelessness and vulnerability which the Infant Soul once possessed but lost in the course of fragmentation. This new guilelessness results from an unprotected openness combined with a wisdom gained through ten thousand years of earthly experience. An Old Soul can touch the hearts of other people by letting the eyes express all the feelings and by establishing a fearless eye-contact. We don't mean that every Old Soul permanently and constantly possesses this vulnerable and guileless expression. We only mean that it can have it when it is free from distrust arising from the fear of being subject to all the terrors of a hostile world.

For the Old Soul religion means basically a totally personal creed and a rejection of all the established forms of belief and dogma. Belief will be replaced by inner certainty, but before achieving this certainty a soul must experience a great deal of uncertainty. It seeks that which unites. It senses the godly principle within itself but doesn't know how to comprehend it.

It seeks connection to the whole of its Soul Family and the AllOne but finds help only in a few other people, in nature, or within its own heart. The desire is overwhelming for a new security which has little in common with the security sought by the Infant and Child Soul, but this desire is seldom satisfied. The Old Soul knows for sure that everything manifest, including its own existence, is interwoven by a great and loving intelligence and it wishes to be transported by this spiritual force. But it senses that it is not easy or a matter of course to gain such complete trust for an incarnated soul. Therefore, many lives in this last cycle are spent in a tension between the desire for an endless unity on the one hand, and discord over the fact that the truth of the divine oneness cannot immediately (and seldom over a longer period of time) be sensed, on the other. The soul in this late stage of development in the physical world perceives the divine at all times and in all places in a kind of pantheism. But it suffers from a sense of being shut out, a state of being it can hardly understand. This sensation can be explained by the discrepancy between an inner knowledge and a perception of reality which is limited by all too human fear.

What does the Old Soul fear? It fears the disintegration of all it has been during the past ten thousand years, of its body, of its identity, of its ego, although paradoxically this is all it constantly strives for. It is afraid of decomposition and transcendence but practices it daily. It is frightened by the realization of the new intimacy with the divine in all manifestations but doesn't desire anything but this. It knows now almost everything one can know towards the end of the circle of incarnations but seeks refuge in apparent ignorance. It feels wise after the accumulated experience of a hundred different lives in a hundred different bodies but complains about its inadequacy. Its standards of loving are high but it condemns itself for every act of unkindness. It wants peace but can't attain it as long as it doesn't accept the fact that it differs fundamentally from most others. It senses the pettiness of all problems but poses a great problem to itself. And despite of being convinced that all facets of its existence are based on the decisions of its immortal soul, and that no one else decides which move to make in which direction, in all humility it fears the consequences of such a clearly defined reality.

The closer an Old Soul comes to the end of all incarnations, the more clearly the natural laws of existence become apparent. The readiness to love grows inexorably. The unconditionality of this love becomes a central interest to the Old Soul, a love which no longer has a single object like a child or a spouse for its feelings. For the Old Soul wants to and must realize that everything, even desires and hopes, are ultimately chimera of bodily existence. That explains why it can't take seriously the dramas, ecstasies and tragedies of human relationships. Love is now directed toward many people. It doesn't want to spend a whole life with just one person, although it's more inclined to emotional faithfulness than Younger Souls. It is hardly prepared anymore to invest a great deal of energy in maintaining an unsatisfactory marriage or prolonged tedious friendship. It prefers a partner with whom it can maintain a relationship without a great deal of psychological effort, or it chooses relationships which allow a great deal of personal freedom and possibilities of development. The narrow concentration of feelings on a single person and the children which result from such a union, is a form of relationship which Young and Mature Souls above all choose in order to experience love. For as soon as a soul reaches this last part of its incarnated development, exclusive personal ties will mean little to it. The Old Soul exudes its love, which more and more frees itself from earlier possessive emotions, on all fellow beings in its immediate and more distant environment and indeed on animals and trees, without reserving it for a particular person. And if sometimes it's not able to achieve this, the desire is certainly there.

The third achievement, which is now undertaken with great readiness, is a calm ability to be alone, to do without constant company and sexual satisfaction, not because of a lack of ability to establish relationships, but because of the knowledge that all forms of contacts and relationships have been explored and experienced in many lives. It's no longer necessary to have children in order to have crucial experiences. It's much more desirable to find oneself in love with existence, to allow the collected energies of one's own psyche to flow, and to concentrate on relationships with children, elderly people, a number of good friends. The only prerequisite is that these people have a vibration and energy field which allow the energy of the Old Soul to flow. Then it pours out its warmth and love unconditionally on all those who wish to refresh themselves on this.

Until now we've described the faultless portrait of the Old Soul, but we would like to return once more to its fear, which often results in two-thirds or three-fourths' of its life being marked by severe discord and a dispute between the limited human personality and the unlimited soul identity.

The Old Soul now leaves behind the bustle which made it so nervous in the previous two stages. It senses that it only has a few things left to do and to experience. It doesn't want to be rushed by anything or anyone any longer. The great motivations of the past, the search for money, fame or fortune, no longer affect it. If it takes the trouble to learn a demanding profession it is only so that, with its help, it can achieve a few important personal goals, for instance to aid in a certain way its soul siblings, or to resolve karmic debts which couldn't be resolved in any other manner. But it would prefer not to have to make any efforts anymore. It enjoys more and more being dependent once again, to let others care for it, or to pursue a peaceful, almost meditative activity, which no longer involves seeking success or which results in the bitter disappointment of failure.

A person with an Old Soul usually has many gifts and talents. The many abilities gained during earlier lives are latently and unconsiously at his disposal. Therefore, he often doesn't know which inclination he would prefer to follow. And it's often a pleasure for him to be supported by a social network or his family, or to be supported by the work of fellow men. And sometimes it doesn't matter to him if he sits on a street corner and begs, or lives without a roof over his head as a homeless person, to no longer be restricted by any guidelines or authorities. So you will often find Old Souls among those whom you believe you must pity. Rarely will a person at the end of his incarnations correspond to the picture you would expect. He is not always blissful and wise, he is in no way healthier than Younger Souls, he is also not always relaxed and friendly at all times. It's possible that you'll meet such a person in a phase in which he is at peace and free of fear, but these phases will be the exception and not the rule.

Wisdom, goodness, calmness, candour, humility and helpfulness are surely more accessible to Old Souls than to Young Souls. Nevertheless they often to dissolve too soon. The ego sees its last chance to assert itself. But if dissolution occurs, the Old Soul experiences with great pleasure and awareness. On the other hand, it is exactly this which causes a not inconsiderable amount of its torment. For, in contrast to a Younger Soul, it knows that melting into the AllOne is possible and has personally experienced it, if only for a few seconds. Therefore, it plunges into a void at the the loss of the beloved ego which until now seemed to make its identity. Memories of safer states of being are there, but the safety of a well-defined personality is being threatened. The new emptiness experienced in this cycle is not easy to bear but it must be endured.

Ecstatic participations in the AllOne will now happen more frequently on their own without any aid from meditation or drugs, special exercises or techniques. The Old Soul is tired of methods and their application. It tries once more one way or another, but senses that the delightful stillness, the true ecstasy, the precious agreement with the vibrations of cosmic love, lie beyond all efforts. Fulfillment lies within itself, and in its courage to cross over the barriers of its fear. The closer the end of the journey approaches, the more the small and great moments of ecstatic union with the whole on the level of energetic connection, and transcendence of self and character will take place as a matter of course.

Even if an Old Soul's body is still inhabited, energy layers will constantly be separating from the body. Achieving a state of reverie no longer means an inattentive, unconscious, distancing oneself from, and transgressing of, the everyday personality, but something consciously experienced as moments, hours or days of the highest ecstasy. This occurs because one truly perceives unity. It is the experience of being united, of harmony, love and peace, instead of being guided by desire for spiritual thrills, or from a vague mental idea that fantastically altered states of consciousness like out-of-body experiences must happen if only one listens to the right master or has practised diligently. Although Old Souls are often divided within themselves and painfully feel a conflict between their limited bodily manifestation and their intellectual-spiritual consciousness, all Mature and Old Souls can see very clearly the soft, light gleam, the bright light which surrounds such beings the closer they near the end of their incarnations and their final goal. This specific charisma can be perceived as a warmth or an aura. It is independent from the subjective state which is reflected in the psyche or body of a person with an Old Soul. But whoever has the fortune to encounter an Old Soul in the fifth, sixth or seventh stage of this last Cycle at a moment of peace or reverie will have an unforgettable impression of the potential which has been released. It's good to know that this very state of being will one day also be available to him.

What is often called »enlightenment«—either a temporary or permanent state—is latent for souls on the last steps of this cycle. It can happen at any time now. And when we say at any time, this means that a soul in this stage of its development will be able to view, without the use of any so-called enlightenment-inducing methods, the glowing brightness of its own perfection without being blinded by that vision. It will afterwards never be the same and, in most cases, will not sense any great desire to further inhabit a body. But it can happen that depending on the duties assigned to a soul by its Soul Family, a certain amount of time must still be spent in the actual body in order to spread that glow and to allow others access to it. However this happens, the essential cannot be communicated. But the ultimate knowledge of what has been viewed and recognized as enlightenment, can be, as best as possible, described and taught. If such an experience as enlightenment should occur before the last life, before the seventh step of development in the last cycle, this doesn't shorten the cycle of incarnations as many believe, because the sixth and seventh steps have their own indispensible qualities and must be experienced. They pursue goals and offer insights or lessons of love which are independent of the aforementioned enlightenment. They must be lived. A completion of any incarnation circle is not dependent on the temporary realization of the AllOne, and also in no way on the final resolution of all karmic debts. It will only be concluded when a capacity for love in an all-encompassing way is achieved, sensed, experienced and lived. And since love is experienced until the very end in contact, and in intimacy, with other embodied souls, it is necessary until the final moment in time for an Old Soul to be prepared for encounters which can provide it what it can't achieve with its own powers since that isn't possible in the physical world.

Several advanced lost civilizations were created by Mature and Old Souls. Included among these were the Megalithic and Egyptian cultures. While telling you this, we caution you against equating technical and impressive intellectual achievements principally with a high number of Old Souls. The above-mentioned cultures had populations made up of about 70% of Old Souls but the actual technically-brilliant achievements were made by the smaller number of Young and Mature Souls. For, as you've learned, Old Souls care little about external things. They no longer desire to influence the world, to create huge building structures or canalization systems. They don't need the temples as places for adoration. But they realize the need of Younger Souls for places of worship and can see to it that these needs are fulfilled in the very best way. They do want to put at the disposal of those who are still working hard, who desire to make an impact on the material world and who struggle with their problems, their experienced intellectual potency, their transpersonal contacts, their inspiration and their spiritual wisdom. In such a way they even make life on earth more comfortable for themselves. You often ask yourself how something like the Pyramids could possibly be constructed if not by aliens or half-gods. We assure you, it is possible for humans and it isn't difficult, but must remain unimaginable until the number of Old Souls on your planet surpasses 50 %. And when individual nations or peoples again reach a high proportion of Old Souls, a completely different potential will be opened which hasn't been available for thousands of years.

B. The Two States of Being

Energy 6

The Transpersonal Soul

When almost all members of a Soul Family have completed their path and the majority of this family is now forever in the non-bodily dimension, it can happen that the united energy, which is in the third territory of the Astral World, will take the opportunity to use a body to again manifest itself, not as an individual soul but with the united and familiar power of many hundred souls. As a collective, it then occupies the body of a soul sibling who has just completed its last incarnation, that is, the seventh stage of the Old Cycle. This very rare phenomenon represents the archetypical energy of the Priest's Soul Role. Its principle is consolation.

Although this only occurs under exceptional circumstances, it is the way in which a meaningful part of soul development may be realized. The Transpersonal Soul is no »normal« person, it is not even »human« in a strict sense. It is the combination of one human body and several hundred individual souls inhabiting it. Freed from the five physical soul cycles open to all souls and all bodies, here is a soul community, which as a rule doesn't seek anything other than to return from the Astral World in order, because of a special love, to help a particular soul sibling in its development. This Transpersonal Soul is capable of unusual deeds in the physical world. There will usually be no more than five or ten such newly-ensouled bodies in the world, who, each in his own way, take an Old Soul under their wing. This soul may be from the same Soul Family or a related soul from the same Soul Tribe.

Regarding the Transperonal Ensoulment one can no longer speak of an incarnation Cycle as before, since the manifestation of such a collective soul power does not extend over a number of lives. It is not even a reincarnation in the strictest sense. One should therefore be cautious in using the term »life« for this particular being, since the soul-collective which occupies the dead body of a soul sibling the very second after he completed his in-carnations, fills this body with a vibration and a new life which has little in common with that of an individual soul.

To its fellow men it appears that here is a person who was deathly ill and who, through a miracle, recovers, but who appears to be incomprehensibly changed. This person you had known before is totally transformed. What has occured in reality is the unobserved death and the unobserved occupation of one and the same body by a new group of kindred souls. This often occurs at night, when it's not noticed by relatives.

You are familiar with the occupation of a body by a soul only in connection with a newly born body. If following the departure of the soul an adult or old body is suddenly filled with the power of its whole Soul Family, the charisma is correspondingly altered. You'll probably think that the personality is now different. We point out, however, that following such a transformation, that body no longer has a personality as it once did. The personal power seems to be immensely strengthened, but in reality it has disappeared. The newly-ensouled body is surrounded by a strange radiance and light which almost everyone can perceive.

Transpersonal Souls possess the highest sensitivity imaginable. They mostly perform a teaching activity which no longer is tied to words and mental content, but results from a direct energetic transference. Only a few fearless Old Souls come near them since most people find this unusual energy field neither attractive, and aren't drawn to it, nor can they profit from it. Adepts who surround the teacher, mostly siblings from the same Soul Family, build an energy circle around that center of power, something which stops unsuitable »spiritual tourists« from being touched by that overwhelming yet delicate energy field. Others feel fearful, alienated and irritated by the field and develop resistance or enmity while confronted with something they don't understand, and they are not to be blamed for it.

But those who are touched are able to transfer and transform their knowledge and feelings into words and teachings. But they must rarefy and purify their extraordinary experience in order to make them understandable.

The Transpersonal Souls serve at the same time to show small groups of eager individuals the last possibilities of opening and merging under physical conditions with the AllOne, and at the same time to allay their natural fear of the disembodied regions which await them after their last incarnation. Although the desire to leave the body behind for the last time is overwhelming for very Old Souls, a nameless fear arises at the same time at the prospect of leaving behind a form of existence which it has experienced and often enjoyed over many lives and many thousands of years. Since the soul siblings who are in the Astral World have already made this leap into the void, they can show and prove to their siblings who are still in the body that, while their form of existence changes, they don't cease to exist. In this way consolation takes place. The priestly energy around Transpersonal Souls allows them to be perceived as truly holy men or women, when in fact they are no longer human.

Energy 7

The Transliminal Soul

Another rare soul manifestation unites not the Astral World, but the Causal World with your Physical World in a powerful, unbelievably rich and effective way. It only seldom occurs in the course of the universal development history of Souls. Transliminal Souls are teachers and leaders of entire Soul Nations. This phenomenon concerns not only one, but many disembodied, reunited Soul Families who are now existing in the Causal World but who, out of a love for themselves and for humans, decide to inhabit the dying body of an Old Soul who has finished his last incarnation. His individual soul moves on to the Astral World where it belongs and joins his own Soul Family. But a new type of ensoulment takes place. It differs from that of the Transpersonal Soul in that it is not members of one's own Soul Family who occupy the dead body, but more highly-developed entities unknown to the departed soul. These entities of several thousand once human souls are unable to act, lead and influence on the planet earth without a mortal frame which can accomodate their total energy. For high energies in a human form lessen the fear of transformation in »normal« humans. This is the archetypical energy of the King's Soul Role. Its principle is leadership.

Transliminal Souls, who can cross over all barriers and know no limits, manifest themselves in various epochs. This seldom happens and only when it is absolutely neccessary for the spiritual development of large groups of souls. While Transpersonal Souls help assist the transition of large groups of souls from one Soul Cycle to another, for example from the Young Cycle to the Mature Cycle, an association of Transliminal Souls in a seemingly human body uses all its strength to assist. Especially whenever a legion of Old Souls attempts to make the big leap into the final, disembodied region. This happens only once about every two thousand years.

This is not a life form but an ensoulment of a former living body by a Causal entity of at least seven thousand Souls. This also means that Transliminal Souls are freed from the usual limitations that apply to humans who are inhabited by an individual soul. The body of the Transliminal Souls consists of flesh and blood as before: the heart beats, the eyes see, the mouth speaks. But this body is neither vulnerable nor mortal. It doesn't age, it knows no sexual needs, it must neither partake of nourishment nor eliminate. It's function consists solely of providing guidance when legions of Souls have lost orientation. They bring about an immense energetic change in all people who see it, touch it and listen to it or even hear of it even hundreds of years after its appearance on earth.

The ability of such a super-human body, newly-ensouled by the powers of the Causal World, also consists of being able to materialize and dematerialize at will, for the Causal World is freed from the laws of time and space. Such a body can appear at any place on earth, as long as this is considered necessary and helpful, but will not be visible to all people. Only those who possess an energy structure which enables them to make contact with the overwhelming energy of the Transliminal Soul will be able to recognize the stunning soul force which is present in this body. To all others it must remain camouflaged, as it would cause their energy system to fuse.

This process represents a great sacrifice for the Soul Family of the person who has just died, since it prevents it from transformation into the Causal World of consciousness. It must remain on the third territory of the Astral Plane for an indefinite period. But this sacrifice is made out of love for the whole humanity and the AllOne. The soul of the departed one is transformed, but his family cannot complete its final reunification in order to, with increased energy frequencies, cross over into the Causal World, because the reunification of the Soul Family can't take place before the last soul takes final leave of its body forever and has broken all connections with its last incarnation. All further development processes must wait. These last, after the final incarnation of a soul fragment, longer than between individual lives, since once more the whole course of all past incarnations is evaluated. Moreover, when the last fragment has completed its final incarnation, the Soul Family wants to study, observe and understand everything that has occurred to all its siblings during the course of all their incarnations and the meaning it all conveyed, the love that was experienced, the insight that was gained. This takes longer than the planning and clarification between lives.

The whole course of incarnations must be evaluated. The experiences must be integrated. And as long as the last soul fragment is in some way attached to its body, this isn't possible. When you as humans want to describe the greatest expression of awareness in a human body, you refer to Buddha-awareness or Christ-like-awareness or a Krishna-awareness, and these concepts describe very impressively what the Transliminal Soul displays. You should always make a clear distinction, for example, between Siddharta, the person, and the mortal frame of this person which was occupied by a Transliminal Soul, just as you should differentiate between Krishna, the person, and the Krishna-awareness, or between Jesus and Christ. But when you as a normal human being try to attain this same type of awareness, you'll inevitably run up against the limits of your possibilities as incarnated individual souls. You'll certainly find reverent joy in the idea of surpassing those limits, and maybe this longing will please your ego. But it's more important to us to tell you that those of you who now live on the planet earth, are being touched by the awareness of a Transliminal Soul and will experience that influence even when you don't realize it.

Transliminal souls choose an embodiment in order to directly raise the awareness level of the entire population of a planet. And since this is an energetic occurence, it can't be undone or cancelled. This always happens when a large proportion of the earth's population of Old Souls departs from the planet and thus a new soul era begins. The Infant Soul fragments which are now newly dispersed on earth don't begin their path of awareness at the same place as the previous wave of ensoulment, but at a place where the Transliminal Souls have created suitable conditions the new fragments will need for the coming ten thousand years of their incarnation cycle.

It makes a considerable difference if an Infant Soul began its path fifty thousand or twenty thousand or ten thousand years ago. The planetary and cultural conditions it came across will have been formed and prepared by many other Souls. The myriads of incarnated and then excarnated Soul Families have done their work on the planet. Each fragment has made its contribution so that awareness and love can develop and experience is gathered. Therefore, it's important to understand that what has been created in former times is not lost but forms a basis and will be a benefit for all those who are beginning their path and come after you.

Development Stages

⑤
5th Stage
I become restless

②
2nd Stage
I seek stability

Expression Level

⑥
6th Stage
I need peace and harmony

①
1st Stage
I gather new courage

Inspiration Level

⑦
7th Stage
I apply what I've learned

③
3rd Stage
I become active

Action Level

④
4th Stage
I reap the fruit

Assimilation Level

The Seven Stages of Development

Each of the five Cycles of Soul Development in the body consists of seven Stages of development. Development happens by some inherent necessity just as the program for the entire circle of incarnations is prescribed by necessity. Souls essentially follow the same law as plants or bodies. An oakling develops from an acorn and then inexorably into a fully grown tree. Eventually it dies. It cannot choose to become a rose or a dog. In the same way souls develop from the first stage of the Infant Cycle to the seventh stage of the Old Cycle. We compare these five times seven stages to a biological-genetic program of a plant or a living being which follows its path from its creation or procreation until its natural death, from the first cell division until dissolution. This occurs without any special effort or hard work, without constant self-awareness. The path leads on its own to an increased ability to love and to more awareness. This is the goal, to experience forms of love and awareness unknown in the Astral World and enrich the AllOne by this experience gained during physical existence. This is the purpose and the sense of human lives.

Every stage of development takes a minimum of two lives, but also often three or four. The soul remains in one stage until it has had all the experiences which mark this stage, until it has experienced the corresponding fear and has conquered it, until it has developed the awareness structure appropriate to this stage and fulfilled the duties and tasks that, together with its soul siblings, it planned for this section of life.

In each new Cycle the soul begins again from the first Stage. The first Stage of the Infant Soul, of the Child Soul, Young Soul, Mature Soul and

Old Soul have something in common. It feels unsure, weak and helpless after having left behind the astral homestead or conquered the seventh stage of the previous Cycle with its security and fullness, with its satisfaction and fulfillment. None of the thirty-five steps may be avoided or passed over. Whoever pursues a Goal of Acceleration in one Stage will feel a natural impulse to slow down in the next Stage. The Stages are subject to a pulsating rotation between extroversion and introversion. The Stages 1, 3, 5 and 7, the uneven ordinal numbers, are clearly aimed more at the outside world, the contact with active life, than are the Stages 2, 4 and 6, which are dedicated to gathering new strength, integration and overcoming.

A transition from one Stage to another, from 7 to 1, from 3 to 4, from 5 to 6, rarely occurs during an incarnation. This happens usually in the Astral World. The precondition for crossing over to the next Stage of Development is always a phase of reflection and assessment combined with insight, a desire for change, a great strain and consequent relaxation. Concretely, it can be noticed that a change from one Stage to the next is usually accompanied by a seemingly overwhelming life crisis, by severe illness, coma, loss, pain, a feeling of unbearable meaninglessness, abject depression and anguish. In this transitional period it seems there is nothing more to justify continuing to live life the way it was. Souls seek to avoid this unhappy experience, but once in an incarnation cycle it may be appropriate.

The transition to the next Stage of Development can be compared to going through a wall of fire with the consequent loss of skin. A person who, during his earthly incarnation, moves from one Stage to the next, after some years, when the »skin« has healed, feels greatly changed and as if he had been reborn. After such a crisis a great sensitivity at first develops in view of the massive changes in the energy vibrations since the transition is, in the first place, a change of frequency, and the body must acclimate itself slowly and carefully to the new vibration. Therefore, most souls prefer to complete their initiation into the new Stage in the Astral world. It's easier there to overcome the unaccustomed vibration frequency. The disembodied soul siblings help draw a balance and other astral authorities assist in gaining insight.

Soul fragments take as much time and space as they need in order to understand each individual Stage, to gather the planned experiences, and to anchor themselves in the insight achieved. That's the reason why there's such a difference in the number of individual incarnations in the entire five cycles with their seven stages. Some need 80 lives to reach the final Stage, some 110. There is no pushing, no pulling and no need for haste. In view of the entire incarnation cycle of some ten thousand years on earth, no Soul is in a hurry.

A soul while out of body between lives has little fear but great freedom and natural inner determination in persisting on its own individual path. The soul siblings are naturally and lovingly ready not only to wait, but to support the unusual development of each fragment until everything has been experienced and all possibilities have been explored.

Each of the seven Development Stages within an individual Soul Age has a motto.

Energy I

Stage I

Motto: I gather new courage

Wherever you are, whether you are in your first incarnation or have just crossed over the last great hurdle which allows you to pass from the Mature Soul Age to the Age of the Old Soul, it's good to realize that all beginnings are difficult. Each of you needs an especially great deal of courage on the first Stage of the new Development phase. It takes so much courage to incarnate in a human body for the first time, to confront the difficulties of incarnation and to accept them. It's frightening for everyone to confront new soul challenges, and at the beginning of a new Stage—whether it is the transition from a Child Soul to a Young Soul or if a Mature Soul is entering the Old Soul Stage—the soul needs a corresponding amount of time in order to become accustomed to its yet unfamiliar energy world. On the first stage of this new segment of lives, it will often long for previous conditions. It will feel torn between all that's left behind in the previous seventh Stage but now no longer appropriate, and that which lies before it and about which it knows nothing except that it is new and will be difficult, although interesting.

You can compare this stage to the time you began a new job and faced new duties without knowing what exactly was expected of you. You have a general conception; you have many plans and made promises. But you don't know if you're really prepared for what awaits you, whether you'll succeed, and whether what you've planned will actually occur. And sometimes you'll feel insecure and wish that you had never given up your old position. It represented security for you even though it was a little boring. It no longer gave you great happiness but you knew what you were doing. The old methods of behavior which you acquired over a long period of time are still partially valid but can't really be relied on anymore.

You gather new courage and must tell yourself every day: »It will work out somehow, I'll manage.« This phase is of special importance for it sets the base for further developments. Nothing is wasted, not even a moment of doubt or anguish, but much will be created for which you are now setting the course.

Consider once more the example of the new job. The conditions which you create today will have to serve you for a long time. The contacts which you make in the first few days will leave lasting impressions. The new Soul Age will now become for you a workplace for many years and lives to come. It will be beneficial for you to take time to look around and investigate the various areas of responsibility. And everything that you now begin leisurely and with consideration, with joyful courage and prudence, will also lead to a happy ending.

Each soul, therefore, takes more lives for its first Development Stage in the new cycle than for the following ones. On the average, it takes two or three lives to complete a stage, but four or even five lives may be appropriate in the first stage. These can be brief or long lives. It doesn't depend on the number of years, but rather on the quality and the relaxed period of insight one spends after each life on the Astral Plane in order to become familiar with this new period of the first Stage of your new Soul Age. This Stage has the archetypical energy of the Helper/Healer. Its characteristic is feeling helpless and seeking help.

Energy 2

Stage 2

Motto: I seek stability

While the first stage was a time of insecurity in which you were confronted with many new things, since you had to become accustomed to a number of unknown factors, the second stage serves as a period of settling in the place which will now be your home. The most important purpose of the second Stage is the detailed work, the complex sounding out of your possibilities. It's all the same if you're a Young, Mature or Old Soul—the second stage provides the possibility of anchoring yourself or putting down roots. Only now will it be clear to you where you are and who you are. This will be much more obvious than in the first Stage. You'll have the first insight into the meaning of this new phase of lives and your willingnesss to remain here, to examine everything, increases. Your curiosity and interest in what is awaiting you will become even greater.

In this second Stage of Development, you have the feeling that you've arrived. While you're not yet at your final goal, at least you've reached a secure rest stop which allows you to have new experiences. You've arrived and now you begin to look around and to explore this new place. You've become accustomed in the meantime to the altered, higher energy condition. This is a result of the first Stage. Now you can make yourself at home.

The second Stage is a phase of peace following the turbulence of the first stage, which was marked by many set-backs in the area of awareness. This second Stage lets you become aware of tranquility and stability as potential benefits. We're not referring here to events or to relationships but only to the willingness of your awareness, no matter which Soul Age Cycle, to accept what must be learned in this Cycle. The acceptance of what is strived for will become greater and a person feels secure in his desires and needs.

The second Stage is usually not one of great turbulence. There's no place here for drama or tragic events. Grief, however, will play a bigger role. Grief means the ability to accept what is. To grieve doesn't mean to reject and should not be confused with resignation. Solidity, a resolve to be where and who one is, characterizes the second Stage. A feeling of loneliness, which marks the soul's experience at the beginning of the second stage, leads directly and indirectly to a new view of »others«. The soul will feel a new energy in its willingness to experience and shape oneself and the world. In the second Stage, a person abandons his infant-like egocentric attitude. He can now devote himself to »others«. The other person is a mirror, a fellow human being, he is understandable, close and identifiable. This ability will be solidified at the beginning of the third Stage.

A further factor, something unpredictable, will enter into the equation. No matter which Soul Cycle, whoever is in the second Stage will have to spend two to three lives developing ways and means in order to create security and inner stability, for he must prepare for the third, very turbulent stage. Compared to the previous Stage, it is mainly toward the end of the second Stage when you come into contact with fear and concern increases over the slight Development fever you observe. A vague but exciting notion of what is awaiting you will be there. Your Soul decides to take appropriate measures to clarify your condition.

Your existence in this first stage of development can be compared to a permanent place of residence from which you can make trips to sights near or far away without losing your point of reference. You look around, you learn new things and meet new people without losing your trusted environment. You find new soul friends who are having similar experiences and with whom you can exchange views. You explore all the possibilities, the advantages and disadvantages, which your new inner residence provides.

The strong determination to remain where you are is decisive in this phase. For the security which your expression of will creates also opens up new inner perspectives. The second Stage is creative, for it corresponds to the archetypical energy of the Artist. Its principle is shaping and inventing. Only because you are surrounded by great tranquility are you capable of discerning the fine, almost imperceptible inner feeling of unease. You have a slight incarnation fever which serves as an indication that sooner or later you must seek the reason for this spiritual indisposition.

Energy 3

Stage 3

Motto: I become active

When a person is well-anchored in the second Stage and has created a foundation of contemplation, peace and stability, he is prepared on this basis to once again emerge and to risk advances in areas he hasn't encountered previously.

To return once more to the allegory of the work place: after a person has become acquainted with his new job and feels secure, he can introduce improvements not only in his narrower area but in the interest of the whole firm. He can invest, take risks, and because of the security of being solidly anchored, puts out his feelers in order to learn new things and experience adventures which can only be meaningful if he doesn't lose his footing but can positively integrate into his work what he has learned during his adventure.

The third Stage is characterized by a certain courageous lighthearted-ness, a multitude of interests. Many things will now be explored. Each life in this Stage is characterized by a large number of talents and abilities which are interweaved and connected to each other. Lives become risky adventures. This is a period of gathering impressions, a time of more or less careful ex-periments. This is also a time in which a Soul all too recklessly makes mis-takes in order to learn from them. It is understood how important it is to take real risks and to deal with the set-backs, the disappointments, the difficul-ties which ensue from a true risk. The third Stage is connected to the arche-typical energy of the Warrior, with all its characteristics. Its principle is fighting and winning.

Security doesn't mean much during this time. It only serves as a starting point to make experiments possible. Its only purpose is to provide a means to set out on adventurous journeys. These trips can have as their destination the outer or inner world, but the significance of the third Stage lies, in the first place, in integrating the security of the second Stage with the readiness to achieve something totally new, to conquer unexplored territories and to broaden one's horizon.

The third Stage is a phase of great excitement. It can be compared to what a person feels when he leaves his parental home for the first time and makes his first journey to a foreign country. He has never travelled alone before, he will experience everything possible. Existential loneliness will also appear for the first time in its clearest form and its creative powers will develop. Rapid advances, serious set-backs, the wave-like movements of fate and your own psychic sensitivity are now objects of your inner examination.

On this third Stage of Development many unexpected things occur to you. Victorious conquest of new artistic, industrial, scientific or spiritual fields can give way to utter failure and defeat. This Stage is highly agitated but on the whole successful. Creativity alternates with long phases of stagnation. If it weren't for this stagnation, you wouldn't be able to explore anything new. Many projects on a grand scale will be planned but not carried out. You now depend to an increased degree on the support of other souls and your incarnated soul siblings, for only through energetic cooperation can all the high-flying plans and the predominant projects of the solitary fragment be brought to fruition. The third Stage, therefore, also represents an opening to the outside world. The »I« and the »other« have, since the second Stage, been in a solid relationship, they are predictable and can be integrated without fear. The opening to the outside happens now because the soul fragment admits not only the »other« into its awareness, but also »them«, the chaotic, unknown collective of other souls even outside the Soul Family or Tribe connections. The solitary fragment draws together the collective power of many fellow men as well as the awareness and support of the Soul Family in his actions and inner processes.

The third Stage of every Cycle is characterized by a creative chaos. While you thought you had found yourself and your identity in the second Stage, all that will be put into question in the third Stage so that unforeseen and unpredictable events can occur, so that changes can take place which none of you would have consciously brought about. Chaos, disorderliness, unpredictability and adventurous excitement mark this phase. However, a long-term plan and a target are developing behind the foreground of these experiences which later, in the fourth Stage, will come to fruition.

Energy 4

Stage 4

Motto: I reap the fruit

The fourth Stage of every Soul Cycle symbolically shows a person as he returns from his adventurous travels and must again develop a sense of quiet security.

He will become peaceful and centered. The fourth Stage serves to assimilate all the impressions, to view all the pictures, to relate what he has experienced, to choose what he wishes to retain from all he has learned and to give shape to the varied visions which fill his spirit, to analyze and integrate them. It is like sorting photographs from an around the world trip after one's return home. The best will be stuck into an album.

This phase is marked by contentment over one's experiences and, at the same time, a joy over a safe arrival home and pleasure over the fact that nothing has been lost and now much that is new has been added to his life. He finds what was tried and true in former Stages has not been lost but has been enriched.

The fourth Stage is one of reflection and of contemplation, a time of passing on knowledge, impressions and experiences. Those who are in the fourth Stage can now, to a significant degree, be helpful in motivating others to undertake a trip to unknown regions.

Just as a person in the fourth Stage can be a great friend and healer for those on the second stage, who aren't yet prepared to make a great journey but are slowly approaching that third Stage, so can a person on the third Stage be especially helpful to those on the first stage. The Soul in the fourth Stage has so much to relate, has understood so much of the laws of his Soul

Age Cycle and of all that he has experienced, that he can be, without verbosity, an instructive example for those who plan the same things he has already done and only need some encouragement.

The conditions of the fourth Stage are more calming rather than excit-ing. Introspection is more important than contact with the masses, although contact is of great significance since without it people on the fourth stage would not succeed in communicating and passing on their experiences. But contact takes on completely new forms. There is the possibility of teaching, the possibility of supporting, the gaining of insight in every respect. And no one in this stage will want to withdraw from these duties no matter what their life circumstances are or what kind of psychological or matrix structure they have. This Stage has all the characteristics of the Scholar's energy. Its principle is learning and teaching.

People on the fourth Stage of each Soul Cycle experience for the first time moments of true satisfaction and fulfillment, for they reap the fruits of their spirit of enterprise and their courageous exploratory trips of the third Stage. They know what they have, they settle down for a cosy winter time with the barns full of provisions, and they realize that they have successfully con-cluded an exciting and sometimes dangerous journey. While they are resting, remembering, integrating and enjoying, they are teaching people what they know. They prepare for further trips which will lead to still more unknown and unexplored areas.

Energy 5

Stage 5

Motto: I become restless

On the fourth developmental Stage of his long spiritual journey, the person returned home in order to rest and tell others of his experiences. The fifth Stage now allows him to make new and more daring plans. He realizes that he hasn't seen everything, although his journey was exciting. Now he finds out from others, who have already explored inner places, which although unknown to him, appear very attractive, that it is in no way impossible to reach those mountain realms and that it will take some effort.

And a person on the fifth Development Stage of each Soul Cycle becomes restless. His soul longs for movement, for an awakening, for fresh air and exercise. However, he's not sure whether he wants to again take on the stresses which he remembers very well. Therefore, he is interested to a high degree how to avoid unnecessary waste of energy and also motivated to question everyone who has been up there, how he should prepare for his new journey, what he needs, what his inner and external provisions should be. Above all, he is curious to find out what he can experience there.

The fifth Stage makes one curious and eager for knowledge. It can be compared to the time in which a person plans an adventurous hike in the Himalaya or an exploration trip to some indigenous tribe in the Amazona region. The future traveller not only looks through travel brochures but carefully studies customs of every area he wishes to explore, learns the language, gets vaccinations, and studies the history of the people and the geography of the land. Such preparations take a great deal of time, for if all these things are learned only from books and not from questioning those who have already been there, the theoretical knowledge will not be well-anchored. Communication is the principle of this Stage; its basic energy is that of the Sage.

Nevertheless, a person on the fifth Development Stage has a strong tendency at first to learn everything second-hand. He reads a great deal about the spiritual experiences of others. He studies the writings of the masters and enlightened teachers who have explored that inner world. Only toward the end of the fifth Stage is the soul prepared for direct contact with a lively, fresh personal impression from this region.

Then he is suddenly seized by the desire to travel and the lengthy, careful preparations encourage him to risk a trip. He decides to do what he has long wanted to do and he begins to cast aside all doubts, decides to take one risk after another, plunges in and lets himself be carried away by a jumble of events. The initital caution is transformed into recklessness. Something absolutely new must happen. He realizes that his increasing unease and restlessness can only be calmed by great activity. It's now or never!

Perhaps someone who's been an accountant in a small firm until his fifty-third year, decides to go to an Indian ashram to spend the rest of his life there, or a woman abandons her uneventful life as a widowed housewife in order to become a committed politician. What it is that brings the personalities out of their shell and leads them to a storm of applause, commitment and a life of public dedication depends on the Soul Age Cycle. It's characteristic, however, that after many years of shy, retired behavior one no longer shows any restraint, and the dynamic of the fifth Stage will often be reflected in a surprising outcome. A Soul in the fifth Stage of any Cycle will be a person who spends more than half of his life in seclusion and then suddenly will sense an unbelievable strength within himself noticeable in all areas of his life.

Here we also see spinsters and bachelors who spend many years alone and, at an advanced age, begin an overwhelmingly deep and strong relationship which often has a karmic background. We also find those who late in life become involved in artistic activities, who begin a new profession, who, as pensioners, attend a university and happen to make important discoveries at an age when their peers play golf, or settle in foreign countries in order to experience the insecurity of adventure.

These people also serve as examples to their soul juniors in this Stage. They have a stimulating effect, even if they upset many people. But they're not really conscious of their role. They're only surprised that those who have less courage or whose souls are in a phase of rest, admire them. They themselves are motivated by a strong, inner power and don't realize that they're doing something unusual which challenges others to imitate them.

People on Stage five of every Soul Age are strong individualists. They withdraw from all customs and activities of the masses. They desire something different, something new, but for a long time don't dare to make their dreams come true. This late dynamic corresponds to the restlessness which paves the way for it. These souls find happiness late in life and experience their lives as clearly divided into two parts in their energy perception. It's as if they were two people in one and the same life. They barely recognize themselves when they arrive in the second phase of their development.

They're not willing, after their leap into the unknown, to return to those who don't dare take this risk. Therefore, they often break with their past and from those whom they knew in the first, more quiet and conventional phase of their development on the fifth Stage. But it's noticeable that after the great leap, which is both exciting and calming at the same time, they start having many contacts with those whom they met lifetimes ago, during the third Stage of their Soul Development.

The fifth Stage is filled with the power of restrained expectation and released tension. The liberation after a long, tedious period of waiting for something to happen is unbelievable and has a long-term effect. Much which seemed to have been postponed forever will now be accomplished. And since the fifth Stage, when it's successfully dealt with, takes a lot of energy and leads to a certain natural weariness of the soul, a new phase of retreat and contemplation follows in the sixth Stage.

Energy 6

Stage 6

Motto: I need peace and harmony

There is calm before the storm, and there is calm after the storm. There is tension and anxious expectation before the tempest. Then, however, there is great relaxation even if the sensations are still in turmoil from the memories and feelings which can gradually turn into a lasting state of harmony. The sixth Stage of every Soul Age Cycle is comparable to this silence after the tornado, while the fifth Stage in the first phase describes the tension before the great leap and the turmoil which must naturally accompany it.

The sixth Stage is marked by a strong feeling of relief over all that has been achieved. This is a time of harvest, not in the sense that harvesting means a great deal of work, but rather that a person can truly rejoice over the fruits of his soul's accomplishments. A time of rejoicing can't be reconciled with constant threats. Nobody's capable of both relaxing and being tense. But it's necessary at this Stage of Development to really learn how to relax and trust and forget about the past in general. Therefore, many people now turn to meditation, whether they be guided or not, techniques which are promoted by foreign traditions or fashionable gurus or which belong to one's own native traditions.

Meditation in every sense, even spontaneous contemplation, fills a soul with peace and harmony on the sixth Stage. This can be an hour spent on a bench at the edge of the woods, a concert, sitting at the bedside of a sick child, as well as a concentrated form of physical activity which leads the mind to a certain train of thought and helps prevent jumping from one thought to another. There is also a large number of meditations practised by many whose education or character seldom or never allows a moment of peace in the course of a day. We're not referring to people in the west but to human beings in general. Just as an African farmer, who must work hard from dawn to dusk in order to earn a living, is in meditation either when he walks behind his oxen and plows his field or when he is sitting by the fire at night, it is possible for others on the planet to carry out certain rituals which are accompanied by meditative arousal and a subsequent relaxation.

A person who's reached the sixth Stage of any Soul Age will prefer to incarnate in cultures and countries which offer a traditional, secure possibility for a contemplative life. For example, this might be an area where eskimos live, or areas far from large cities, where there is much natural harmony with the surrounding environment, climate and agriculture, in places where families still live together in large well-ordered clans and who resolve conflicts in such a way that not all responsibility or cares are placed on one individual.

For conflicts don't please a person who is in the sixth Stage of his soul's development. He can't always avoid them, however he shuns them since he's already experienced enough of them during most lives in his particular incarnation cycle. He now needs a harmony which is more than superficial. Therefore, he'll prefer to choose ways of living which will cause comparatively little friction with his fellow men. Being solitary, he often prefers to remain single to avoid being confronted with the conflicts of a partnership. This is not a deficiency or a sign of neurotic behavior in this Stage, but rather a deep, inner need. Nothing is more important to a person on the sixth Stage than to find true harmony within himself which in turn creates harmony with nature. This also in no way means that a person lives without contact or human companionship but it is pleasant for him not to have constant stressful contact or to lose himself in someone else since in this phase he has no interest in solving problems or in being confronted with considerable inner efforts.

If we refer to the all-encompassing image of a life journey comprising many incarnations, then this is a period in which a person sets out on a prolonged vacation which at first is devoted to rest. This isn't a time to learn a great many new things, to go sight-seeing, to become excited or to seek adventures. The purpose of this vacation is rather to gather strength and regain the spiritual health which was either exhausted or lost during the stress of the great leap forward in the fifth Stage. Such a vacation, free from all the tension and rigours which the vicissitudes of life on other Development Stages so abundantly provided, is a well-deserved reward for all the trouble the soul took on when it applied its ultimate power for the leap in the fifth Stage and jumped over the precipice of its own fear-possessed self.

A vacation entails much happiness. As long as a partnership or marriage offers in the first place such harmony, it will in no way be spurned. But a person on the sixth Stage will either separate from his partner if the relationship becomes too difficult, or he'll look for a partner who also seeks lack of conflict without withdrawing from a partnership entirely. The work place of a person on the sixth Stage, regardless of the culture in which he lives, should provide him a correspondingly peaceful frame since he will feel ill at ease if he is presented with too much stress. The inner vacation serves the purpose of opening up to higher inspiration. Imagine a person falling asleep one evening on a beach and having an important dream. In this same way the inspirational forces of the Astral and Causal Worlds of conciousness can reach a soul in the sixth Stage of Development whenever he's in harmony with himself and his environment. This is the archetypical energy of the Priest's Soul Role. Its principle is consolation.

Of course the sixth Stage also has a troubling side. A person who seeks and really needs peace and harmony often allows himself to be put under pressure and then loses sight of his goal. He often becomes the supposed victim of all who seem to want something from him which he neither wants to offer nor to fulfill. However, one can observe that he finds himself in a discrepancy between his own needs and that which his psyche has created based on personal ideals or social norms.

So a person in the sixth Stage of his Development may grow up in a milieu in which diligence and an unremitting readiness to be active are highly valued. This person then feels forced to deny himself and his own needs for peace and quiet harmony in order to please others. A person on this sixth Stage is also tired of being subjugated to the requirements of his religious upbringing. But he happily says his prayers in order not to be viewed as a luke-warm agnostic whose convictions don't mean much, because he doesn't want to be blamed by his community.

The person on the sixth Stage also seeks inner peace and harmony. This means that the requirements of his world view and faith are always created anew and must meet the demands of the present situation. He is, therefore, a person whose spirit and psyche appear from time to time flexible as well as vacillating. This adaptability is one means of ensuring inner balance.

When it isn't possible in any other way to achieve this peace and harmony, a person in the sixth Stage is prepared to spend a great deal of time alone. The figure of a hermit can be found in all cultures and societies. This may be a scientist who works in a field which doesn't depend on the presence of a team, as well as a single-handed yachtsman who spends weeks and months alone on the sea. A coal-miner who lives in his forest cabin or an old woman who only leaves her apartment to shop and doesn't miss the company of her fellow men can also be people on the sixth Stage. A hermit's life is not always motivated by religious belief. He is simply possessed by the desire to be left alone, to be left in peace, to find an inner harmony which would only be disturbed by others.

This whole phase, which often lasts a little longer than other stages, serves to work through, register and digest all the excitement that the first five Stages of experience and development with their increased activity brought about. The sixth Stage with its entire spiritual development can be compared to a month's vacation following eleven months of hard work.

Only when the restful phase with its reflective and calming processes is completed, can the seventh Stage be tackled. This last Stage has an integrating ability to utilize all that which was learned during the long, work-filled journey of the Cycle and to apply the knowledge from the sovereignty of understanding, practice and experience.

Energy 7

Stage 7

Motto: I apply what I've learned

The seventh Stage of each Soul Development cycle is again one of labor. Now the time has come in which the application of what has been learned is no longer viewed as a difficulty, duty or challenge, but rather a fervent desire to apply all the skills and abilities developed in former times and to create something which before now was achieved with difficulty and could only be completed imperfectly.

The seventh Stage is one of activity. But its work is not that of an intern or journeyman but that of a master craftsman. He who masters his trade and what he can create or influence, not only in a material sense but also intellectually, approaches his work in a relaxed way, and the result is superb.

The master craftsman works with ease and sovereignty since he masters his material as well as his instruments and theory and since he also unites an idea with his work, which develops independently. This is the fruit of his training, his efforts, but this is also the fruit of his experience and his now-achieved security. Security creates freedom from fear.

This is trust in the wealth of one's own experiences, a self-confidence which can also tolerate insecurity, which remains flexible rather than rigidly maintaining the status quo. It enjoys a security which is pleasureable and corresponds to the delight of a person who takes swimming lessons in a pool, develops trust in being carried by the water and will soon swim in the sea and high waves. The person may withdraw from the threatening elements for a time but will then gather new courage to perfect his swimming ability, take more lessons and finally will develop a technique which allows him to move in the water like a fish. He's confident of his ability to swim and no longer fears drowning unless he encounters something with naturally hinders his ability.

The seventh Stage is characterized by applying what the soul has learned. And it has learned so much, during a Soul Age Cycle of more than two thousand years and more than 15 lives. It has so much at its disposal both in content, meaning and structure that, from abundancy and often over-abundancy, it doesn't even know what to choose at first in order to experience the joy of that which has been achieved, the joy of mastery. The wealth of possibilities is at first confusing. So many talents are apparent, so many skills, so many proved and tested aspects of one's own being, that confusion arises which results not from a fear of being incapable but from the realization of being capable of everything.

The life of someone who is in the seventh Stage of his Development Cycle is characterized by abundance. Such a person will first have to sound out his many and diverse talents, also his ability to judge people and to overcome problems, before he makes a choice. It should be a consolation to him to know that he will have several lives to exhaust the wealth of possibilities and their application. And it would be a shame if he capitulated before the multitude of treasures available to him in order to avoid making a decision about which experience to choose and to utilize.

One person may choose to unite music, mathematics and meditation, another will combine an acting career with leadership and the exercise of power through his examples. Another will finally lead a life of leisure in order to devote himself to the upbringing of children, reading and writing, which he couldn't reconcile with each other until this time.

We've only mentioned the combination of three abilities here, but often it can be ten, twenty or more. It's characteristic in the seventh Stage that a synthesis and integration are strived for. Previous tensions in former lives full of conflicts are transformed into an enriched conflict-free positive expectation which allows originally disparate elements to be happily combined. It's not a renunciation but a combining of previously conflicting and contradictory desires which characterizes this Stage.

The need to combine many things with each other can lead to the behavior of a jack of all trades, producing a person trying to do too many things at once, with the superficiality which accompanies the feeling of elation of those who can do everything. We've already spoken of the necessity of making a choice, but choice assumes the responsible examination of one's own possibilities which is not dominated by the fear of renouncing or missing out on something.

Whoever is plagued by the Chief Characteristics of Greed or Impatience will find it more difficult to chose from the wealth of his potential than someone who is stubborn and is anyway scared of what is too insecure. A self-deprecating person, on the other hand, doesn't make enough use of all that is offered and given potential. Those who are arrogant use their abilities as a weapon against others and against themselves. The Martyr overworks since he wants to prove to himself and others that he is the most selfless, the person who practices Self-Sabotage does everything he can but avoids the liveliness in his actions and the joyfulness.

So it's clear that the Chief Characteristic of fear colors or clouds the ability to apply what has been learned and needs to be applied. This inner conflict is constantly present in this Stage. The seventh Stage brings to completion the soul's Development Cycle and therefore it is concerned not only with abilities, talents and experiences in the outer world but above all with the learning process relating to love and fear of a given cycle. The seventh Stage is the one which allows a person more intensively to deal with love and fear, to admit the wealth of his reactions.

Problems will be resolved easily. The soul now knows all the advantages and dangers which the current cycle presents, he realizes that love and fear arise out of certain attitudes and behavior. And while the person is not free of difficulties which confront him again in this stage, he now deals with them in a different way because he is in a phase in which he isn't entangled but has achieved a beautiful clarity and awareness.

He is more aware of his possibilities and limitations than those who are in other Stages. He applies what he has learned during the whole cycle and finds his fulfillment therein. He knows what he knows, and is more or less painfully aware of what he doesn't know. Because of his experience he appears to himself and to others reliable, self-confident and peaceful-not because he has withdrawn or constantly strives for harmony, as in his lives in Stage 6, but because he's in a position to experience the ups and downs of life, the pain and joy, powerlessness and power without clinging to one pole or the other.

The contradictions which marked the first Stages are now gradually resolved. In the seventh Stage the soul and the person are in a position to recognize what connects and unites. Therefore, people now often have a broad overview and a sense of humor those in other stages aren't capable of having.

Distance and admittance, being close and far away, seclusion and the complete readiness to submit to the demands of life in human society-these are things which a person on the seventh Stage can unite within himself and sense with happiness how he himself becomes united. He does the work of a King. Everything he does for himself, he also does for the society of all men and all souls. There is no longer any separation here.

The seventh Stage ends each particular Soul Cycle. And when something draws to a close, one must say goodbye. Parting is always accompanied by melancholy and often sadness. Regardless which cycle comes to an end, the first, middle or last, the soul feels bound in love and gratitude to the past but also already strives for the future in the knowledge that it must move on. It can't linger. Its desire is irrevocably aimed at the exploration of new dimensions.

The Seven Developmental Themes of Mature Souls are:

Mature Stage 1: Experience freedom in dependency
Mature Stage 2: Forgive injustice to yourself and others
Mature Stage 3: Serve an unjust master loyally
Mature Stage 4: Renounce something essential out of love
Mature Stage 5: Entrust life and destiny to others
Mature Stage 6: Erase the barrier between guilt and innocence
Mature Stage 7: Recognize the potential and the limits of will-power

The Seven Developmental Themes of Old Souls are:

Old Stage 1: Act against conventional morals from inner conviction
Old Stage 2: Honestly admire yourself, dispense with the admiration
             of others
Old Stage 3: Combine precise introspection with active results
Old Stage 4: Unite your well-being with the welfare of the community
Old Stage 5: Follow a path unwaveringly without knowing where it leads
Old Stage 6: Impress by being, not by doing
Old Stage 7: Receive without giving, give without receiving.

The Seven Cosmic Energies

We use the comprehensive term »AllOne« as a name for the Godliness of all that is and in order to explain the seven cosmic basic energies of which it consists. Everything that is, is created from these seven basic energies. Together they create a unity. Although we differentiate between a material reality and a non-material, transcendent reality, all energies in both spheres are organized basically in these seven different elemental aspects which, taken together, again produce a whole.

The concept of energetic shaping, which we express through seven non-mathematical symbolic numbers, is of fundamental importance, for the principles which are linked to it will be found everywhere. The seven energetic basic principles shape the whole material and non-material world of experience and being. They determine the Soul Matrix of every single incarnated human just as they determine the cosmic order.

All numerological systems created by man claim to reveal a hidden truth, a secret lying deep beneath the revelation, but they reflect only the material reality, not the comprehensive transcendent reality. You'll find out more about the truth of transcendent reality in mythical and mystic traditions as well as sufficient proof of that which we want to tell you about the higher reality and its structures through the principle of the number seven.

This theoretical statement can only become concrete for you if you observe and experience the effects the seven different energies have on your own life and on the lives of others. In this respect, the MATRIX offers direct access.

The concept of the seven universal energies is of such central importance to us that we want to provide a simple, comprehensive introduction to it. These energies develop on various levels which, on their part, interact with each other. In order to make this clear we want to approach this on the level of the seven Soul Roles. We call them Healer/Helper (1), Artist (2), Warrior (3), Scholar (4), Sage (5), Priest (6) and King (7). But these are only words, words which attempt to express in human language the corresponding energies. Other human languages express the same energy through correspondingly different verbal concepts.

An example is provided by Energy 1: In some English speaking countries the word Healer has a high, almost holy connotation and reputation; in others it is quite the opposite—something dubious and unreliable, like a charlatan. As an Archetype and complementary energy to the Priest (6), the word and function of Healer is of course correct. Every primeval society has a place for this inherent role as for the other six. But when it comes to »being a Healer«, many people today prefer to employ the word and concept of Helper, although that noun is artificial and slightly pale and certainly does not denote an Archetype in the strictest sense. Basically, both are the same. Healers and Helpers as Soul Roles representing Energy 1 both heal the wounded in body and spirit. The English word Slave, though sometimes used in an archtypical sense for the Energy 1 Soul Role, is so revolting to people living in the 21st century that it must be discarded for psychological reasons.

On the level of Soul Roles the Archetype of the Healer/Helper expresses Energy 1. Further related Archetypes which express the same Energy 1 are: Self-deprecation, Delay, Reservation, Stoicism, an Emotional Center, an Infant Soul. We would like to provide some additional concepts which are helpful in understanding Energy 1: soft, caring, tender, harmonic, unifying, emotional, speechless, comprehensive, supportive, slow, simple, heartful, touching, unobtrusive, restrained, relaxed, healing, nurturing, receptive. A sky blue colour renders the characteristic of Energy 1.

The Archetype of the Artist represents Energy 2 on the level of Soul Roles. This is an intellectually-oriented person who likes to play with life. Other aspects of Energy 2 are: Self-Sabotage, Rejection, Caution, Skepticism, an Intellectual Center, a Child Soul. Vivid aspects of Energy 2 are: happy, witty, lively, playful, volatile, imaginative, pictorial, transcending, artistic, confrontational, mental, thoughtful, creative, aesthetic, exciting, original, lively, amusing. The colour of a yellow butterfly would correspond to this energy.

Energy 3 is represented on the level of Soul Roles through the Archetype of the Warrior. Other Archetypes with the energy 3 are: Martyrdom, Submission, Perseverance, Cynicism, a Sexual Center, a Young Soul. Concepts of Energy 3 are: powerful, enlivened, effective, energetic, vitalizing, defending, protective, convincing, focused, courageous, persevering, persistent, devoted, active, goal-oriented, loyal, candid, ready for action, direct. Blood red is a colour corresponding to this energy 3.

Energy 4 is expressed on the level of Soul Roles by the Archetype of the Scholar. Other Archetypes with the Energy 4 are: Stubbornness, Standstill, Observation, Pragmatism, an Instinctive Center, a Mature Soul. Suitable concepts for Energy 4 are: instructive, thorough, attentive, instinctive, knowledgeable, determined, clear, just, neutral, distanced, functional, at peace within oneself, observing, forming, practical, protective, orderly, balanced, pausing, experience-oriented. A colour corresponding to Energy 4 would be grass green.

Energy 5 is expressed on the level of Soul Roles by the Archetype of the Sage. Other Archetype aspects of Energy 5 are: Greed, Acceptance, Power, Idealism, a Spiritual Center, an Old Soul. Additional concepts for Energy 5 are: connecting, expressive, comprehensive, communicative, satisfied, goodly, idealistic, conciliatory, sociable, talkative, collective, authoritative, powerful, wise, comfortable, luxuriant, generous. Sunny yellow would be a colour corresponding to energy 5.

Energy 6 is expressed on the level of Soul Roles by the Archetype of the Priest. Further archetypical aspects of Energy 6 are: Arrogance, Acceleration, Passion, Spiritualism, an Ecstatic Center, Transpersonal Ensoulment. Concepts which express Energy 6 are: inspired, transcending, enthusiastic, trustful, quiet, serious, sensitive, uplifting, compassionate, vulnerable, charismatic, passionate, moving, comforting. Ocean blue is a colour that corresponds to this energy 6.

Energy 7 is represented on the level of the Soul Roles by the Archetype of the King. Other Archetype examples of Energy 7 are: Impatience, Dominance, Aggression, Realism, a Moving Center, a Transliminal Ensoulment. Suitable words to describe Energy 7 would be: dignified, courageous, sovereign, patient, perceptive, tireless, dynamic, far-reaching, structured, integrating, responsible, mobile, radiating. Purple is a colour corresponding to the energy 6.

After a little training, the Soul Pattern can be sensed by every person within himself and in his relations with others. But it's also easy to observe the seven basic energies in abstract areas: differing weather conditions, works of art, musical masterpieces, political moods, inventions and scientific developments as well as religions. Classic Buddhism, for instance, displays the balanced, almost scientific ordered structure of the scholarly Energy 4, Islam is governed by the active Warrior-Energy 3, Christianity has as its basis the charitable Healer/Helper-Energy 1, Hinduism mostly emanates the priestly Energy 6.

Your Individual MATRIX

An individual MATRIX describes the complete, personal, individual soul pattern or network of seven basic Archetypes which a soul assembles before any incarnation in order to adequately fulfill its goals, projects and desires for development.

Various goals require differing preparations. The SOUL MATRIX is the equipment to meaningfully master a certain life, promoting growth, knowledge, insight and love. The MATRIX is, at the same time, the incarnated soul's development plan.

The Soul Pattern is weaved anew each time. The loom and the threading, however, remain. The Soul Age can be compared to a loom. It is an unchanging, reliable instrument which, nevertheless, is subject to an aging process. The white threading is the Soul Role, which doesn't change no matter which pattern is chosen for a specific life. Colours and materials, the other five Archetypes, are ever new. They depend on the individual soul's plan, on certain necessities, on the soul's desire for experience and its ability to love.

Every human possesses a soul and therefore has a Soul Pattern or MATRIX. It is like a colourful garment, which is worn for the duration of an entire life and then removed when the soul again departs a body. The garment is placed into the astral closet because it is immensely precious. When you remember a previous life or through medium contacts, your past incarnation, it can be re-activated like a theatre costume.

A Soul Pattern consists of seven individual Archetypes, five of which can be chosen at will and combined with two predetermined fixed points, the

Soul Age and the Soul Role. These five elements are the Chief Characteristic of Fear, the Development Goal, the Mode, Mentality, and Reaction
Pattern.

The numbers within a MATRIX element bear their own distinctive
energy. Energy 2 is completely different from energies 1, 3, 5, 6, 7 or 4. All
variables of the MATRIX which possess the number 2 are, on the other
hand, an expression of one and the same basic energy. The principle of the
numbers as an allegory or an archetypical energy marks not only the Soul
Pattern but all spheres of the cosmic, universal order. Therefore, when a number such as, for example, 4 is assigned to the Soul Role of the Scholar, it can
be supplemented by all other elements with the energy number 4—Stubborness, Standstill, Observation, Pragmatist, Instinctive Center, Mature
Soul—and in such a way results in the pure energetic Archetype of the
Scholar or the archetypical energy 4.

A planned individual Soul Pattern, however, will never represent a pure
archetype since that wouldn't make sense. In order to grow, a soul needs to
experience and come in contact with energies which differ from those of its
essential Soul Role. While the individual MATRIX shows the same Soul
Role in each life, the variety of every individual Soul Pattern in each individual life provides the opportunity of experiencing all that is of essential importance and instructive and which is connected to the energies of other
essences and Archetypes.

The energy pattern of a soul with the essence of a Sage can in one
of his lives create, for example, a MATRIX with the fear of a King
(Impatience), the goal of a Priest (Acceleration), the Mode of a Sage
(Power), the Mentality of a Priest (Spiritualism), a Reaction Pattern of a
Healer plus Warrior (Emotional-Sexual). This MATRIX can also be
described as a pure energy pattern by the corresponding numeric symbols:
5 7 6 5 6 1/3. The Soul Age and Developmental Stage should also be
added, for instance, Young 3, Mature 7 or Old 2. In the case of a Young

Soul third stage the complete MATRIX for that particular life would then be: 5 7 6 5 6 1/3 3/3

A further possibility of describing this MATRIX briefly would be through the key words: «An impatient sage with the goal of acceleration, the mode of power, a spiritualistic mentality, an emotionally-centered, sexually-oriented Young Soul in the third stage of development.» Or: »A Young Soul, stage 3, a powerful sage and impatient spiritualist with the goal of accelerated development and an emotional-sexual reaction pattern.«

In another life that same Sage Soul might chose the Fear of a Priest (Arrogance), the Goal of a King (Dominance), the Mode of a Priest (Passion), the Mentality of a Priest (Spiritualism), the Reaction Pattern of an Artist plus King (Intellectual-Moving) and still be a Young Soul third stage. The corresponding energy pattern would then be: 5 6 7 6 6 2/7 3/3. Or, put into words: A shy, yet sometimes talkative person, withdrawn and proud, very sensitive to offense, who exerts a hidden dominance through manipulation and indirect communication, who is passionate in a secretive way and very gullible when flattered on an intellectual level.

A double or triple number of certain energies, such as the three times 6 in our last example, leads to an emphasizing and intensification of certain archetypical basic energies (Priest energy in this case), which can give specific accents to the essential Soul Role energy of the Sage.

Even the Soul Age and Development Stage have an energy quality, and a Young Soul on the 3rd level possesses a double Warrior quality to complement the energy of MATRIX. In yet another life, this same Sage soul could chose the fear of a Scholar (Stubbornness), the goal of a Warrior (Martyrdom), the Mode of a Scholar (Observation), the Mentality of a Sage (Idealism) and the Centering of an Artist (Intellectual) with the Orientation of a Healer (Emotional). The Soul Age could advance to Stage Young 4. The cypher would then be: 5 4 3 4 5 2/1 3/4.

Through this almost unlimited diversity and flexibility in conjunction with other aspects of the individuality, the human soul is able to experience everything in the course of his many incarnations and to make all contacts with other souls that seem necessary and which contribute to his development and unfolding. Also, this diversity of experience helps every individual soul to understand other souls despite the basic fragmentation and existential separateness from the whole and from its Soul Family. It allows forgiving for the pain he causes himself and others, and to connect out of authentic experience.

Each of you, therefore, has at his disposal a SOUL MATRIX, whether you realize it or not. The seven Soul Roles: Healer/Helper, Artist, Warrior, Scholar, Sage, Priest and King, are Archetypes which together encompass all the possibilities of spiritual and material development, the soul's transpersonal history and the total potential of mankind.

The constant essential Soul Role is also chosen, but this choice is subject to criteria other than the choice of the individual variable MATRIX elements. The criteria for the choice of one of the seven Soul Roles or essences are so closely connected to the purposeful necessities of the entire cosmic order that it fulfills higher functions. Imagine that of the billions of people who presently populate your earth, the billions who've died and the endless billions who are not on the planet at the present time but are preparing in the Astral World for new incarnations, or who have already completed their incarnations, all possess one of the seven Soul Roles. And when you consider as well that souls in a different guise also populate other worlds, other planets and are developing there within one of these archetypical Soul Roles, then it becomes clear to you that these essences must be suitable for an endlessly broad range of functions and needs.

And yet, there are only seven Roles, which are equally valid for all. If you embody one of these, it means that you share it with billions and billions of other ensouled beings in the entire universe. The essential Soul Role is, therefore, on one hand, your personal characteristic, which in your time and space allows you to discover life from a particular, individual perspective, and, on the other hand, creates an archetypical relationship with all those on earth and in the universe who possess the same essence as you.

The Soul Role will be combined each time with the Cycle and Stage of the Soul Age, in which your development takes place, and with the five other variables which at this point become your personal, unmistakeable and absolutely unique pattern. Each one of you is both bound to a universal whole and is also absolutely unparalleled, not only in respect to your genes, face, personality, or fingerprints, but also with regard to your Soul Pattern.

The fact that the MATRIX of a person contains a singular identity at a certain period of his development through the ages, in a particular body at a given point in human time, is desirable and meaningful as a contribution to the endless diversity and the endless unity.

Existence itself, and especially human life, is meaningful and ascertainable only if each individual soul can be distinguished from other souls. Distinction and definition are possible when there is a broad mutual basis. You establish a relationship with your fellow man by comparing yourself to him and simultanuously distinguishing yourself from him through the fact that you are both human beings, with human bodies, a human spirit, human ways of behavior and needs.

The more different life in the evolutionary process is, the less you are able to establish a relationship. It would be extremely difficult to establish a relationship with a snail or a fungus. But for humans the MATRIX provides the basis, the solid yardstick, on which you can judge and understand yourself in comparison to others.

Once the Soul Role has been established it remains valid throughout all dimensions of time and space. It continues long after you have left your human, mortal body behind. It remains valid in the Astral as well as the

Causal world of Soul Development and consciousness. It imprints the structure of the Soul Family, it determines your contribution to the AllOne, it will never desert you until the end of the universe.

Each individual soul preparing for a new incarnation, decides first on the Development Goal and then on the other MATRIX-variables, which it chooses to combine in order to reach the Development Goal. On the Astral Plane, after the soul has recovered from its last incarnation, drawn a balance and discussed its just completed life with other souls, it weaves together a highly complex pattern of physical, spiritual and soul characteristics.

Advancement in the Soul Age depends on the result of a physically lived experience. There is no advancement in growth on the Astral Plane between lives, although there is assessment and new planning. The Soul Age advances to the degree that a person fulfills his or her MATRIX. This doesn't mean that someone who fails to love gets stuck and doesn't advance in his development. He'll move forward more slowly and in detours, but there will be nothing standing in the way of his ultimate fulfillment which could be regarded as punishment or atonement.

No person and no soul on your earth will want to be always negative or »bad« throughout his lives. Therefore, over the course of time, there's nothing wrong about the differences in souls whom you meet in the body and whom you consider negative or unaware, or those who, in contrast, strike you as enlightened, loving and aware. Time does not play the same role in the development for which a soul strives as it does for embodied beings who are bound to time and space.

It's irrelevant to the AllOne if a soul needs seventy, eighty or a hundred lives to reach its fulfillment and reunite with its Soul Family; it proceeds on its own path, follows its own rhythm, its individual needs and desires, in unconscious harmony with superior necessities. This fact eliminates the need for you to condemn yourself or your fellow human beings for alleged blindness, for lack of vigilance or unlovingness, which may seem exceedingly unpleasant and disturbing but which are not of such decisive importance in the advancement of the soul as you might mistakenly believe.

The MATRIX is complete only when all seven elements are united. None can be omitted, but of course the MATRIX alone is not sufficient to create a meaningful life. In addition to the MATRIX, which is indispensable, there are other elements of choice, for instance, the cultural background, the parents, the preparedness to resolve karmic debts and to arrange meetings with soul companions who — in a beneficial or painful way — support each other in reaching the Development Goal.

Since the Soul Pattern changes from one embodied existence to the other and each time is created anew in the Astral World from the fortynine individual elements and the thirty-five possible levels of the Soul Age, each individual soul is capable, in the course of its incarnations, to explore all variables and basic energies, to become acquainted with them and to experience the whole frequency range of their positive or negative forms.

In your former incarnations all of you already became acquainted with all seven Modes, with all seven Mentalities, with all the body Centers and their Reaction Patterns, all Chief Characteristics and Development Goals. Therefore, you have at your disposal, in your collective-psyche and in your soul's memories, detailed knowledge, comparative possibilities, a willingness to forgive, an ability to understand why a person acts or reacts in a certain way. Because of this, you can empathize with your human companion, and comprehend his decisions and behavior, if you desire to do so. For almost all of you have basically experienced in previous lives the experiences which he's having at the moment. And you have the right to expect from your fellow man that he understands and accepts you to a certain degree, if not in every point, because he's done and thought what you're now doing or thinking. We point this out to you to draw your attention once again to the fact that you are not as alone and isolated as your fears might make you believe.

But it's not only from past experiences, from earlier lives, that you know much—if not all—about the five variable elements of the MATRIX. In the present individual life you create new experiences from the multiplicity of your MATRIX. Nevertheless, the actual Soul Pattern, which each of you especially chooses and shapes from the seven possible variables, retains its validity, just as one illuminates with a spotlight an individual painting from the many works of art in a museum in order to better observe it.

In the course of the many incarnations an increasing self-awareness occurs completely on its own and a natural, unstoppable movement ensues toward more love, a longing that leads and guides. Because of this it can't fail to happen that your possibilities and abilities become more conscious to you in increasing Soul Ages. It is certainly desirable to seek more clarity and more understanding; but introspection, self-analysis and intellectual awareness are not given to everyone and are not every person's goal. Our messages are aimed at the optimal usage of your personal SOUL MATRIX and should relieve and protect you from being overburdened. Humans are wonderful creatures. Being human contributes to the evolvement of the AllOne. There is abundant time and energy at your disposal.

The Poles of Your MATRIX

The MATRIX with its soul pattern is but a plan, a blueprint as long as it has only been drawn up and not lived. But as soon as a soul chooses a body and begins to inhabit it, this plan comes into effect and begins to materialize. With the act of incarnation new laws come into being which we've described as the principles of duality and polarity. And at the same time tension is created. The poles of the individual MATRIX variables build their energy fields.

Each variable of the individual soul MATRIX possesses a plus and a minus pole. Plus and minus poles represent the extremes of love and fear. They are the termini on a broad range of possible actions and reactions. This doesn't mean that you only have the choice between the positive or negative pole. Quite the contrary: in the course of your days and nights you'll find yourself almost always in a relatively limited midfield and only seldom will you be extremely unloving or overwhelmingly loving.

Above all don't reproach yourself when you realize that you tend a little more toward the negative poles of your MATRIX variables in certain situations, since experiences with the effects of a unloving, fearful reaction are a helpful means and an indication that you have distanced yourself from love. But love is just as accessible to you at any time as is fear. It's up to you which way you choose. There's no one who'll punish you for alleged mistakes and aberrations or who'll reward you for successes. You and your soul alone determine how the consequences are manifested. It's your soul and your psyche who want to learn from this. There is no reason to try to always be loving and good, to always move in the high realms of the plus poles. For no person on earth is capable of doing this and it also isn't meaningful since that futile effort would slow the learning process. What is important is ensuring constant pulsation between the plus and minus poles. This creates an intensity enabling the learning process and proves that you are alive.

As long as a soul is in a body and in this way pursues its development, the whole wave length of possibilities takes place in the field created between the poles. We are referring to a tension between the respective plus pole and minus pole. If we speak of plus and minus, we know very well that you will, of course, associate this with a concept of good and bad. Therefore, we would like to help you better understand that the plus pole of a MATRIX element is in no way good and the minus pole in no way bad, and that the point is not to avoid contact with the minus pole in order to maintain almost constant contact with the plus pole.

The tension created is necessary. Whoever attempts to constantly avoid the minus pole reduces the tension that makes it possible for him to reach the plus pole. Learning is possible only as long as energy flows between both poles, only then can the force field of an individual increase and vitality be maintained. Only when a person dies is the tension released and that means: As long as you're alive you'll repeatedly come into contact with the respective minus pole, and only then can the pendulum move toward the plus pole. Because of this we urge from time to time: don't try to be always good! And you can naturally and self-evidently assume from this that it is impossible, even under unfavorable circumstances, to always be bad, to always act and react from the minus poles of one's MATRIX.

Therefore, don't worry about coming to a halt but let the energy swing freely between the poles. The frequency heightens only through the to- and fro-movement. Coping with the tension between the poles increases your consciousness. And what we call love will be achieved through the natural alternation between the poles, but this won't occur if you're frantically involved in trying to avoid the minus pole.

The words used to denote the poles, »positive« and »negative«, are, in our view, neither a quality characteristic nor a value judgement. We're aware, however, that it's difficult for you to free yourself from the illusions of your experience and your language. We therefore ask you to take our advice to heart. Of course it's necessary to understand that—with the exception of the plus pole of the characteristics of fear, which are always dominated by fear, but disguise themselves sometimes as false virtues—all plus poles of all MATRIX elements are imprinted with a loving, relaxed energy. The respective minus poles draw their energy, in contrast, from fear.

Love and fear can be described neutrally as manifestations of certain energy frequencies. Expansion and contraction, relaxation and tension, mark these phenomena and are just as normal as the muscle contractions of your heart. The tensing of the heart muscles is not »bad«, the relaxation of the pumping movement is not »good«. Just as here a necessary function is fulfilled, the compression and relaxation of the energy fields through the alternating movements between the poles is a necessary function for vitality and growth. And we say once again: love is not »good« and fear is not »bad«. Fear belongs to life on earth just as does love. Pulsating means being alive.

If you would like to begin sharpening your view of the law of polarity and for the endless possibilities of behavior and reaction which are contained in the corresponding energy field, then you'll realize that you very seldom stay in the potential extremes of the poles. As a rule you'll move more in the middle range of this field of tension. If you discover through self-examination that, because of tension and necessity, you move more toward the minus pole than you would like and at the same time the movement toward the plus pole is slowed because of an energy blockage, and you want to lift this blockage, you must first of all realize that the energy field in which the plus pole is located is always accessible. It exists, it belongs to you, it does not lie outside your reach. The blockage often occurs because you don't trust yourself to explore that other half of the energy field.

Your psyche fears the unknown and wants to be led extremely carefully into new areas of experience. As soon as you sense that new possibilities threaten to overwhelm you, take into consideration the present condition of your psyche and don't overwhelm it, otherwise it will be automatically filled with new fear and negative tension will be forcibly increased. Reassure it, lead it back to familiar territory, but show it mentally, as through a panoramic window, by an inner dialogue or a conversation with other people, the beautiful landscape of relaxation and love that belongs to you, in order to awaken a desire to stroll through it. It often suffices to speak to your fear and tell it: »We don't want to eliminate you, but we know that we can gain access to goodness, mercy, imagination, service to mankind, certainty, the powers to lead and persuade. Let's try it.«

If, however, you criticize, berate and debase yourself for your mistakes, inabilities, discrepancies, you drive all your MATRIX-variables into the field of their minus poles, just as a shephard dog herds his sheep, and it will be difficult for even one solitary sheep to escape through the barrier to the field of love.

We advise you fundamentally to do nothing but carefully and lovingly observe yourself in respect to the inner confrontation with the poles. And occasionally it can be helpful when you write down all your shadows from the minus poles in their totality in order to realize that while the shadows belong to you, you don't represent the shadows alone. And if you then note down all of your plus poles it becomes just as clear to you that this is the other aspect of your being, your potential, but that the energy of the plus pole is richer and warmer. Both aspects symbolically portray your body in flesh and blood, you'll reap entirely new and helpful realizations. As long as you possess a body, you'll also have shadows. A person without shadows isn't alive. Therefore, happily accept the knowledge that the plus and minus poles of the Soul Pattern belong to you just as breathing in and out does.

How to Explore Your MATRIX

If you choose to use what we've presented to you, there are three fundamental ways to explore the MATRIX. The first, quickest possibility of discovering your soul pattern consists of asking a medium, who's competent
and knowledgeable in the subject matter, and to deal with the message you
receive. This approach produces a sudden release of new realizations, a
thoughtfulness, and often also a revulsion and a rejection. In general this is
fruitful and connected to the habits of the psyche, which in turn lead to
repercussions on the conscious anchoring in the soul pattern. If you discover
your soul pattern correctly in this way, you'll depend on yourself to a great
deal in the digestion and observation of your own soul growth program. If
the investigation of the medium leads to wrong results, you will feel utterly
confused.

Another method we recommend is making contact with the soul pattern
as a chance to establish an honest, inner, contact with one's own self. And, as
you know, this self reveals itself more easily, more quickly, and more clearly
when one works in conjunction with another person who's just as curious
and honest about discovering himself or herself as you are.

We recommend that you don't read this book alone but together with a
group of people who are close to you or who share a similar interest in their
soul structure, so that you don't depend on your own suppositions, on helpless speculation and wishful projections. This approach to the thorough
exploration of your soul identity will take some time, but this time will
be amongst the most fruitful periods of your life. At first, you'll be able to
discover a great deal in others and others will be able to identify certain

characteristics in you. In such a way your knowledge will mature. The intense communication, the careful observation, the novel candour which result from a mutual exploration of the individual elements of the MATRIX by members of a family, a group of friends or participants in the MATRIX exploration groups, are of inestimable value and result in shedding new light on life.

The third method of using our information is appropriate for all who tend to be drawn to an adventure in the hope that they'll be well-prepared for all detours which might occur. Those who are acquainted with the methods and techniques of divination or who are experienced in the interpretation of oracular signs and at the same time possess a grounded knowledge of themselves, can use these possibilities in finding out about their Soul Role, their Chief Characteristic, Development Goal and other aspects of the MATRIX. We refer in this context to the Tarot, I Ching, astrology or the pendulum. One can also ask the powers of the higher self or a spiritual disembodied master about the respective aspects of the soul pattern. But one must take great care that the desire for self-idealization, the longing for a final confirmation of the fondest desire of the ego, doesn't color one's perception.

We'd like to compare these three possibilities of determining the MATRIX to three different approaches to a high mountain region. The first path is wide and comfortable, it stretches out before you like a highway, and you travel it not on your own but reach your goal because you're supported by the appropriate tractive power. This broad highway is heavily travelled by many people, but you'll be less interested in the beauty of the landscape than in the ascent of the mountain. The main point is to reach the top, whether or not you decide to leave again after a brief look at the panorma and a few puffs on a cigarette. If, however, you decide to make a pause at the summit to absorb the atmosphere there, you'll be enveloped by surprising, happy and overwhelming aspects of your own being. And this sojourn will become an unforgettable experience. You'll come to love this place and will seek to return to it as often as possible in this life.

The second approach can be compared to a trail that's easily recognized, has been travelled for hundreds of years and preserved and marked by many people. You'll seldom travel this trail alone but your progress along it is a result of your efforts. No one drives you, no one carries you. You'll perspire, you'll have to stop and allow yourself longer periods of rest. And if you pause along your path, there will always be something important and beautiful to view. With every step and at every point of rest you'll feel an inner relationship to the earth on which you stand and to the landscape which surrounds you. When you reach the summit, you'll be filled with a satisfaction, a joy at the achievement, a pleasure at viewing the panorama which can't be compared to the surprise one experiences after having been driven to the summit. The experience of the wayfarer is anchored in the patient, longer-term efforts from which his life experiences and changes have been drawn.

The third way can be compared to a mountain-climbing trip. You must secure yourself with ropes and hooks. There are dangers and emergencies, strains, agitations, the danger of falling and the necessity of complete concentration. You find yourself on the steep face of the mountain, and will have to focus on the next anchorage point. There's hardly any time to observe the landscape and its beauty, but the challenge you face because you chose the steepest path and are always in danger of slipping, because you find your joy in climbing and not sitting on the summit, is incomparable and possesses its own beauty. You focus your intention on the dangerous solitary journey, and, even if others are tied to your climbing rope, each person must with the utmost responsibility take care of himself.

If you safely arrive at your goal, you'll have experienced that which will differentiate you from others on the path. You know of the dangers, and possibilities of overcoming them, you can tell of adventures that will amaze others, but it will also be clear to you that your striving to storm the summit of self-knowledge is tied to great efforts which aren't to every person's taste.

Envision your individual soul pattern as a terrain, which, depending on your individuality, according to your needs, wishes and possibilities, can be explored and experienced in differing ways: alone, with a guide, or with a group of like-minded people; carried, accompanied, or on one's own; quickly or slowly, superficially or thoroughly. Don't forget, however, that beyond all your own efforts, you're operating in an energy field and that this energy field develops through its own interplay with you. Just as the higher you climb in the mountains, the more you're affected by changed climatic conditions, fresher air, differing air pressures, so, too, develop the energy fields of the MATRIX. And the fact that you're exploring this terrain will help you complete this experience. You can trust that relatives, loving souls, who are not in the body, watch over your progress, and guard you like a mountain rescue service, which is prepared for all emergencies to stand by you and, if necessary, to conduct a rescue operation.

Now we would like to provide you with a few hints that will help you find the right connection to the individual elements of your MATRIX. It consists of seven Archetypes.

If you observe the seven Soul Roles and their principles, remember that they don't describe the ephemeral but the essential. And if you want to find out which role is yours, pay attention to that which—in the present and past—evoked the most authenticity, the most inner satisfaction, the most positive radiance, the warmest feelings of love. Your essence is not what you would like to be in order to fulfill your ideal but what makes you happy. If it's possible, observe the fragments and information, the memories and suppositions which tie you to earlier existences, earlier lives, and draw indications of your Soul Role from these experiences and teachings.

If you're trying to identify your basic fear with its Chief Characteristic, and this means the greatest barriers, the unconscious hindrances, the secret difficulties, you must use exactly the opposite approach. Observe the seven fears and that which causes the most fear and disgust among the seven, that which arouses the most revulsion, the most contempt and the most anger, that which you most of all wish to avoid, that which embarrasses you and for which you believe the highest punishment awaits you—this is most probably your basic fear. And don't forget—the Chief Characteristic is a mask which hides the basic fear. Greed, for example, masks a desperate fear of privation, Stubbornness an abysmal fear of the unpredictable. This mask is like a protection necessary to shield you from recognizing the feeling of oppressiveness, the angst and the chasm.

Whichever plus pole of the chief characteristic you consider the highest virtue is also a guideline on which you can orient yourself. For the greatest virtue like modesty or selflessness, when it's rooted in fear, turns into a false virtue, into a vice masked with noble traits, that makes you and others unhappy even though it promises to save you from disaster.

The Goal, on the other hand, contains the decisive aspects of your life theme. Everything that you learn and become, that which is the center of your consciuous and unconscious efforts, your development and your spirituality is clearly defined by your development goal. And when you seek from among the seven goals the theme, one which the most frequently, the most clearly, with the most relish and the most pain causes a resonance in you, then you'll in many cases have discovered the right goal. Again, it's important to be honest with yourself, to take care that this isn't simply a fulfillment of your ideal pretensions nor something set by others' standards, but only that which your soul has undertaken to learn. And since the will to learn is nourished by the ancient powers of the Godly, it is easy to discern through its clear, unmistakeable and unlimited multi-faceted aspects. It is the leitmotif which your soul has chosen for its present embodied existence.

The Mode is the source of your power. Try to determine which mode makes you feel well, grounded, integrated, which mode communicates naturalness, spontaneity and a feeling of sincerity within yourself. You are the way you are. And every attempt to block the sources of your own power and to quench your thirst on other, foreign waters, will weaken you or rob you of the possibilities of living out your goal. Don't even try to seem passionate when in truth you are cautious or reserved. Don't hide your power in order to make believe that you are harmless. Don't train yourself to be more aggressive when your best and most efficient mode to deal with people is caution. When, in contrast, you strengthen your very own mode, your life will be enriched through invisible currents which contribute to everything developing in a easier, faster and happier manner.

The Mentalities describe the seven basic mental attitudes a human can have. They represent an unmistakeable and unchangeable ability to observe and categorize the world and its manifestations. If you want to understand the Mentalities, ask what you're striving for, which ideas you've developed about the right way to live. Think also, however, about which kind of people you most often come into conflict with because they have a completely different approach to life. At the same time, remember contacts with people which made possible a direct, amicable mutual understanding and ask, on the basis of your knowledge of human character, which of the seven mentalities this person represented the most clearly. This is the best way in which you can determine your own mentality.

The Mentality as part of the MATRIX doesn't reflect the acquired habits of a family, race or group, it does not reflect the outlook of a period or society, but rather your own way of looking at what is occuring within and around you, your conception of truth and your conception of reality and your world vision. Therefore, in the search for your basic mentality it's valuable to ask the crucial question: »If I could change the world and could influence the views, method of thinking and perspectives of mankind—how would I do this? What would I want to do? How would I want everybody to be?«

The Reaction Pattern, which consists of the two primary active energy centers in your body, shows the connection of the powers of your soul to those of the psyche. You can easily determine your reaction pattern when you consider which chakras can be most quickly or most often opened, from which dimensions you react most immediately, but also which zones and regions of your body are the most sensitive, where tension and pain are the most noticeable, which situations wound you and where you feel threatened. Can you quickly categorize events or do you need a long time to digest that which has occured? Are you often speechless? Do spontaneous notions and creative solutions arise out of erotic fantasies or sexual activity? Which feelings are evoked or blocked when you're extremely active? It pays to ask these questions and also to ask those close to you how they feel and how their chakras react to the activity of your own energy centers. An emotionally centered person will never find it easy to express feelings verbally, a person with a moving center will be moved and moving also emotionally or intellectually or sexually, and often is not at all a sports person. But someone who is, for example, emotionally centered and oriented in the moving chakra will be able to realize much clearer what he or she is truly feeling when acting or running or banging doors or smashing plates —instead of staying mute inside.

The physical reaction pattern is directly ascertainable and easy to observe. When looking for it, it's unimportant whether the centralization or orientation create the Reaction Pattern in the correct sequence. It is of greater importance to find these two components and observe them in daily life. Then it will soon be possible to determine the priority of one over the other.

The question about the Soul Age follows last but the Soul Age is the decisive launching point of your inner journey. The Soul Age, that which you've arrived at, is not the result of free will but rather the result of a thousands-of-years-old process of increasing cognition and subconscious experience. However, it's to be expected that an Infant Soul, a Child Soul or a Young Soul neither wants nor is able to deal with freedom of decision and the implicit responsibilities. Therefore, it's probable that most of those who are interested in the Archetypes of the Soul, our teachings of the constants and variables of soul development, and who can open themselves to this tool of observation, are already in the Mature or Old Soul cycles.

We would like to return to our symbolic description of the approach to the high mountains and to supplement it with the questions: do these mountains lie in Africa or Asia, are they close to your home town or far away? Does the summit rise directly from sea level or must you first wander through deserts and low mountains, through strange lands and unknown zones to reach it? Is there perpetual snow on the top of the summit or is it still green? Are you equipped to scale the summit?

All these considerations relate to the launching point, the Soul Age. An observation of the five Soul Ages, which must be lived in the human body, shows that, with increasing age, the demands become ever more complex, subtle, that they require more preparation and more experience. Because of this, many of you overestimate your possibilities of scaling the highest summit. They start climbing the peaks in tennis shoes. We mean in this context that most of you who are interested in testing our patterns of the soul will view themselves as very, very advanced souls but are not. Only a few of you are in fact approaching the end of your incarnations. Your soul knows, however, very well what lies behind it and what awaits it in the future. It knows what it knows and it senses the areas it wants or is able to penetrate. There can be no possibility of an error which would be a disadvantage and which would hinder your development. If it helps you to view yourself as a little younger or a little older than your soul actually is, go ahead and do so. It's no disgrace to be a Young or Mature Soul. To possess an Old Soul is not a merit.

Here the observation of the seven levels or stages of development is of special significance. Only the connection between cycle and level will evoke a true resonance, the vibration of truthfulness, the reflection of being understood and understanding oneself. The key questions can be: »How great are my feelings of isolation, my longing for cosmic union? Of what do my problems and conflicts consist? What desires do I have for relationships and solitude? Which illnesses plague me? What do I need the most?« And all this not because of some neurotic disturbance, but out of the deepest need of your soul.

We repeat again and again: you are the way you are! And if, with the help of the Archetypes and the MATRIX, you understand yourself better, this does not alter your true identity. Casting a glance in the mirror from time to time isn't a question of vanity but arises from the desire to test your own sense of self and to develop objectivity. But if you look into the mirror, don't be too critical of yourself. A glance into the mirror of your soul is a special occasion to love and value all that is contained there at the present time. Make time and take time. And allow time to work for you as long as you're subject to its law. As humans you have time, and as humans you are operating within a space. These are the axes of your MATRIX. It's up to you what kind of life you'll create for yourself.

The Energy Structure of the Number 7

In addition to the action and functions of the plus and minus poles, which characterize the individual MATRIX elements, another aspect comes into play in the Physical World which makes the MATRIX understandable. This isn't polarity in the sense of a plus and minus pole, which creates an indissolvable force field, but rather another aspect of the physical or material world: Duality.

This duality makes an imprint in the sphere of the MATRIX through an inner order in which the seven individual aspects of an element are divided into different categories. The principle of duality combines, respectively, two aspects of the MATRIX in a special energetic way so that three pairs are created, for example Sage (5) and Artist (2), Priest (6) and Helper/Healer (1), King (7) and Warrior (3). They represent complementary aspects of the same, but are not the same. The fourth element forms the dormant neutral point from which two groups with the numbers 7, 6 and 5, as well as 3, 1 and 2 unfold like wings. The number 4, the Scholar, therefore, stands alone. It is not dual in the same way as the others. But its duality is within itself; it has two faces, it represents the principle of assimilation and remains neutral.

Positions 7 and 3 represent the principle of Action, 6 and 1 that of Inspiration, 5 and 2 that of Expression. Thus Expression, Inspiration, Action and Assimilation describe the four basic development and growth possibilities or, as we call it, the four Levels of Being Alive. And if a soul is creating a spiritual plan in the Astral World in preparation for a new incarnation, he'll choose individual elements from the various levels which, as a rule, will have a main emphasis. It isn't necessary that all four levels of growth be taken into consideration in each life, but at least two usually are. In addition, a person who's subject to a particular part of duality can learn to a great extent from others.

So an Artist learns from a Sage, a Warrior from a King, a Priest from a Healer/Helper and vice versa. A passionate person learns from a reserved person, the reserved one from the passionate. The respective dormant aspects of the number 4 have the task of observing, calming and assimilating. The neutrality of the number 4, which doesn't have a counterpart, allows the respective integration of great movements which arise through the tension within the duality process.

Each MATRIX element consists of seven individual variables. The dimension of soul reality, which is described by the MATRIX, is characterized by the principle of the number 7, which represents its entirety. And even if at first glance it appears inconceivable, the entirety of all seven-times-seven MATRIX variables contain respectively all possible aspects of human development. Seven is the symbolic number of entirety. It extends beyond everything earthly and human, and is, in this sense, a spiritual number and at the same time an expression of distinctly-defined energies.

As you suspect, there are other dimensions of truth and reality beyond what you discern in your everyday life, in the material world. When we use the term reality in the transcendental sense, we refer to dimensions beyond your Physical World, dimensions like the Godly or your own soul which can only be experienced during a temporary transcendence of your Self.

Now, strain your mind in order to discover the number seven in your daily life, and you won't be able to find it. Of course you're confused. But then you'll discover that the numbers of your earthly world are the three and the four. You'll encounter the number seven only in symbolic, religious, mystical, magical and fairy-tale spheres. You won't find the seven in the area of reality ruled by three and four. Seven can only be found beyond the material, beyond the physical. The reality which is subordinated to the number seven, which is ruled by it and which reacts to it, is not of this earth or planet or material world. This transcendent reality, which is also, but not exclusively, spiritual, breaks down into seven partial spheres. But the seven is an entirety which is aware of its integral whole at all times. If it touches the physical on earth or in another place in the universe, the seven will manifest itself through the numbers three and four. Therefore, in the MATRIX there are three dual pairs, but four spheres of realization. The individual soul fragment, however, can choose for a specific life-time only one of the variants from a MATRIX element like the Goal (Acceptance or Rejection or Acceleration, etc.), or the Mode (Passion or Caution or Power etc.) if the spiritual plan is to adequately meet the requirements of the future incarnation.

We've said that the Sage can learn from the Artist and the Artist from the Sage, the Priest from the Healer and the Healer from the Priest, the King from the Warrior, the Warrior from the King. The Scholar learns from everyone. Basically, however, all archetypical energies which form one wing, namely 1, 2 and 3, differ from the archetypical energies 5, 6 and 7 of the other wing and, therefore, special impulses can be received from them.

The archetypical energies of the Artist (2), Healer/Helper (1) and Warrior (3), all belonging to one side of the duality are directed within; they are receptive, withdrawn, passive, not per se but in relation to the energies of their dual Archetypes, the Sage (5), Priest (6) and King (7). The latter are outgoing, dominating, giving, active, far-reaching. They relate to one another like the male and female principle, like Yang and Yin, they correspond like willpower and willingness, making events happen and letting them happen, pushing and resisting.

These concepts are intended to help you understand how two wings which project from the energy 4 relate to each other. It's known that nothing can fly with one wing only. Both wings are essential in their interaction.

Therefore, a MATRIX will, for good reason, always combine elements from both sides, even if not in every life, in an almost symmetrical manner.

The neutral position 4 unites all others and creates peace from the movement. Energy 4 integrates all that the other energies manage to achieve. It lives from the duality but is not dual. The neutral position unites the »I« with the »you«, the active with the passive, the introverted with the extroverted.

When all is said, the main thing is to understand the principle of 7 in its manifest duality of 3 and 4. You can understand the 7 only symbolically, as an entirety. It always disintegrates into structures of 3 and 4 when it seeks to make itself tangible to you.

About the Authors

Dr. Varda Hasselmann was born in 1946 and brought up in Germany and Italy. She taught Mediaeval Studies for fifteen years at Göttingen University, receiving her doctorate there in 1978 with a thesis on Arthurian Verse Romance, published in German and later translated into English (*The Evolution of Arthurian Romance*, Cambridge University Press, 1998). She has also published numerous articles on Arthurian subjects, Tristan, hagiographic legends, courtly literature, iconography, Middle English lyrics and 19th century French novels. After lecuring widely in Europe and the United States, she was being considered for chairs at the Universities of Lausanne, Neuchâtel and Leyden until, in the early 1980's, following several years of intense spiritual experience, she decided to leave her academic career in order to pursue her spiritual interests. She discovered her talent as a trance medium and has since devoted her life to the study of the nature of the human soul. In Dr. Hasselmann's words: »As before I write, teach and lecture, but the fascination of the Arthurian Autremonde found its counterpart in a quest for the even more mysterious, inner otherworlds.«

Frank Schmolke, a college instructor and family therapist, was born in Würzburg in 1944. He studied English and German literature, pedagogy and art history at the universities of Hamburg, Munich, London and Göttingen, where he received his degree in 1973. He worked at the English Department of Göttingen University until he left his teaching career in 1991 to join Varda Hasselmann in the exploration of the teachings about the soul transmitted by the causal entity they call the »SOURCE«. Both speak fluent English.

»If anyone had told us that we would one day be involved in writing and lecturing about material received from a causal source of information, we would have laughed at them. We met when we were students and married in 1972. We were both involved in promising careers, we studied and travelled, loved art, literature and good food and were completely normal people. We knew nothing about esoteric topics and insist even today that we simply consider ourselves people who, in middle-age, were touched by an inexplicable power and began to explore the possibilities and limitations of contact with transpersonal sources of information.«

Now, more than thirty years later, their shelves are filled with thousands of tapes and recordings of information received from the Source during trance sessions in which Dr. Hasselmann, Frank Schmolke and the Source form a productive triangle. Frank Schmolke leads Varda Hasselmann into the trance and poses the intellectually-penetrating questions. She provides the vehicle through which the Source transmits the messages in energetic form and which her mind then translates into words in a precise and poetic language. Together they lead seminars where they introduce the participants to the teaching of the SOURCE. Varda has also published a successful novel: (The Soul of the Papaya) and other books.

Through their numerous publications, seminars and lectures, Dr. Hasselmann and Frank Schmolke have become well-known both in their native Germany and other parts of Europe. A documentary about their work was televised in Germany, Switzerland and Austria. As Dr. Kurt Hoffman, a former professor of philosophy at Harvard University, former director at Bavarian television and producer of the documentary writes:

»The SOURCE provides a comprehensive teaching about the soul which is just as much of interest to psychologists, priests, doctors and teachers as it is to spiritual seekers and esotericists.« (From the German publication »Esotera«, February 1998.)

Seven more books about the soul, based on information they have received from the SOURCE, have been published in Germany and have found a wide resonance, especially with psychotherapists. They have been translated into Portuguese, Russian, Italian and Hungarian.

For more information see www.septana.de
Or contact:
Dr. Varda Hasselmann/Frank Schmolke
septana@t-online.de

Terry Willey
15902 Bay View Drive
Brookings, Oregon
OR 97415 USA
541 469 65 90
willeyt@wave.net
Terry Willey, a journalist, translated this book.
She is intimately acquainted with the material.

Dr. Bob Hooper
Hütteldorferstrasse 257 d/6
1140 Wien/Austria
Karin.Hooper@chello.at
Tel. 0043-1-95 65 622
Dr Hooper is a psychotherapist working with
the Archetypes of the Soul.

Notes

CPSIA information can be obtained
at www.ICGtesting.com
Printed in the USA
LVHW032359061218
599438LV00018BB/391/P

9 783442 220007